S0-CEW-244

Reel Conversations

Reel Conversations

CANDID INTERVIEWS WITH FILM'S FOREMOST DIRECTORS AND CRITICS

George Hickenlooper

A CITADEL PRESS BOOK
Published by Carol Publishing Group

Copyright © 1991 by George Hickenlooper

All rights reserved. No part of this book may be reproduced in any form, except by a newspaper or magazine reviewer who wishes to quote brief passages in connection with a review.

A Citadel Press Book
Published by Carol Publishing Group
Citadel Press is a registered trademark of Carol Communications, Inc.

Editorial Offices: 600 Madison Avenue, New York, N.Y. 10022
Sales and Distribution Offices: 120 Enterprise Avenue, Secaucus, N.J. 07094
In Canada: Musson Book Company, a division of General Publishing Co., Ltd.,
    Don Mills, Ontario

Queries regarding rights and permissions should be addressed to Carol Publishing Group, 120 Enterprise Avenue, Secaucus, N.J. 07094

The interview with David Cronenberg appeared in slightly different form in *Cineaste*, Vol. XVII, No. 2.

Portions of the interview with Louis Malle previously appeared in *Cineaste*, Vol. XVIII, No. 2.

Carol Publishing Group books are available at special discounts for bulk purchases, for sales promotions, fund-raising, or educational purposes. Special editions can be created to specifications. For details, contact: Special Sales Department, Carol Publishing Group, 120 Enterprise Avenue, Secaucus, N.J. 07094.

Manufactured in the United States of America

10 9 8 7 6 5 4 3 2

Library of Congress Cataloging-in-Publication Data

Hickenlooper, George.
    Reel conversations : candid interviews with film's foremost directors and critics / by George Hickenlooper.
        p.   cm.
    "A Citadel Press book."
    ISBN 0-8065-1237-7
    1. Motion pictures. 2. Motion picture producers and directors--Interviews. 3. Film critics--Interviews. I. Title.
PN1994.H48   1991
791.43--dc20   91-13145
                                                         CIP

FOR SUZIE AND FRANKLIN
and in memory of
JOHN LINCK
(1964–1986)

CONTENTS

ACKNOWLEDGMENTS

To the directors and critics who gave me their valuable time to participate in this book, I am eternally grateful. I am considerably indebted to Suzanne D'Mello, who both tolerated my long absences and copyedited many of the interviews. I would also like to extend my gratitude to Bruce Shostak and to Citadel Press for their patience while I juggled two film projects. And special thanks to my agents Peter Miller and Jonathan Blank, in addition to Kevin Burget, who introduced me to the agency and who participated in both the Dennis Hopper, Peter Bogdanovich and Michael Cimino interviews. I'd like to add a very special thanks to Bruce Venezia for encouraging me to go ahead with the project while Marty Greenwald and Lee Kasper supported me during my short stay with Image Entertainment. Also a very warm thanks to David Kipen, who helped me converse with Louis Malle, to Jan Walton, who transcribed much of the book with a broken hand, and to Trevor A. Tarr, who let me take refuge in his Altadena home for almost a month.

Finally, I would like to offer my gratitude to the following who, in various important ways, were instrumental in the completion of my book: Howard Lavick, Sam Bottoms, Timothy Bottoms, Steve Foley, Frank Marshall, Alan Parker, Les Blank, Norman Jewison, Marshall Brickman, John Harris, Shana Hagan, Jeffery Schwegger, Joann Carelli, Paul Federbush, Burk Bilger, Jennifer Nelson, Jordan Mechner, Sebastian Holderman, Debbie Traubnik, Julia Judge, Mary Radford, Fred Roos, Dough Claybourne, Eleanor Coppola, Michael Roemer, Rick Hayes, W.M. Grimes, Kary Antholis, Brent Williams, Cindy Chastain, Kathy Gilbert, Bill Boll, Tom Frei, Robert Dean, Joyce Lilley, Christina Hare, Patricia Siegel, Chris Sievernich, Tim Gallaher, Doug Hart, Bob LaBrasca, Michael Lassell, Yasmin D'Mello, Dolly D'Mello, Kirk Okimoto, Kate Rubin, Shannon Kugler, Antonia Bogdanovich, Polly Platt, Bob Gale, Curt Columbus, George Zaloom, Les Mayfield, Catherine Meyers, Michael Greer, Jay Miracle, Denise Gigante, Rusty Lindemann, Chris Morrison, Charlie Lewis, Kelly O'Neal, Mario Cutajar, Steve Goedde, Chris Curtis, A.J. Deeman S.J., Mike Beugg, Tom Hagale, Don Zirpola, F. Joe Schulte, William George, S.L.U.H., Barry Spikings, Shelley Browning, Anna Reisman, and the folks at ZM Productions, Carol Publishing Group, *Cinéaste* magazine, *L.A. Style*, the Louis B. Mayer Library at the American Film Institute, the Academy of Motion Pictures Arts and Sciences Library, and New York University's Tisch School of the Arts. In conclusion, a special thanks to my father and mother, who have always encouraged me with my every endeavor.

FOREWORD

Sitting around chatting about film, politics, or even the weather can be festive, particularly in the right company. My hours spent with David Lynch, Martin Scorsese, Oliver Stone, Peter Bogdanovich, Andrew Sarris and the others who generously gave me their time for this book were inspiring to say the least.

Having been raised not in a theater family but rather in a theatrical one—my mother introduced me to guerrilla theater and her antiwar dramatics when I was the tender age of seven, while my father spent much of his time as a struggling playwright—I became fascinated by drama, particularly on the silver screen, at a very early age. Weekly slide shows of Vietnamese children after napalm droppings and dramatic political satires performed out of the back of flatbed trucks became events at the neighborhood Peace Union, a community service dedicated to nonviolence which my mother considered educational for me while my father thought I might have more fun at the movies. Consequently, much to my mother's dismay, my father took me to see a double bill of *The Wild Bunch* and *Five Easy Pieces* at the old Festival Theater in Palo Alto. The evening traumatized me for life and for the past nineteen years I don't think a month has gone by when I haven't dreamt about Karen Black or the Mexican Army. So, for me, simply going to the movies has became a visceral reminder of my war-torn childhood.

What eventually developed into a passion for films, and ulti-mately for filmmaking, drew me to my first meeting with a major American director at the age of seventeen. Determined to conquer Hollywood during a summer in Los Angeles, I carefully mapped out my plans and passed quietly into the old MGM lot where Steven Spielberg was overseeing his production of *Poltergeist*. Be-lieving that the popular young director would appreciate my de-termination, the same kind for which he was rewarded during his youth, I was promptly thrown out of the lot in tears.

Unwilling to be discouraged, I took the bus across town to what was then American Zoetrope Studios, where, slipping right past the guard, I made my way into the offices of Francis Coppola. There I found the legend himself rummaging through the flotsam on his desk. Immediately, I presented him with a caricature I had drawn of him directing *One From the Heart*, which I had concocted on the bus ride over. He rewarded me with a warm smile, some lunch, and a wonderful day at American Zoetrope, which at the time was a potential paradise for filmmakers with innovative ideas and a plethora of aspirations. That afternoon I was inspired like never before, and though American Zoetrope did not survive the following year, I felt determined to follow Francis Coppola's example in my desire to participate in a kind of open forum, where filmmakers could get together and explore new ideas through some kind of dialogue. So, perhaps, I tried to use a little of that inspiration in the creation of this book.

I hope you'll appreciate *Reel Conversations* for the discussions, which were friendly, casual and, I believe, intelligent. I hope they function as a celebration of those who were interviewed.

George Hickenlooper
April 1991
Pasadena, California

I

The Americanization of Auteur

ANDREW SARRIS

The Patriarch of Modern Film Criticism

Auteur is one of those delectable French words that has been rolling off the tongues of film critics now for almost thirty years. The word simply means "author," but for all practical purposes in English has come to mean "film director." Introduced to America by film critic Andrew Sarris in his controversial essay "Notes on the Auteur Theory" (*Film Culture*, Winter 1962–63), the expression was first used in the 1950s by French film theoretician André Bazin, critic/director François Truffaut and their comrades at *Cahiers du Cinéma* (then the world's most renowned cinema magazine). The concept of auteur, then and now, is to regard the director as the primary creative force behind a motion picture. Sarris considers it a policy, rather than a theory, that ranks one filmmaker's vision over another, as he illustrated by creating a pantheon of directors in his book *The American Cinema*, a listing of auteurs rated according to the significance of their work.

Whether one embraces the auteur theory as a director's privilege or dismisses it as undemocratic, it was true that Hollywood directors hadn't been given their due since the early silent days of D.W. Griffith and Erich von Stroheim. During the height of the industry's Golden Age in the 1930s and early 1940s (for a conservative minority that Golden Age was still the silent era of Griffith), it is ironic that the great pioneer directors of the sound era (among them Preston Sturges, Ernst Lubitsch, John Ford, Josef von Sternberg, Fritz Lang, Billy Wilder, Frank Capra) were not popularly recognized for their work at the zenith of their careers. During the heyday of Hollywood studio grandiosity, when mogul and star were king, the contribution of the director, along with the writer, generally went unacknowledged by both the studio and the media.

Though the names of filmmakers like Alfred Hitchcock, George Stevens and Cecil B. De Mille have always been as recognizable as the stars they immortalized on screen, it was the folks at *Cashiers du Cinéma*—after years of examining the significance of the director's contribution to film, particularly in Hollywood—who inspired Andrew Sarris to write "Notes on the Auteur Theory." The essay was meant to award the director artistic deference. Within months Sarris's essay stormed through the then unappreciated and unassuming profession of film criticism. Perhaps those who preceded him (critics like James Agee, Robert Warshow and Manny Farber; also virtually uncelebrated in their time) needed someone like Sarris to fire up a torch for an industry in the dark about its filmmakers, and a literary establishment blind to film analysis. Consequently, Sarris proved to be the catalyst for a polemical bonfire that provoked a number of attacks on his auteur theory, most notably by Pauline Kael in her eloquent diatribe, "Circles and Squares" (*Film Quarterly*, 1963). However, Kael, by severely reprimanding Sarris for calling the lesser works of the bigger named directors better than the finer works of lesser named directors, only succeeded in fueling the fire, putting enough heat on the dispute to entice the media to notice Sarris's argument and to adopt his policy as a new way of looking at film. The Sarris/Kael quarrel also made the profession of film criticism look sexy to any young member of the literati with aspirations to print criticism. Consequently, it wasn't long before there were as many new film critics as there were auteurs—a job and a concept which began suffering from codependency the moment Sarris cast his eyes toward France.

After 1969, when Dennis Hopper's *Easy Rider* burst onto the scene with incredible economic success, a new generation of Hollywood directors (Francis Coppola, Martin Scorsese, Bob Rafelson, George Lucas, Peter Bogdanovich, among others) who entered the profession in an industry now conscious of both film history and Andrew Sarris ironically became more celebrated in their time than the pioneers from whose work they had learned their craft. These nervy young filmmakers became not only new viable economic forces for the studios, but also the new industry superstars, receiving creative and political carte blanche like no other generation of directors before them. Hence, in the wake of the deteriorating studio infrastructure, the power in Hollywood began shifting from the commodity of the star to the director. The auteur had finally been given his due by Hollywood, and soon the word itself became assimilated into the American vocabulary.

In light of this development, I would now like to be so audacious as to suggest that the years 1969–1980, a period ending with *Heaven's Gate* (the culmination of the Hollywood director's excess and consequent political downfall), constitute Hollywood's second Golden Age or its third (for those who still haven't forgotten the magnificence of the silent era). Subsequently during the Third Golden Era, this new group of filmmakers, working in an environment now conducive to the notion of auteur, created an impressive oeuvre (*The Godfather, Five Easy Pieces, The Last Picture Show, Taxi Driver* and a score of other films). But that level of output had diminished considerably by the 1980s with very few exceptions (David Lynch, Barry Levinson and Spike Lee stand out as the few original, mainstream auteurs during the Reagan years). The 1980s was a decade that saw a major power shift from director back to star, studio and ultimately agent. The decade also presented an interesting change in the state of film criticism: the advent of the television critic and his growing influence.

Recently film critics Andrew Sarris, Roger Ebert and Richard Corliss participated in a heated debate in *Film Comment* (March–August 1990) on the current state of film criticism. Corliss, the founder of the magazine, feels that the profession of print criticism is being seriously compromised by the popularity of the television critic. Ebert, who is featured on his own television show, believes the air waves have made criticism more accessible to the general public. And Andrew Sarris? Well, after his recent well-publicized departure from the *Village Voice*, he agreed to meet with me and discuss his career, the auteur theory, my premise and the current state of film criticism. I joined Sarris in New York, where the graying patriarch of modern film criticism has lived most of his life as a cineaste.

HICKENLOOPER: You grew up in New York. Was there a particular film that moved you in your youth?

SARRIS: I think it was probably *Gone With the Wind*, because I'd never seen it when I was a kid. My parents thought it was a little too risqué—you know, carrying her up the stairs and all that stuff. And consequently, when I finally did discover Vivien Leigh, I went just crazy about her. I wrote in an article about her that I'd seen *That Hamilton Woman* seventy-eight times. I was pretty much hooked on the movies by then. Unfortunately, I was up against a lot at Columbia [University] because the faculty discouraged us from writing about film. They thought that James Agee was enough and you really didn't need anyone else. Movies were not taken that seriously.

H: Were you also trying to write fiction at the time?

S: I was more of an essayist. My big thing was rhetoric. I've always been a great speaker and I was very interested in politics, and my father was always talking politics and ideas—the very crude kind, the Victor Hugo kind. So my writing started out as something very grandiose—awful, stupid. I wrote nothing of consequence, but I still felt I was a writer. And I had the perfect ingredients. I had a mother who spoiled me rotten and a father who scared me to death. And between the two of them I thought I was it. I knew that I'd either become fairly prominent or I'd become a bum, but nothing in between—nothing normal or mediocre like having a job and working from nine to five. I eventually managed to scramble a very undistinguished B.A. out of Columbia, then I went to graduate school in dramatic arts. I tried to direct a scene, but I couldn't figure out how to get the people on and off the stage. I thought that was the most boring thing I could think of. So I guess I felt the irony was that I absolutely had no trace of talent to direct anything. I'm the classic critic, you know. I know the way, but I can't drive the car, so to speak. So I went back to dramatic literature and into writing, essayistic writing. And I was pretty good, but I wasn't getting anywhere.

H: What was film criticism like around that time?

S: It was very anti-Hollywood. I mean, the interesting people looked down on Hollywood, and yet they were fascinated by the medium themselves. It was a popular art. People weren't using the term pop art, because the thing was you were insulting the seven lively popular arts. But there was a social interest because this is what ordinary people did, as opposed to the high arts, which affected only a tiny subculture. So movies were, therefore, much more relevant socially than the theater and literature were. But in general, criticism was much more of an analysis of film then, completely allegorical, descriptive. Outside of a few of the great ones, it wasn't very exciting. And I certainly never thought I'd make a living out of it. I didn't know exactly what I would do.

H: When did you first learn about *Cahiers du Cinéma?*

S: My close friend Eugene Archer was in Paris on a Fulbright scholarship in 1958, and instead of studying, he spent all of his time at the French Cinémathéque where he met all the *Cahiers* people. And he started writing me lengthy correspondences about what he was seeing, which was everything. And I was keeping up with everything here and catching up, but there were a lot of things that I caught that he had missed. And I remember he wrote me one letter, and he asked me, "Who the hell is Howard Hawks?" That was the first time I heard those words, which eventually critic Robert Fulford used for the title of his book, *Who the Hell Is Howard Hawks?* Of course, everybody knew who Hitchcock was. The big argument about Hitchcock was that the French took him more seriously than we did. But Hawks, nobody really knew who he was. I was vaguely aware of Hawks's personality. I had heard of Lauren Bacall and Joanne Drew and Ella Raines—the Hawksian types of women with husky voices—but I didn't think that Hawks was an artist the way John Huston was. Hawks was still very elusive, his work was very difficult to describe. However, he was utterly and absolutely pragmatic and very American for the French. I mean, I even have very complex views of Hawks right now.

But anyway, Archer wrote me about the fellows at *Cahiers du Cinéma*. I had never read *Cahiers* but I had heard about it, and I had heard what their views were and what they were propounding about American film. They had very definitive views. For example, they were the ones who discovered John Ford's work. To them *The Grapes of Wrath* was it. They didn't like Zinnemann and they thought Stevens was obvious with his eccentric classicism and his overdeliberateness. They had very strong reservations about John Huston, but liked Kazan. And the thing is that none of them understood English very well and therefore they weren't blinded by the scripts. I thought the real acid test was *Rebel Without a Cause*, because if you listen to the script, it's full of all this social worker crap. But if you look at the film, it's mythological, it's beautiful. That's what they were writing about, but when you write you're supposed to write about ideas. So I think they were a little bit at a disadvantage seeing the American films with subtitles and by not knowing English very well.

H: Do you think that that had anything to do with *Cahiers'* emphasis on the director and de-emphasis on the writer?

S: Well, actually, the attacks that Truffaut made usually had more to do with the French cinema than the American, and he was frequently attacking some very fashionable French screenwriters. Now, the auteur theory was not a theory. It was a policy. You know, I recently noticed in *Variety*, they just announced the pictures for the New York Film Festival, and they listed them alphabetically by director rather than by country or anything else. I think there's an irony about that.

I think screenwriting is the weak part of American movies as it turns out. In other words, I think if I were to take the levels of achievements in American films, acting, directing, set designing, cinematography, music, I would say that these people are much more effective on the whole. Of course, there are exceptions. There are writer-directors. When I watch a film I always look for screenwriting. I'm very conscious of where films come from. An unfortunate line or a brilliant line is a crucial point with audiences, but they're not always aware of everything else. Movies are a collective art. However, that does not mean that everybody who contributes to building a cathedral is responsible for the design of it. I say that is bullshit. I mean, to be an interesting work, somebody's personality has to come to the fore so you have style. You have to find the human element in it. That's the point. That's what people find difficult to say, and they thought it was like teamwork. But narrative, dramatic art, isn't a question of teamwork. It's somebody's story, and it's somebody's feeling that comes through if it's any good. Now that's the catch. Two of my worst enemies, besides Pauline Kael, were Hollis Alpert and Arthur Knight. And they've received awards for directors' views in criticism. I never have because directors don't like me, and I don't like most directors. I mean, by creating this pantheon of directors in *The American Cinema*, by saying this handful of directors are great, I'm saying the great majority of them are just traffic managers, bums and hacks, which is what I believe. I believe most directors are not worth talking about.

H: Were you aware of the kind of impact your essay would have?

S: Not fully. And that's the thing that surprised me. I was surprised and shocked. You know, when you're not making any money for years, and most of the time I didn't get any money from *Film Culture*, though certainly it was one of the things that made me, and then you get all this attention, it feels odd. I had no idea I was being read until one evening a producer came up to me and said I'd opened Pandora's Box. Now all of Hollywood was going to have to deal with "auteurs" rather than with directors, who were simply there to hire. Now they were artists.

H: Were you prepared for Pauline Kael's retaliatory essay, "Circles and Squares," the following year?

S: I was completely amazed that I would be attacked that way. I was flabbergasted. And I wish I had had my essay reprinted after hers, because I think what happened was that more people read her piece than ever read mine. I think if they'd read it, they'd see the disclaimers, modifications and so forth. It has flaws. She picked them out. It wasn't a perfect piece of writing by any means.

H: Pauline Kael and you have been called the Katharine Hepburn and Spencer Tracy of film criticism for having made the profession sexy. Does that flatter you?

S: Well, not really. I'm uncomfortable with it because I'm not someone to make jokes about. And, you know, Pauline Kael is no glamour girl and I'm not much to look at. As Ronald Colman said to Cary Grant in *Talk of the Town,* "You're no oil painting yourself." But more importantly, I feel uncomfortable with it because I know how to distinguish myself from Pauline as a critic in the sense that she makes herself the center of her piece. She makes it the job of the filmmaker to astonish her, and if he fails, you know, "Off with his head!" Some say that that's honest at least, but I don't think you should write it that way. I think the function of the film critic is to try to understand what the artist is doing and what he is feeling, and how he is conveying it. This is true for Pauline only when the piece satisfies her. What I do is subordinate myself to the art. The art means more than the artist. It is this work which is a thing of beauty forever, and it's my job to explain why and who. What I do journalistically to this extent is to say, "Well, this is how I see it, and you may see it differently, and I have to give it to you so that you can calibrate it and relate it to your own experience."

H: Michael Wilmington, a critic at the *Los Angeles Times,* believes that Kael's essay "Raising Kane" [*The New Yorker,* 1971] was as much a diatribe against Orson Welles as it was an oblique attack against you and the auteur theory.

S: It may have been, but it was really more of an attack on Welles because Welles was considered an auteur by everyone. I mean, Welles was an auteur before there were auteurs. And that was part of his downfall in Hollywood. What she was saying was, "Look, everybody thinks Orson Welles wrote *Citizen Kane,* but what about Herman J. Mankiewicz?" Well, Herman J. Mankiewicz was there. I mean, he wasn't denied credit for the movie. And he got an Oscar for it. I mean, who knows anything? What she was trying to imply was that Welles had gone around claiming credit for everything and taking credit away from other people. But the fundamental flaw with that essay was that she never bothered interviewing Welles. And that was disingenuous. I mean, if she just wanted to resurrect Herman J. Mankiewicz she should have written about his work rather than doing it through tearing down Welles. Now, as far as I'm concerned the great Welles film is *The Magnificent Ambersons,* not *Citizen Kane.* And with that film, you could do the same thing with author Booth Tarkington. You could say, "Well, it's Booth Tarkington. Some of the best things in *The Magnificent Ambersons* come right out of Booth Tarkington's novel." But you know, Pauline wants it both ways. She wants it that *Citizen Kane* is great because of Mankiewicz, and Welles never made anything that good again because he didn't have Mankiewicz, but what else did Mankiewicz ever do? *The Ladies Man?* Not very memorable. So Welles, as erratic as his career was, certainly seemed more artistically consistent. And this is the point I wanted to make about Pauline. To make her argument stronger she has to establish the complete uniqueness of *Citizen Kane*. And she's doing the same thing she accuses everybody else of doing by enthroning Orson Welles with *Citizen Kane*. Because if you say that this is the only thing that Welles did, then what is your argument? Well, the argument is that *Citizen Kane* was not a commercial success, that it was a little bit more successful certainly than *The Magnificent Ambersons* and all his later films. And so what? You know, *Citizen Kane* was much less successful than *Gone With the Wind*. Does that make *Gone With the Wind* a better movie than *Citizen Kane*? If Welles could make great films without Mankiewicz, and I think he did, then her argument doesn't have the force it did. But she won't acknowledge that. She wouldn't acknowledge the greatness of *Ambersons*. I think she doesn't think it's great. And there I disagree with her completely.

H: Do you think that's because of the ending RKO imposed on Welles?

S: Well, it's flawed. But *Kane* is flawed. *Kane* is not perfect.

H: The late 1960s and early 1970s were said to have been a very hopeful time for directors working in Hollywood—when directors were at the height of their power. Personally, I like to refer to this period as Hollywood's last Golden Age—a period that was highly influenced by your introduction of the auteur theory and which continued throughout the late seventies and early eighties, ending with films like *Heaven's Gate* and *Raging Bull*. What are your thoughts about this?

S: Well, that's like if Karl Marx could be alive today and walk into the Kremlin, or run into Josef Stalin—he might have second thoughts. Look, I'm a historian, I'm not a prophet. And I'm not an activist or a revolutionary. I don't want to change movies. In fact, if I wanted to change movies, I'd go out and make them. But I never had the slightest desire to make movies, even to write them or write stories for them, so I just sit in my bemused way and look. Now I do think a great many directors became self-indulgent during this period and I think that they're oversimplifying the power. There was a whole drug culture in the sixties and seventies, and a lot of these directors just went completely crazy. And it was an interesting question. They didn't accept any limits of any kind. Perhaps that's why the films of the thirties and forties are considered such classics, because they were filmed in a rather controlled environment. When you look at the great books of literature, how many of them were done in society that was rather constrained? Is *War and Peace* less of a novel because Tolstoy couldn't indulge in frontal nudity? I mean, come on! You know, people are babbling. There's a lot of licentious babbling going on in the name of freedom of expression. And it has nothing to do with anything else. And I certainly am not going to say that all this auteuristic fervor and ferment, of which I was a part, was designed for the greater glory and edification of Michael Cimino, Martin Scorsese, Francis Coppola, Peter Bogdanovich or any of the directors working during that period. I mean, that's not the end that we sought. Certainly, I don't think Cimino is as bad as everybody says. I think there are interesting things in his movies, particularly *Heaven's Gate*, which is certainly not the worst movie ever made. It's ridiculous to say it is. You know, this movie cost a lot of money. But so did *Ishtar* and so did *Howard the Duck*. No one bothered writing books about those movies. You know, just because they cost a lot of money and didn't make much money doesn't mean they're the worst things ever. That's nonsense. It's the height and the prominence of the people involved with them and the publicity that goes with the people. So everybody's waiting for them to die.

H: Roger Ebert was recently lamenting the loss of university film societies, that young people no longer want to see obscure films, or discuss films.

S: Well, life changes. I mean, I no longer go to the Glenwood and take my friends to see a triple feature. Things are always changing.

I was doing research on von Sternberg, and I was looking up an interview with him in 1925 in the *New York Times Sunday Magazine*, and I was fascinated to see what people were talking about then. And I came to this other thing in the magazine that said, you know, Paris was no longer what it used to be. There's a big article in the magazine section, and it said that all these phony Americans like Gertrude Stein, Ernest Hemingway and F. Scott Fitzgerald were over there and how the real Frenchmen had all left the city. So Paris isn't what it used to be. New York isn't what it used to be. Movies aren't what they used to be. But that's what people were writing in the thirties, forties, fifties, sixties and seventies. So every generation hates itself to a certain degree. I mean, into the next millenium they'll be saying movies are really going to hell, they're awful, the industry is awful, all these awful people making money and other people are starving to death, and so-and-so can't get this project off the ground, and so on and so forth. The so-called Golden Age of the forties was a period when Orson Welles and Preston Sturges were driven out of the industry. What's so golden about that? I mean, they keep talking about hype, hype, hype. But that's journalism. Journalism has to constantly fuel the alarm, apocalypse, whatever. Look, I think there are as many good films coming out now as there have ever been, and I know this because I don't have time to see everything I want to see. And that doesn't even count the retrospectives I want to catch up with. So I don't know what everybody's yapping about.

H: What about film criticism? In a recent issue of *Film Comment* [May–June 1990], Richard Corliss was lamenting over the state of film criticism and how print criticism in particular wasn't flourishing as it used to.

S: I think there are more outlets for critics than there ever were. As I indicated, I think one of the problems is there are many more writers on film then there used to be, and I think that during the sixties, when film studies were at their peak, we propelled out a lot of professional critics who now can't find work.

H: Corliss feels threatened by the television critics.

S: Well, I mean TV, that's rather low on the chain. A lot of political people feel threatened by TV, by the sound bite, by somebody saying "Read my lips." But whenever anybody says "Read my lips," I say, well, what about "Tippecanoe and Tyler Too"? You know, that wasn't much more sensible. Television is a fact of life, and millions of people look at it.

H: But do you think television is affecting journalism? Many magazines and newspapers now have these new, easier to read, faster formats coming out.

S: Of course, and it's sad, but that's because magazines and newspapers want advertising. Magazines want two million readers. When I first went into the Army in 1952, I thought there were three cultural levels of people. There were the people at the top who read Marcel Proust, and there were people in the middle who read Somerset Maugham, and then there were people at the bottom who read Mickey Spillane. And I thought those were the three cultural levels, roughly. I went into the Army and I found there were few people, a really tiny group of people at the top, who read anything as profound as Mickey Spillane, and then there was a slightly larger group who read comic books, and then there was the vast crowd of people who didn't read anything. Now, think of the most vulgar thing you can think of on TV, the most vulgar game show or the most stupid soap opera, whatever. And it's probably a cultural advance for most people. I mean, everybody says, "Oh, look at what television is doing!" People are talking about kids today not knowing where Saudi Arabia is or not knowing where Wisconsin is. Well, they never did! However, those of us who did grow up with radio, like me, like a lot of people I know, were all bright talkers. Because, you know, you were always imitating things on the radio, imitating sounds. We were aural, verbal. One of the bad things about television in that sense is that it makes conversation superfluous in an odd way. You don't imitate what it does, because it provides the imitation. It provides its own parodies. It supplies its own irony. It even comments ironically on what it's doing. That's why I tell my students what I'm trying to do. I'm trying to cut through that hypnotic haze that television creates, so they can see how they're being manipulated. You know, but that's like saying to girls, "Don't listen to that good-looking guy with the fast line and the smooth car and the great moves and the right rock music on the console. Don't let him throw you down on the floor and take your clothes off and sweet talk you. I mean, be strong! Say 'No' as Nancy Reagan says." I mean, come on!

H: Specifically in terms of film criticism, what do you think of shows like "Sneak Previews" or "Siskel and Ebert"?

S: Well, when all's said and done, I think Gene Siskel and Roger Ebert are probably very useful. I mean when they come out and support a smaller film that doesn't get much advertising money, that's very positive. And I say more power to them! They try to apply standards. They try to explain what they do. They may be a little facile in some respects, they don't give the total analysis of everything, but people in television don't want the total analysis. They don't want too much. And I enjoy seeing the clips of things, and I like to see what their reaction is to them. I certainly don't accept it as the last word, but I don't accept anyone as the last word.

H: Do you think that the auteur theory was the catalyst for over-discovery?

S: Well, it was part of a lot of other things that happened. It was part of the general ferment, shake-up. And the controversy did a lot of good. I think the recent arguments in *Film Comment* between Ebert, Corliss and myself were an attempt at some of the old polemics, but the angle isn't there anymore. The fury is not there, or rather it's very diffused. There are not as many feuds as there used to be, or the feuds are much pettier. It's possible that Corliss and Ebert are closer than Ebert and Siskel, but I know them both. I know most of the people involved in these things. They're all pretty sharp, and intelligent. They're all jockeying for position if there is any left.

H: Well, why isn't there as much argument or fervor as there was?

S: Because we are all much smugger. We all play by many of the same rules, whereas both Pauline and I were outsiders. And we were provincial. And we were really sort of screwballs.

H: So, as you said in your recent piece in *Film Comment*, you believe that the auteur theory is alive and well?

S: I believe that the feelings that gave it birth are still surging everywhere. It's there looking at everything, and it doesn't discriminate. It's not rigid, it's open to things, and it remains today in the way a lot of people look at film.

H: Any plans to write your memoirs in the near future?

S: By the time I'm ready, I should be dead or everybody else should be dead. So either way, I can tell the story as I like without worrying about it. No, some day when I become really famous I'll get together all the unpublished pieces of my writing. I'm not as efficient as Pauline is. Pauline has published her laundry lists by this time. I have huge amounts of stuff and some day I'll get it out there.

Books by Andrew Sarris

1966 *The Films of Josef von Sternberg*
1967 *Interviews with Film Directors*
1968 *The American Cinema*
1970 *Confessions of a Cultist*
1973 *The Primal Screen*
       The John Ford Movie Mystery
1978 *Politics and Cinema*

MARTIN SCORSESE
Means of Redemption

The fact that Martin Scorsese grew up in New York has had a profound effect on the kinds of films he makes. His environment, his history, the fact that he grew up in a rough, Italian-American neighborhood are parts of a collective emotional experience that saturates his characters. They are so plugged into real-life urban experiences that the images and actions of Scorsese's active imagination will stir the viscera of anyone who watches his films.

Born November 17, 1942, to parents who were children of Sicilian immigrants, Scorsese grew up suffering from asthma. Forced to stay indoors, he developed a passion for drawing and painting which became a love for recreating stories on paper that he had just watched on screen at the movies. "My father would take me to see all kinds of movies, and there was kind of a thrill to it because you always wondered how the Catholic Church was going to rate a film. You know, was I committing a mortal sin or just a venial sin by seeing this movie? But, of course, whatever it was you'd still have to go to confession," he adds with a slight guffaw.

While considering the priesthood as a possible vocation, Scorsese at the same time had begun making amateur films with his close friends. When he wasn't accepted by the Jesuit-run Fordham University, he enrolled in New York University's film school where professor Haig Manoogian nurtured his passion for filmmaking. At NYU Scorsese made a number of impressive student shorts,

17

culminating in his first feature, a difficult four-year endeavor titled *Who's That Knocking at My Door?* (1970).

Moving to California in 1970, Scorsese looked up his old friend Brian De Palma who helped introduce him to a group of young, aspiring cineastes that included Francis Coppola, George Lucas and Steven Spielberg. "We had all gone to film school," says the director. "So as a generation we seemed to be more ciné-literate than any generation before." Getting work was difficult, but eventually he was hired as an editor on a rather ambitious concert film which became the Academy Award—winning documentary *Woodstock* (1969). The following year Scorsese's luck turned even better when he was hired by B-movie king Roger Corman to direct a feature. His experience making *Boxcar Bertha* (1972), a low budget exploitation film with resonances of *Bonnie and Clyde* (1967), culminated when he enthusiastically screened the film for film maverick John Cassavetes. "After the showing, John took me back into his office and said, 'Marty, you just wasted the last year of your life making a piece of shit. You're too good for this crap. You're more talented than that. Make something that means something to you.'" The following year, Scorsese battled to get financing for a script about a character named Charlie, a small-time hood, and his friendship with Johnny Boy, a wild derelict who drags him into trouble.

The struggle ultimately produced *Mean Streets* (1973), starring Robert De Niro and Harvey Keitel in a compelling look at life in a tough New York neighborhood. "*Mean Streets* was my attempt to put myself and my old friends on the screen, to show how we grew up, how we lived, what the whole way of life was like in Little Italy." The film was highly acclaimed at the 1973 New York Film Festival and later in the Directors' Fortnight at Cannes. Cassavetes saw it and approved. The success of *Mean Streets* secured Scorsese's future as a director, a career that has consistently produced a diverse, yet emotionally charged body of work including such films as *Alice Doesn't Live Here Anymore* (1974), *Taxi Driver* (1976), *New York, New York* (1977), *Raging Bull* (1980), *The King of Comedy* (1983), *After Hours* (1985), *The Color of Money* (1986), *The Last Temptation of Christ* (1988) and *GoodFellas* (1990), in addition to number of commercials, documentaries and a music video.

"Making films is like a religious experience for me. It consumes me, my whole life," adds the director. "However, I don't want you to think that's all I'm capable of talking about," he says with a brisk chuckle.

HICKENLOOPER: Many of the filmmakers of your generation, [Francis Coppola, Steven Spielberg, George Lucas, John Milius] went to film school and became major forces, economically or artistically, in the American cinema. How is your generation different from the earlier generations of Hollywood directors who didn't go to film school?

SCORSESE: That's an interesting point because I think we're talking about a generation that literally didn't have film as a major or subject at all. I don't think the generation before us had the opportunity of going to a school where they taught film. I mean, what was beautiful about the generation before us is that they created film as an art form. They did it by trial and error and literally working in the field, and their aesthetics came from having worked in the American theater, European theater, or having been writers and then coming here to make films. Or, even having come from selling shoes on Orchard Street and then coming out to Hollywood and selling films and getting a sense of theater, and having a sense of what people want. Whereupon you get, I think, the heads of the studios mixed with the creative talent who are teaching themselves through theater—like Von Stroheim coming from Europe, and Zinnemann, Wilder, Lubitsch and Lang and all those guys coming over from Germany in the thirties. So what I'm trying to say is that there was a background for the creative side that came from anything but film and they had to make a new language in film. And on the economic side, there were people coming in who were used to selling things. You'd sell things in the street. What I mean is that people were selling things in order to survive. That creates an edge. That creates a passion.

H: How do you think Andrew Sarris's essay "Notes on the Auteur Theory" changed commercial filmmaking in Hollywood?

S: Well, I don't think it really did. However, I do think it dramatically changed the way we looked at movies. I grew up on American movies, of course. I saw many of them because of my asthma. I would be parked in front of a movie screen or a TV set, and on television in the early days, 1948 on to the early fifties, there were lots of British and Italian films, and so when I grew up I began to notice other kinds of filmmaking and I started to go to the Thalia theater here in New York and see Russian films and all these different films. I sought out all these pictures that were playing around and did my own learning, in a sense, while I was in high school. And by the time I came to the university, which was around '60 to '62, it was kind of beaten over your head that the only serious filmmaking was foreign. And so for two or three years it was almost a shame to say that we liked anything American, yet we grew up on the American films. The first name I saw on films that I consistently liked was the name John Ford. I didn't know what he did, I didn't know what a director did, but there was a consistency, anything signed with John Ford. I knew that there was a consistency in the poetry of his images that I really enjoyed.

So at the time I guess I enjoyed the American films just as entertainment. And so when Sarris's theory, which he borrowed from the French, came out in '62, it suddenly made me realize, yes, there is room for all kinds of filmmaking, and the more important or serious filmmaking is not necessarily foreign, like Bergman, Fellini, Antonioni or Renoir. But rather we have a whole treasure trove of incredible wealth from the American cinema. And in a sense, D.W. Griffith is the one who started it all anyway. Quintessentially, it's the American art form. But, just in a funny way, to put everything in it's place, there couldn't be any Woody Allen without Bergman and Fellini. So it all blends together. But there was a great snobbery in the early sixties, and maybe there still is about "important films" or "serious films" and serious filmmakers as opposed to the traditional American filmmaker. And what Sarris's essay did was to make us realize that directors from Vincent Minnelli to John Ford to Howard Hawks to Sam Fuller were all valid filmmakers who had a certain amount of grace and a certain personality that was showing through the work, and that was creatively very difficult because the films were essentially created in a studio assembly line, factory situation. And if you can get a personality through something that is imposed upon you, you could do something genuinely artistic by remaining consistent as much as possible. What's important is to go back to film and create your own little universe there—you know, be like some folk artist away in the corner working where nobody bothers you. Sometimes that could mean going to Europe to work where filmmakers like Don Siegel and Orson Welles felt that they could get appreciation for their new work. I even think that's the reason why Hitchcock went back to Britain to make *Frenzy*. He became disappointed with Hollywood in the late sixties and it showed in his work.

H: It seems like many of the directors of your generation represented the height of the Hollywood director's political powers.

S: Yes, it probably started with *Easy Rider* and then shifted back to the studios or whatever in 1980 with *Heaven's Gate*. But directors had a great deal of authority from the early seventies up to the mid seventies, up to and including *Raging Bull* in 1980. It opened ten days before *Heaven's Gate*, and it was from the same studio, United Artists. And I had a great deal of freedom with *Raging Bull* while making it. And since the *Heaven's Gate* situation it's been difficult. But then again, it's never been easy, let me put it that way. To a certain extent with Kubrick and a few other directors who can do anything they want, the situation hasn't changed. Some directors can maintain all the power they want. Unfortunately, I'm not one of them. But I think in their cases when the studio signs on to do a picture with someone like Kubrick, they are getting a certain kind of product and it's worth a certain amount of money to put it in the budget, and you get a certain kind of return, and therefore they get a certain amount of freedom. It's all become very pragmatic, I think.

H: I know that you dedicated *Raging Bull* to your former NYU professor, the late Haig Manoogian. Would you talk a little bit about his influence on your work?

S: Well, the key thing about Haig Manoogian during 1960–65, when I was involved with him as a student, and later on when he helped me finish my first feature, *Who's That Knocking at My Door?*, was the inspiration he gave me to make films. When I first saw him lecturing about the history of film, it was so fast and so strong, and had so much energy and was so interesting that it seemed like there could be no other subject in the world. He was exclusive and very immediate with the student audience. And he did it in such a way that he was able to weed out by the end of the semester all the students who had joined the film history class thinking that they were going to get two and half hours to rest, because every other week they showed a film and they figured they could take the course for two or three credits just by watching a couple of movies, you know? Manoogian got rid of them fast. And he was very very single-minded about it. And he hooked me in that way; made the importance of film, the history of film meaningful to me. And by the third or fourth semester, the second year of the university, I took production courses with him, just elementary production courses. And what I learned from him was the most important lesson anyone can learn about filmmaking: to make films about what you know. Don't try to stretch out and do a light Viennese comedy, or try to pull an Ernst Lubitsch or an early George Cukor. I mean if the film isn't you, it isn't you. Unless you're a professional director of the old school—who was able to do anything, like during the Golden Age of the thirties and forties when one week they did a costume film and the other week they did a western and they were able to handle each one somehow, and in some cases retain a personality to each genre—don't try it yourself or it will more than likely seem phony. You should just do films about what you know. He was very passionate about that. His inspiration and passion inspired us to actually make films. When he spoke, he really made you think that you could actually go outside, line up your shots, and shoot. That's a very, very serious thing to say because you could conceivably lay it all out on paper for years, but to succeed you actually have to go into the field, you've got to put the camera down, you've got to look through the lens. That's when you realize the enormity of what you've taken on. Because it's madness. It's like a craziness that takes over. And he gave us that inspiration to stay mad [laughs].

H: *Who's That Knocking at My Door?*, *Mean Streets*, *Taxi Driver* and *GoodFellas* are all set in tough New York environments, and it seems like they all grew out of your own emotional experience.

S: Well, I suppose that even my short films that I made at the university were from my own experience. One was a satire of gangsters, more in the tradition of *The Roaring Twenties*. But it wasn't just a gangster film. It was also a combination of what I knew from my own neighborhood growing up, and where I still was living when I was a film student. So that when it finally dawned on me to do things about what I know, I mean, that's what I knew. But then I took a turn into a dramatic arena, in a way, rather than comedy, which was *Who's That Knocking at My Door?*, and Haig saw me through for the three or four years it took to finish film school. And the film was never quite finished to my satisfaction. I always considered it still a work-in-progress and it was like a sketch. And it had all these other scenes and I had this whole other story I wanted to tell that eventually became *Mean Streets* about six or seven years later. And when I did *Mean Streets* in '73, when I finally got the money to do it, I didn't think it was going to be released. I thought, doing these things about what I know, who really cares about them, especially with *The Godfather* out there. I believed *The Godfather* was more on an entertainment level than on a level of mythology. But for the guys in *Mean Streets* or in *GoodFellas* that was not the case at all. So *Mean Streets* I didn't think anybody was going to see. And finally when it was released, Warner Brothers bought it right away. I was very, very surprised and I was very happy about it.

But you have to understand that when *Who's That Knocking at My Door?* was finished in '69, I was working on *Woodstock*, and the guys at William Morris who used to represent me said, "Marty, you have to understand that this picture isn't going to draw them in." And they were right. Here we were in 1969, at the height of the sexual revolution, and I had just finished a film [*Who's That Knocking at My Door?* began shooting in 1965] about a guy who loves a girl so much he won't make love to her, because he respects her. And I realized that I was on the outs. In other words, I realized I was so far out of the issue, I was so far out of the mainstream, that it was absurd, and I couldn't hope for any of my pictures to get any public recognition. And *Mean Streets* was just another try at that. I just keep trying at what I feel most comfortable with and I take those chances. And *Raging Bull* was another struggle that succeeded in getting off the ground mainly through De Niro's persistence and vision to help me through to make the decision to make that film. And then I began, after a few years, to see my side of it, my angle, you know, how I could fit in. You know? And, of course, the same is true with *GoodFellas* too, which is totally experimental in a way. I mean, *GoodFellas* has all the things that I did back at NYU. In fact, looking back at it now, *GoodFellas* really has a lot of the techniques and things I did in the short films.

H: In the book *Scorsese on Scorsese* . . .

S: All lies [laughs].

H: In it you talked about filmmaking as being a kind of redemption. I was wondering if you might elucidate?

S: That book is interesting because we had to pare down a great deal of what I said. I think what I meant was that I keep becoming attracted to themes where I'm trying to work out elements of my own, things I'm obsessed with, feelings or emotions that mean a great deal to me in my own life. And that through the process of making a film, maybe there's a way of exorcising those feelings or working them out and coming through feeling better, or I should say, coming out of making the film a better person. But at the same time, I really think that doesn't necessarily work in the long run. But I must say that every time I go into a project, I do it for that reason. I go into it genuinely. And, of course, you always find out that it doesn't work, but that's life.

H: Before you embarked on *Mean Streets*, you went to Los Angeles. What was that like being a New York expatriate in Southern California?

S: Well, that was twenty years ago, 1970, and I was twenty-seven, so I also started life on the outside late. Like a lot of people when they're teenagers, they do that sort of thing, they get away from home, but not for Italian-American-Sicilians. You get married and at the age of twenty-one you have a kid right away, which is what I did, and that's how you get out of the home. And so I was living two lives until the age of twenty-seven, but I might as well have been fifteen. To be thrown out in California for the first time on my own, alone, with only a few friends—Brian De Palma helped me a great deal—was a very difficult experience for me, very lonely. Harvey Keitel came out to do some work, to try and get some acting jobs, and he stayed with me for a few months. But I was very lonely. I was still a baby in a sense. I had to learn to live alone. But it took about two or three years, until I was making *Mean Streets,* before I felt a little more at home in Los Angeles. It's not necessarily the city's fault. It was my own learning to grow. The asthma was very severe at that time. I think the emotional strain manifested itself through that asthma. Now the asthma's gone, you know.

H: Elia Kazan said that while he was in Los Angeles he felt insulated and that while he was in New York he felt like he could walk out on the street and have life confront him head-on—it made him feel more alive.

S: Well, there's no doubt. I think one of the problems you can get into in Los Angeles is the fact that there are so many details to filmmaking and selling films and publicity. The more you insulate yourself from that the better it is. The more you stay on course with what you want to say, even if it's an entertainment film, or strictly entertainment, I should say, the better off you are. The minute you begin to worry about what the people at the next table over in the restaurant feel about what you are saying, because they can overhear you, it could be dangerous. I think you just have to stay true to yourself, and that depends on the person. Because movies are the main thing in Hollywood—to live, breathe and eat them everyday is not a good thing for me. Because, you know, I live, eat and breathe them everyday myself, but in my own way, and I can always step into a whole different world outside my cutting room.

H: Do you have any thoughts about what's happened to your generation of filmmakers? I know that you're friends with Spielberg, and I was wondering if you had any thoughts about their work and the direction it's taken as opposed to yours.

S: I can't see the direction they're taking. Steve and I are pretty good friends and we're hoping to be working together in a company to create more activity in independent films in America and Europe. The thing with Steve—but you see, I can't quite tell. I'm so busy doing my own stuff it's very hard for me to see. I know De Palma's work is becoming much more formal, much more accessible to an audience. Now what do you tell me, that's good or bad? I can't tell. I think his films are quite extraordinary. I think the same with Steven. The way Steven puts something up on the screen nobody else can—image after image. I can't tell. We wait for you guys to let us know if we're off course.

H: I've noticed that throughout your career you've worked on smaller projects—documentaries, television commercials, a music video—between your larger films. Is that a kind of respite for you?

S: Yeah. I don't know whether I'll be able to do it in the future, but I've done it. Music videos, I don't think I'll do any more of them, and documentaries I doubt very much anymore.

H: Oh really? I love your documentaries.

S: Oh, the one of my parents?

H: They're sort of companion pieces to your bigger films, aren't they? I know that *Italianamerican* is sort of a companion to *Mean Streets*, as *The Last Waltz* is to *New York, New York*.

S: That's true, as *American Boy* is to *Taxi Driver*.

H: Can you talk a little about that?

S: Well, what I used the documentaries for was to become more familiar with clarity, make the clarity more accessible—how you could achieve clarity in a film. In documentaries you're clear with the subject matter and the intent immediately. You know, if there's a shot of my mother and father talking, and suddenly I want to get to another story and I don't want technique—I mean, who cares about fading out or fading in or dissolving so it doesn't disturb the eye—just jump cut it and you're into the next story. And I find that interesting and I was able to translate some of those impulses to feature films. I think the first one to show it was *Raging Bull*—that I think was directly from learning from the documentaries *Italianamerican* and *American Boy*, specifically those two. And then, later on, the commercials I did for money, especially the little stories I did for money, the Armani perfume, taught me a great deal about the length of time a shot will be on the screen and still be perceived by the audience and be understood, digested. And that led directly to *GoodFellas* in terms of cutting.

H: In '73 you worked with De Niro for the first time, and over the course of your career your working relationship has been an unusually strong collaboration between actor and director.

S: Well, we never really set out to make five or six or seven films together. And he's in the next film too, *Cape Fear*. Basically, it became a situation where I liked what he did in *Mean Streets*. It was his idea, for example, to do a little more with Johnny Boy, and that gave birth to the sequence that I adore, in the back room with Harvey Keitel, where he's explaining what he could be—that long improvisation. And I found that to be fascinating. We shot that the last day of shooting. We just squeezed it in and that's a key point in the movie, and it was his insight to feel that his character needed a moment like that so that you see the relationship between him and Charlie. I thought that was really important. And so, after seeing that I really was able to feel his strength as an actor. The next time I worked with him in *Taxi Driver*, I saw the thoroughness with which he approached his character, not only his character, but the entire film. He worried about everything else too, about the look of it, the hairstyle on an extra. And that kind of concern I really appreciated. And when Bob would say something to me like, "Can I try one thing?" or "I have an idea, just let me show you," it was great. Of course, other actors have done that too, but when they showed me, I couldn't find anything new. I wondered what they were trying to show me. Well, Bob De Niro, when he shows me something, or when he has an idea, when something comes right from that visceral part of him, it just comes right out of his soul. You know, I'm surprised that it's always extremely valid and quite good—I usually find it to be pretty much according to what I feel. We're always finishing each other's sentences creatively. We'll put it that way. If we're struggling for words, creatively, he can find them. And that's a pretty rare thing. And we worked together a lot until '83. And on *GoodFellas* he came in and kind of did a cameo for me, even though it's bigger than a cameo, it's the ensemble part of Jimmy Conway. In *Cape Fear* it will be the first time we've worked together in a major role since '83. And the character of Max Gaddy in *Cape Fear* is something that we kind of feel we've approached before, and now we're trying to find a different angle to come at it.

H: How much improvisation did you and De Niro do on *Raging Bull?*

S: After [Paul] Schrader finished the script—you know, the first draft was written by Mardik Martin, who did *Mean Streets* with me and was one of the writers on *New York, New York*—Bob De Niro and I took the script to an island that Bob wanted to go to and we worked for about three weeks, he and I alone. And in that period we wrote the whole script and, in a sense, rehearsed the whole picture, rewrote all of the dialogue, everything. So when we got on the set with the dramatic scenes, not the fight scenes, but the dramatic scenes, we were able to open up each scene a little bit to allow for improvisation between him and Joe [Pesci] or him and Cathy [Moriarty]. For example, the scene at the pool the first time he sees Vicki, there's some improvisation between him and his brother. There wasn't that much really, but enough. The scenes would come alive. It wasn't the kind of improvisation where you say we get on the set and it's like "Gee, I don't know what to do," and we sit around until we come up with it. That was certainly not the case. We had some rehearsals, same thing with *GoodFellas*. We improvised practically every scene, but it was all written. Let me put it that way.

H: In *Scorsese on Scorsese* you said that the Travis character in *Taxi Driver* interested you very much and you were surprised at how the character had an influence on an audience.

S: Yeah, I was very surprised. I really had thought that the movie was just a labor of love, and it wasn't going to make any money, and nobody would really understand it. Instead it seemed to strike a note. The way Bob played it, the way Schrader wrote it, those inner dialogues, the narrative pieces that he did, his actions, all of that really seemed to have appealed to a great number of people around the world, and I didn't anticipate that. I just took it on a purely personal level—what interested me.

H: Was it something you realized before the John Hinckley assassination attempt on Ronald Reagan's life?

S: Oh yeah, sure. I mean way before. We had no idea.

H: Because the book and film had inspired him to do it, were you at all freaked out?

S: Oh yeah. Naturally. Of course. But there's a problem in the Hinckley situation. It seems rather odd that a whole case can be put on the weight of one film, or one book, you know? And another case was the J.D. Salinger thing too. And I find that interesting and I guess it just reflects something I always say, and that I must repeat again, and that is by using something like film in a court case, it reflects something in our culture which is our need to have every end tied up neatly. You know, the rationale is to say, "Well, it's okay he went crazy because he saw *Taxi Driver*, and it's understandable that Mark Chapman shot John Lennon because he read a book, *Catcher in the Rye*. That's what really did it. So it's really okay and we can all sleep well at night now because now we know what did it" [laughs]. You know, it's much more complicated than that. And I'm not saying that the lawyers or the court of law made it appear like that, but when you only take it out of context and you only show a twenty-second spot about it on the news every night, that's the impression that reaches the audience at home. People end up thinking that that's the reason he did it—because of a film. And it's a sad thing to say of our society, but that's the way it is.

H: But perhaps film is that powerful a medium?

S: Film is a more powerful medium on a more subtle level. There was something wrong with Hinckley to begin with. If *Taxi Driver* hadn't existed, or film didn't exist, he might have done it because Beethoven made him do it, or the weather was foul, or his underwear was too tight.

H: Your film *King of Comedy* is stylistically very different from your other work. In that film you shot much of it mise-en-scène as opposed to the rapid montage that characterizes your other work.

S: Well, I felt that it was narrated in the script and some of the script was quite good and it was mainly wall-to-wall dialogue. You could only do so much montage. And at the time everybody was talking about how beautiful certain films were where the imagery seemed more important that the content. So I wondered what it would be like to do a film where the technique of the film is basically 1903 William S. Porter [laughs]. Really. This seemed to be the perfect subject matter for that—all these characters hermetically sealed into their frames, Rupert trying to burst out, and Jerry trying not to let anyone in. And it seemed to me psychologically and emotionally the right movie to apply this technique of restrained camera style, and that's what I tried to do. If you would see it now, it would still be recognized and it would still be appreciated. At that time the film really didn't have an opening. It was closed after a few weeks because of the economics of the situation in terms of the studio. There was a transfer of authority, or power I should say. Sherry Lansing left Fox three or four weeks before the picture opened and the new man came in. So much money had been spent on the film and it didn't equate—the kind of opening it had and the kind of money it was making—to continue pouring money into it.

H: *The Color of Money* and *After Hours* have endings that are more optimistic than some of your other work. Were the eighties a more optimistic time for you?

S: No, it was a very difficult time for me. And I think that *After Hours* and *Color of Money* were like going to a gym and working out every day, and learning how to make movies again, physically, and psychologically setting myself to make films again. And in a way, the hopeful endings were feelings for the hope I had for myself to continue to make the pictures I wanted to make. Maybe *After Hours* and *Color of Money* would not fall into that category, but I had to hope that I'd continue to do it. And it turned out with *The Last Temptation of Christ*, *New York Stories* and *GoodFellas* that they worked out the way I wanted them to be.

H: What drew you to Kazantzakis's novel *The Last Temptation of Christ?*

S: The presentation of Jesus—the way he was presented in the novel as a human, his human nature, the human side of Jesus doubting. I thought that was really interesting. I thought it could be more immediate to people who have that fear, who have that doubt.

H: The film really galvanized audiences, particularly outraging Catholics and Christian fundamentalists. What were you hoping the audiences would get out of the experience of seeing the film?

S: I was really going on more of a religious level than on anything else. I was really approaching it as more of a religious experience rather than making a film, and ideally an audience would feel a sense of hope from the presentation of Jesus in the film. I'm talking about people who are religious in the first place. That's all. The others, I don't know.

H: Were you hoping they would debate?

S: Not necessarily, no. I hoped they would feel better about themselves.

H: Did all the controversy create any tension between you and your family.

S: Well, no. My mother and father were a little disappointed, of course, at some of the media presentation and some of the vitriolic attacks from the clergies, different clergies. Not necessarily the fundamentalists. I'm talking about the Catholic and the Orthodox—you know, different groups. But that's an organization. You have to withstand that.

H: Editing *Last Temptation*, you said it moved you like none of your other films.

S: Yeah, it did, but that's just me. I liked the look. I like Catholic iconography and I wallow in it in the film. I enjoy doing that—a purely personal reaction.

H: How does *GoodFellas* differ from your other work? Do you consciously think it differs in any way?

S: Well, I think the ending is somewhat different.

H: Your homage to *The Great Train Robbery?*

S: Yeah, *The Great Train Robbery*—it's the same movie basically. You know, ninety years have passed and we're still making, basically, the same type of film. And I think that's fascinating. But I think the ending with Henry, his last lines, "Feeling like a fool now. Feeling like a schmuck" I mean, a lot of my movies basically deal with character and there are many scenes in which the characters develop where you see the conflict and the moral conflict in the character. Here you don't see that. Here I tried to use exposition as a device to distract the audience. To get through the film, a two-and-a-half-hour film, very quickly and then gamble on the resonance of the actions of the characters to reveal the character, to reveal the moral character, if there is any. But you're sure there is no moral conflict. They just do it for fun and they deal with it. And that's the experiment in the film. And to people who know that world, it works. People who are more literary, they have problems with it. They feel the problem is in the story. And the beauty of it is that I didn't want to make any story at all. I wanted to show a way of life. And they talk about the violence—people ought to understand that in that way of life there has to be some enjoyment in the violence. There has to be. And I think that's really important. I was making a movie. I wasn't doing a social tract or writing a novel. I was making a movie.

Filmography (as director)

1963	*What's a Nice Girl Like You Doing in a Place Like This?* (short)
1964	*It's Not Just You, Murray!* (short)
1967	*The Big Shave* (short)
1970	*Who's That Knocking at My Door?*
1972	*Boxcar Bertha*
1973	*Mean Streets*
1974	*Alice Doesn't Live Here Anymore*
1974	*Italianamerican* (documentary)
1976	*Taxi Driver*
1977	*New York, New York*

1978   *The Last Waltz*
1978   *American Boy* (documentary)
1980   *Raging Bull*
1983   *King of Comedy*
1985   *After Hours*
1985   "Mirror, Mirror" ("Amazing Stories" TV episode)
1986   *The Color of Money*
1987   "Bad" (music video)
1988   *The Last Temptation of Christ*
1989   *New York Stories: Life Lessons* (short)
1990   *GoodFellas*
1991   *Cape Fear*

FRANCIS COPPOLA

Journey Into Darkness

"I like to come out here early in the morning and jump in naked," says Francis Coppola sitting by the small swimming pool outside his modest Benedict Canyon home. The fifty-two-year-old filmmaker leans back in his patio chair, scratching the side of his graying beard. "It's relaxing and helps get me going."

Coppola's matter-of-fact approach to morning dips is not unlike his approach to making movies. Regarded by his casts and crews as a man of the people, Coppola is unabashedly straightforward when it comes to rendering his vision on celluloid. And it is only *his* vision that interests him, even if that means surrendering the shirt off his back to make the film he wants to make. In the late seventies, Coppola mortgaged everything he, his wife and their three children had in order to maintain full creative control over his Vietnam war epic *Apocalypse Now* (1979). Two years later the entertainment world watched closely as he invested most of the money he earned on that film into buying a studio and building American Zoetrope, a company of "film artists that would make films the way we wanted to make them." Though his next film, *One From the Heart* (1982), failed at the box office and consequently forced Zoetrope into bankruptcy, Coppola (with the support of his family) has never surrendered the fierce sense of independence that has made him one of Hollywood's most venturesome and audacious directors of the last twenty years. His sister, actress Talia

Shire, has called the Coppolas a circus family: "Francis is the high wire act."

Francis Coppola was born on April 7, 1939. As a student at Hofstra College in New York he headed the student dramatic organization and wrote the books and lyrics to several musicals. His passion for filmmaking, however, drew him to Los Angeles where in 1961 he enrolled in the film department of UCLA. Two years later he was enlisted by B-movie mogul Roger Corman to direct *Dementia 13*, a low-budget horror yarn. The job firmly established Coppola as a professional filmmaker. He went on to produce and direct a few other films, culminating in 1967 with *You're a Big Boy Now*, his third feature, which he also presented as his UCLA thesis film. At the same time, Coppola was successfully employed as a screenwriter, working on scripts for such features as *This Property Is Condemned* (1965) and *Is Paris Burning?* (1966) and eventually winning an Academy Award for his work on *Patton* (1971). It wasn't until Paramount reluctantly hired him to direct *The Godfather* (1972), however, that Francis Coppola emerged as one of the world's most respected auteurs.

Though *The Godfather* went on to win the Academy Award for Best Picture, Coppola bitterly remembers how the studio threatened to fire him and tried to prevent him from casting Marlon Brando as Don Corleone. "I was brazen. I wanted to make that film the best way I could, and I knew that could only be with Brando. Otherwise, what would have been the point?" asks Coppola, stretching his left arm behind his neck, the position that has become his signature pose.

Although he lost his own L.A. studio in 1982, Coppola has never stopped working throughout his career: from *The Conversation* (1974) and *the Godfather Part II* (1974) to *Rumble Fish* (1983) and *The Cotton Club* (1984), he has remained prolific. Now the director splits his time between his winery/estate in Napa County and his home in Southern California, where he is preparing his next film after *The Godfather Part III* (1990), which was nominated for an Academy Award for Best Director.

HICKENLOOPER: I understand that you once again had trouble with Paramount, this time while shooting *The Godfather Part III* ?

COPPOLA: Well, generally they were pretty cooperative, but as you know, the budget got really high and all those guys over there got paranoid. And all these new executives who had nothing to do with the first two *Godfather* pictures were hovering around when I decided to cast my daughter, Sophia. They didn't want that at all. They made a big commotion, but I knew she was right for the part so I did it because that's what I wanted to do. You know, the whole reason I did *Part III* was to try to regain my audience. It's the audience who loves *The Godfather* pictures—I don't really care about those movies. For thirteen years I said that I didn't want to do another sequel, but they kept asking me, "Will you do it?" They kept sending me these stupid scripts, so when I agreed to do it, they still weren't really ready for me to do it the way I wanted to. I did some re-shooting in the middle of post-production, and we had some great stuff, yet I felt forced to put it in and cut the movie in less time than I really needed to finish the movie. I was obliged to pull off this kind of post-production miracle or I felt like I was going to be ridiculed. You know, did they want it to be on the same artistic level as the other *Godfather* movies, or did they just want it out in time for Christmas? Well, you got your answer.

H: You've had a film company, American Zoetrope, up in San Francisco since the late sixties. And I know that for much of your career you've wanted to have your own studio.

C: It was always a dream of mine to have my own film studio. When I was a student at Hofstra, I ran a wonderful student dramatic club and we performed plays, musicals, we had our own facilities and we developed new work, and that was something I always really cherished. So when I started working as a director, I thought why not try to apply that to the film industry and base it on how the old studios used to be in terms of cultivating talent and then allowing that talent to actually make the projects, yet more like a collective, much like theater, where people would constantly come up with exciting, innovative ideas and then make them work. And after the financial success of *The Godfather* I felt that I could take that money and create my own studio and maintain full creative control over the films that we wanted to make. And when I found myself in a position to do that, we were very innovative and used *Apocalypse Now* as the vehicle.

H: In 1980 you set up American Zoetrope in a Los Angeles studio where you made *One From the Heart.*

C: Well, I bought the old Hollywood General in L.A., and I really wanted to make it an electronic studio. But that idea went back to San Francisco years before when I wanted to have a studio that had the best technology and the best talent in town—an artistic company that not only had film, but theater, live television, radio and a magazine. These things would all feed one another and only people who really cared about filmmaking would be involved. Of course, money was important to get the projects going, but it would be a company where costs would be kept to the point that the films that came out of Zoetrope Studios could easily pay for themselves.

I wanted to be part of a community of creative people who really had the outlets for what they did. But I never successfully pulled it off. As close as I came, we really never got backed. Maybe what I was trying to do is really impossible. And it's been the double life of trying to be both an entrepreneur and a creative artist at the same time that has caused so many of my problems.

H: Why do you feel that your dream of Zoetrope was never really backed?

C: Well, a lot of reasons. I think the fact that I strongly wanted to be independent always cast me in people's minds as someone who was an outsider, who didn't want to conform to industry standards. It didn't help that I chose not to live in a center, New York or L.A., that I never had the opportunity to become friendly with business people—people who are involved in buying stock or in takeovers. Also I think the fact that the press chose to attack me while I was making *Apocalypse Now* had a lot to do with it. You know, the press and I have never really gotten along. And it really started when they chose to pick on *Apocalypse* and paint a portrait of me as sort of a crazy person and being financially irresponsible, which I don't particularly think is true. If they knew the real facts of how little I was working with, they would realize that I got a lot out of it. And, you know, that just foolishly led me to tell the press what I thought of them, of course, for which you can only be punished. I mean, why didn't they make a big deal about the making of *Super-*

man? That movie cost thirty million dollars too. You know, the thing was that I was making a film about Vietnam. I wanted to address what I thought were some important moral questions, and people looked upon that as a stupid financial risk which, you know, doesn't really say much for our culture and which continues to leave me feeling alienated.

H: Is Zoetrope, as you originally envisioned it, still possible?

C: It would be nice to think so. Certainly in terms of electronic technology it is in the nineties. I mean, Zoetrope was way ahead of its time in regard to that. I was planning a completely electronic studio way back in the mid-seventies. The idea has only recently occurred to most of the bigger studios.

H: You seem to have been very embittered by the failure of Zoetrope in Hollywood. Is it still a dream that you will pursue?

C: Depends on how long I live, really. Maybe one day I could try it again, but it would have to be on a smaller scale. I know that I'm pursuing it a little now, but it's in a form that isn't recognizable. I'm pursuing it by keeping my company up in San Francisco healthy, and by constantly integrating young people in it, and by continuing to improve my base with Hollywood and the film industry in general.

Now, if someone came to me and said, "Francis, there's MGM— would you help us redesign it and launch a project to develop writers and try to work out something so that these things would work?"—I would probably say yes. But whether or not I would go through some of the sacrifice that I have in the past in order to prime it myself, I don't think I would. As I said, I would tend to do it on a much more miniature scale.

H: *The Godfather Part I* and *Part II* and *Apocalypse Now* are considered to be three major landmark films of the seventies, a period which I consider a Golden Age, when the Hollywood director was at the zenith of his political and creative powers. Did you ever sense that there was something unique about that era when you established yourself as an important director?

C: Well, out of that group—Marty Scorsese, Peter Bogdanovich and Billy Friedkin—I really was the first one who became successful. I mean, when I started, Hollywood had no young people at all. You know, there had been Orson Welles twenty-five years before, but since then Hollywood was generally closed to young people. And with *The Godfather Part II* I got rich overnight, but before that, even though I was working, I never felt like I really got any encouragement. You know, I was lucky I was chosen to direct *Godfather* before the novel became a bestseller. I really thought I was going to get fired. Paramount hated my casting choice, they didn't like the way I was shooting it, and I had to virtually beg them to let me get Brando. My attitude became, well, if they fire me tomorrow, then I'll shoot it as much as I can my way today. That's always sort of been my approach to it. Make the film the way you want to make it. I know, because the industry is full of guys who said they would wait to make their own personal film, and by the time they had their chance, they were too terrified to do it.

H: So you never really felt appreciated at the time you were making *The Godfather* movies or *Apocalypse Now*?

C: No, and when you say that *The Godfather I* and *II* and *Apocalypse Now* were landmark films in the seventies, that feels very strange to me because they weren't celebrated at all while I was making them. But I also think there's a paradox to that, because in my work, the stuff that was personally the most painful for me, work that I was supported the least on—the ideas that they made the biggest fuss about and didn't like—are the things that are remembered. You know, the stuff that you really suffer over because it was a little different is very often what years later they like about the work. But I never felt the kind of gratification or immediate success that someone like Peter Bogdanovich felt when he came out with *The Last Picture Show*.

That is a vivid memory. The audience was totally absorbed by that picture in such a fabulous way that when it was over, everyone in that theater, including myself, stood up and gave him a standing ovation. It was one of the most thrilling experiences I've ever seen another director have. But I never had the good luck to experience something like that, except maybe at Hofstra when the cast gave me an ovation. So over the years I've reconciled myself to that, except maybe if I live to be a very old man, or after I'm dead, they may dredge my name up and present me with some Vincent van Gogh award.

H: Do you really think so?

C: Yes, and *Apocalypse Now* was the film that really confirmed my fear that there was going to be no reward in your time for what you were doing—that if you're the kind of filmmaker who's a for- mula director, then you'll get acclaimed. But if you try to step out of that in any way, you know, you're going to get it. It's always the guys who don't have much talent who get the reward and the praise. That's just the way it's always been and always will be. Like I said, *The Last Picture Show* was the only exception that I've ever seen.

H: Frequently in your work you rely on the talents of your fam- ily. Your father Carmine, your sister Talia Shire, your nephew Ni- colas Cage, your son Roman, and your daughter Sophia have all worked with you at some point or another during your career. You seem to surround yourself with your family more than any other Hollywood director.

C: Well, that goes back to my early childhood when my father was a solo flute player for Arturo Toscanini. When I was a little kid, my family traveled a lot. We moved around constantly. I was taken from school to school, house to house, and to me the natural state of things is to be with your family and see them every day, which is what we did. And because of my father's profession we became very involved with his talent. And because of that, we were always perceived as being special. There was something very romantic and glamorous about my family. It was almost like being part of a fairy tale, and we all sensed this and naturally became very close. So I gravitate toward them in my life and in my work.

H: Your wife, Eleanor, frequently accompanies you on location during the production of your work. In fact, during the making of *Apocalypse Now* she kept a journal which was later published as a book, *Notes*.

C: I remember very well. It was a bad time for her, for both of us. I spent a lot of it confused. I was frightened. I had taken every penny I had ever earned, including the futures from both *Godfathers* and placed it all on this mad project. But I was never mad and thought it was unfair that I was constantly being portrayed that way. It was never like that.

H: Because you're with your wife so much, do you rely on her for creative input?

C: No, not really. Sure, we have long conversations about art, and Ellie has great taste in visual art, but the structure of filmmaking and the way I make pictures doesn't really lend itself to her talents as an artist. She's much more visual, a good observer, so she's also a good listener. So yes, if I'm looking for a location or something, she'll often have something good to say. But in terms of dreaming up stuff, that is what I really do.

H: *Apocalypse Now* and *The Godfather Part I* and *Part II* stand out as some of your most impressive work. In your mind, how are those films similar?

C: Well, any of the *Godfather* films, really, and even *Apocalypse Now*—the primary similarity is that in all those cases I'm working with material that I didn't originate. Yet the decision I make with all those films is to really try to make it my own as much as possible. Part of the reason that I'm a little bit resentful of those projects was because I had to spend so many years basically on something that I really didn't want to do.

H: What have you really wanted to do?

C: I would much rather just sit down and write my own screenplay, like I did on *The Conversation* and *One From the Heart*. It's ironic that I've only gotten to do that twice, which leads me to believe that one of my great flaws has been to have a personality that is too political. Rather than going out to find a patron to finance my own films, I've spent a good deal of my career trying to start my own studio and needing a project like *Apocalypse Now* rather than my own project to get it going. So I've always found myself in that odd place of taking somebody else's material and trying to merge it with something that I might have done on my own.

H: *Apocalypse Now* was loosely based on Joseph Conrad's *Heart of Darkness*. During the shooting of that film I understand you went back to Conrad's novel more than screenwriter John Milius had ever done in his original draft of the script.

C: Well, John basically just used the river metaphor. But you know, I thought *Heart of Darkness* was like a magical text that evoked a lot of what I thought about the material and about my own state of mind at the time of the shooting. And *Heart of Darkness* enabled me to satisfy the themes of my own piece in a poetic way. And I felt that John's script was too thick in plot and that Conrad was able to take me out of that and give the material a better sense of a journey into the source of all the madness that was going on around them.

H: I understand that you were particularly unhappy with Milius's original ending, which resulted in your having to improvise your way through the end with Brando?

C: Well, I don't want to blame John for that. After all, I knew what was in the script the moment I touched down in the Philippines. The real wrench turned out to be Marlon [Brando] when he arrived and was unable to play Milius's Kurtz, who was written as this very strong, well-built military combat officer who with Willard, as comrade-in-arms, would heroically take on the enemy, much like the ending of some John Wayne war movie. And Marlon simply couldn't play that kind of character because he had become so fat. In no way did he look the way a Green Beret guy should look. So my first instinct was to portray him as this big sensuous man who had indulged every aspect of himself, and in fact, go the opposite of Milius and more to Conrad.

H: Had you remained faithful to the Milius script up until this point?

C: Well, it was never really about being faithful to begin with. Filmmaking for me has never been about writing a script or adapting a script and then just going out there and shooting it. I believe that the director has to work with more than a script. Having a team of actors and set people, the moods and the conditions of the entire company and each individual, and what people are personally going through, are perhaps the greatest influences on the piece. By throwing yourself into a set of circumstances that are harmonious with the themes of the story, you find yourself living and working in a context that reflects that material. And I've always been impressed with how much what you're going through personally has to do with the themes of the work. Is it a coincidence? I don't think so. Like life, it has to do with the choices you make.

Look at the three *Godfather* films. We went to Italy for a reason. We could have made it in L.A. but we chose to go to Italy, because being in that culture and around that language would influence the movie, enrich it. I like movies to be what they're about. For instance, I wanted *Tucker* to be like a kind of marketing contraption. So that's the style of the movie. And for *Apocalypse Now* I knew that by going to the Philippines, a country that was in the midst of civil war, that had jungles and heat and weather, that by putting us in those real conditions, and not doing it on some Hollywood sound stage with model boats and helicopters or up in Northern California where it might sort of look like Southeast Asia, that by immersing ourselves in a real jungle, it might be more conducive to the conditions of those fellows who were in Vietnam. At the time, people said I was crazy for doing it, but in the end I think it shows in the work. So I knew that while I was in the Philippines, after a major typhoon had wiped out the sets, after the Philippine government kept taking away our helicopters to fight the rebels, and as we moved more and more up that river, that the film was starting to evolve into a different direction. I knew that it was moving more away from the Milius screenplay. So I think that before Brando arrived, I knew that I was going to go more back to *Heart of Darkness* than Milius had ever originally intended.

H: During the shooting of the film, your principal actor, Martin Sheen, had a severe heart attack? How did that affect you and the production?

C: It happened, I think, close to the last month of production, and by that time we had been in the Philippines for well over a year, and I was really trying to get the film finished. United Artists and the completion bond guys were all over me by this point, so I was really ready to hunker down and get it done, and then I got the news that Marty had suddenly had this heart attack. And, you know, my first reaction was the kind of concern you have for a friend who suddenly has a serious health problem. You know, "Is he all right? Is he going to survive?" And I think that I learned very quickly that it was serious, but that he wasn't going to die and there was a lot of hope of a quick recovery. And then I began to think of the implications on the production.

H: What did you do?

C: Well, I first sort of panicked that rumors would start flying, and of course they did, and I knew that that alone could finish me off. And, of course, I immediately talked to the doctor and I talked to Marty's wife, Janet, and I felt that his condition didn't mean that we were definitely going to lose him. And with the rumors going back to the States I feared that U.A. [United Artists, the distributor] might just pull him. And, of course, Janet Sheen had the power to just say he's going home, and then I would have been dead. In a crisis like that I'm usually calm, but when everyone started yapping away I remember becoming outraged, and I think that was misunderstood by a lot of people, the press in particular.

H: One of the most memorable sequences in *Apocalypse Now* is the opening montage in which we see an inebriated Martin Sheen break a mirror with his fist in a Saigon hotel room. I understand that Sheen was really drunk during the shooting of that scene and that he really cut open his hand.

C: Yes, that is true, but you have to understand Marty and the circumstances under which we were shooting. I mean, Marty is a very sweet family man. He's very stable, and at the time I didn't really know that he had any serious kind of drinking problem. I'm generally not interested in knowing about that kind of stuff. But the scene required that his character, Willard, be in a real emotional state. At the time I was interested in showing the levels of good and evil in a person, and I imagined that Willard had done things that no one had ever witnessed, things that he repressed, things that still must be in him. Like Conrad's Kurtz character, he had a side that the outside world would never see. So in talking that way as we set up the scene, Martin wanted to take a drink. And I suggested to him that he should do whatever he thought would help him with this scene. So what happened was that he got loaded, which he did in trying to express a lot of stuff that was inside him, and two things were very amazing to me. One is that I had never seen a stronger human being in that condition when he was intoxicated. And consequently, all that strength on these other psychic levels started coming out, and you know, I knew I was getting interesting stuff, so I wanted to encourage it. We were peeling away layers that I don't think either of us knew Marty had, and I was trying to feed him little cues to relate it to things we had talked about in the preparation, specifically his own face in the mirror. And then he took a shot at the mirror, and I kept the cameras rolling. Then I saw that his hand was bleeding, but, you know, the difficult part for me what that if I had stopped it, then the whole sacrifice of cutting his hand against the mirror would have been for nothing. So I let it go on for a while. I mean, if he had seriously hurt himself, of course, I would have stopped it, but, you know, we kept it going and we got the scene.

H: Conrad's *Heart of Darkness* is the story about one man's journey up a river to find another man [Kurtz] who has gone insane. Is it true that while shooting *Apocalypse*, you, the cast and the crew experienced your own personal journey, somewhat like Willard?

C: For me I think a lot of it had to do with the age—being in your mid-thirties, you're still relatively young and in the process of constantly changing your ideas and views. Also, at the time, I was in a very extraordinary position of power—the *Godfather Part II* had been extremely successful and now I had all this money, my own money, which I had put in *Apocalypse,* and had taken the production to a distant Oriental country with all these people who were willing to pretty much do anything that I asked. And I was flying to work in a helicopter, and after shooting I was living in a kind of little volcano, like a little resort in which I was the only one there, so all of these things did contribute to a state of mind that was a little like Kurtz—you know, it was enough to stimulate the imagination along those lines.

H: When you returned from the Philippines, the film took you almost two years to edit.

C: Yeah, but we had a million and a half feet of film, which was some record, so I knew very soon that we weren't going to be able to throw it together in a couple of months. And I wasn't in a particularly good mood when I got back from the Philippines after spending a year and a half in the jungle. You know, I felt discouraged. No one was encouraging me back in the States. I felt alienated by this culture, by the press who I felt were picking on me because I was trying to do something different. I was also having personal problems, I thought I was going to get divorced, I had a tremendous feeling of guilt toward my kids who had to suffer through a lot of the pain that their parents caused them. I was just extremely depressed, probably medically depressed. It was rough sailing.

H: How did that affect the material you were cutting?

C: Well, I really dreaded working on it. That's what made it take so long. I didn't want to work, I didn't want to do anything. I mean, I went through the motions of it but I was pretty sapped.

H: Now that you've finished *The Godfather Part III*, what lies ahead for you?

C: As you know, I'm going to do another studio picture, *Dracula*, and we're going to do it with a period setting. It's going to be a classical approach to *Dracula* in the Bram Stoker tradition and it should be fun. I'm preparing it now, and Winona [Ryder], who didn't get to be in *Godfather III*, is going to do it. After that, I'm working on an original screenplay for a lower-budget film sort of scaled to *The Conversation*. I think that I'd like to go back to smaller budgets. You know, the bigger the budget, the less freedom the director has. On a fifty-million-dollar movie, you spend most of your time just worrying about the budget, and in a sense what you get from your colleagues isn't a hell of a lot better than what you get on a Roger Corman budget—except for the fact that everything costs so much that you stop thinking about what the movie is and more about how the money is being spent. So generally speaking, I think the lower-budget, more modest Roger Corman-style of film is much better for the creativity of the director who wants to do what he wants.

H: So you don't think a director can be as creative on a bigger studio film?

C: Not until the studios, executives, and even the media are more encouraging to filmmakers. You know, it's real easy to lose your confidence in this business. It seems like everyone is out there to tear you down. And if you want to work, you really can't fight back. So you end up broken-hearted.

My father tells a great story of a cellist who worked for Toscanini. He was the first cellist and he was really a proud man. And one day Toscanini came in, and they were going to do something with a big cello part. He's doing it, and Toscanini didn't quite like it—and he said no, no, no. And he stopped the rehearsal. And the next day, some famous soloist was there, and he did it. And this guy who was the first cellist was there, but you know, three months later he was the second cellist—six months later he was the third cellist, and then he was in the last stand, and then he died an alcoholic. So what does that mean? It means that somehow you have to stop looking at creative people as these kind of cocky, self-assured cowboys. The reason they might do beautiful things is because, like everyone, they're not one hundred percent sure. They're following instincts, and they need not to be lionized— which happens in the other extreme—but just encouraged. They need someone to say, "Do that."

Filmography

1963	*Dementia 13*
1967	*You're a Big Boy Now*
1968	*Finian's Rainbow*
1969	*The Rain People*
1972	*The Godfather*
1974	*The Conversation*
1974	*The Godfather Part II*
1979	*Apocalypse Now*
1982	*One From the Heart*

1983   *The Outsiders*
1983   *Rumble Fish*
1984   *The Cotton Club*
1986   *Peggy Sue Got Married*
1987   *Gardens of Stone*
1988   *Tucker*
1990   *The Godfather Part III*
1992   *Dracula*

PETER BOGDANOVICH
Imitation of Life

A blinking street light sways over a dust blown intersection in Archer City, Texas, a dried up oil town where highways 79 and 25 meet in the mesquite-infested flatlands just south of the Red River. Not much has happened here in the past fifty years with the exception of the birth of one of its most renowned citizens, Pulitzer Prize-winning novelist Larry McMurtry, in 1936, and the making of the film *The Last Picture Show* (based on his novel) in 1970 by director Peter Bogdanovich.

"Sal Mineo was the first to suggest that I read the book. Coincidentally, I had remembered seeing it on a rack in a drugstore. I recalled that the title appealed to me," says Bogdanovich sitting next to his trailer which is parked alongside Archer City's Royal Theater, a stunning visual icon from *The Last Picture Show*. "But then I read the back cover, and I realized that it was about teenagers growing up in a small Texas town and I thought, 'No, that doesn't really interest me.' Orson Welles told me not to do it. He thought that the book was obscene. However, despite Welles's reservations, Bogdanovich's wife, Polly Platt, encouraged him to do it and, a year later, he went to Archer City to begin production. In 1972, *The Last Picture Show* went on to be nominated for eight Academy Awards, after being hailed by *Newsweek* as the greatest piece of American cinema since *Citizen Kane*. Bogdanovich became one of the most sought after directors of the early 1970s.

Peter Bogdanovich is back in Archer City, Texas, nineteen years later, to shoot *Texasville* (1990), Larry McMurtry's sequel to *The Last Picture Show*. A lot has happened to the director in the last two decades. "I feel like I'm going to see the ghost of my former self walking around the corner at the age of thirty," he continues, his hand sweeping through his graying hair. "I'm dealing with material here that changed my life forever. Nothing was ever the same for me after *Picture Show*."

Bogdanovich is a director whose personal life has often drawn more attention than his professional life. Born in 1939 to Serbian parents, he grew up in New York City. An aggressive youth interested in both the theater and cinema, he had directed his first professional play and run several film series at the Museum of Modern Art by age twenty. A few years later he was married to Polly Platt, his friend and collaborator, with whom he was sent by *Esquire* magazine to Hollywood. There the young Bogdanovich would write his monthly film column, a position which provided him with opportunity to meet and strike up friendships with many of Hollywood's legendary filmmakers: John Ford, Howard Hawks, Fritz Lang, Orson Welles and others. These acquaintanceships led Bogdanovich to publish several essays and books about their work, at the same time instilling him with a passion to make his own movies. It wasn't long before the aspiring director approached B-movie king Roger Corman about making his own low-budget film. Despite a limited schedule, the young filmmaker eventually pulled it off—the result was the critically acclaimed *Targets* (1968), the success of which paved the way for Bogdanovich to go ahead with *The Last Picture Show* (1971). The film starred a cast of then unknowns—Timothy Bottoms, Jeff Bridges, Ellen Burstyn, Cloris Leachman and Cybill Shepherd—in a story about youth, promiscuity and despair in an isolated Texas town.

But the making of the film proved to be very traumatic for Bogdanovich. By the end of production his marriage with Platt had broken up over a romance he had begun with actress Shepherd. Despite the sensationalistic coverage of their rather open liaison, Bogdanovich's career forged ahead with the making of *Paper Moon* (1973) and *What's Up, Doc?* (1973). Both films made the director an economic and critical sensation. However, just as quickly as his career took off, it also nosedived. His next three films, *Daisy Miller* (1974), *At Long Last Love* (1975) and *Nickelodeon* (1977), proved to be economical and critical disasters. Soon Bogdanovich found himself Hollywood's favorite commercial and social pariah. And finally, after eight years, his relationship with Shepherd ended.

In 1979, Bogdanovich made a healthy critical comeback with *Saint Jack*, a film based on the novel by Paul Theroux. Then two years later, while he was on his ninth production, *They All Laughed* (1981), his fiancée and the supporting actress of the film, Dorothy Stratten, was brutally murdered. Bogdanovich sank into depression for years until his worsening financial situation forced him to go back to work. In 1985 he made an impressive comeback with *Mask*, a film he made in memory of Stratten, and in 1987 Bogdanovich was informed by Larry McMurtry that a sequel to the novel, *The Last Picture Show*, was forthcoming. Shortly after *Texasville* was published, Bogdanovich began adapting the screenplay, which revisits the characters from *Picture Show* as they enter midlife.

"Dealing with *Texasville* never ceases to be haunting," says Bogdanovich chewing on a toothpick. "It's very strange to be wrestling with material that so closely reflects what is going on in my own life, both now and when I made *Picture Show*."

HICKENLOOPER: What was it like to come back to Archer City nineteen years later to shoot *Texasville*?

BOGDANOVICH: It was the most difficult picture I've ever had to make. I think not just because it was a difficult picture to shoot, but also because of the personal reasons involved, and kind of coming face to face with yourself twenty years ago daily, and with actors who you remembered from twenty years ago. You know, *The Last Picture Show* shot those people at a particular age. I'm not in the picture but I can remember them vividly. You know, I saw images over and over again while cutting the picture. And those images of Cybill Shepherd, Jeff Bridges and Timothy Bottoms are indelible in my mind, and then suddenly there were the actors again. And now they're playing older which is much more odd. I don't imagine it will ever happen again, anything quite as bizarre. It was a strange feeling.

H: Specifically, is there anything in *Texasville* that you can relate to in your life now?

B: Well, I can certainly relate to Jeff Bridges's character, Duane, in the picture. He's going through a midlife crisis. I went through one and it was horrible. And his character is going through a collapse financially as I did a couple of years ago. So I didn't have any trouble following that [laughs].

H: You've acted in your own work [*Targets, Saint Jack*] and I was wondering if you thought an actor's personal life could be affected by the role he or she is portraying?

B: Oh, yes, of course, very much so I'd say. I think actors are always affected in some way by the roles they play. I think Jeff Bridges is a good example. He really gets into his part.

H: Did you ever find that the Jacy character was like Cybill [Shepard] or that the Sonny character was like Tim [Bottoms]?

B: You know, you really can't play anybody but yourself. You can play yourself in the situation up to a point, the characteristics that are written you play, but finally you find the character in yourself, not yourself in the character. You've got to find the character in you. And that's what actors do. So Cybill had to find Jacy in herself and, of course, by doing that Jacy became partially Cybill, just as Sonny became Tim to a degree, and Duane became Jeff. Jeff became Duane but Duane also became Jeff [laughs].

H: How did your relationship with Cybill affect *Picture Show?*

B: Well, there's no question that Cybill inspired a lot of the spark in the picture. She was a tremendous inspiration to me. I think that relationship had a tremendous effect on the picture. In fact, there was a point when I kept asking—I asked Cybill, was I attracted to her or the character? It turned out it was her.

H: How does *Texasville* differ from *The Last Picture Show?*

B: Well, *Texasville* in its time, here in 1990, is an unusual picture. It would be unusual anytime, but probably more so today than twenty years ago or forty years ago. The reason is that audiences of pictures have become much more used to one genre or another, so you have either a comedy or a drama. The thought of mixing comedy and drama, which used to be a kind of sub-genre played very well in the thirties—Frank Capra virtually made his signature a comedy/drama. Funny, funny, funny and then touching or sad and then a happy ending, but nevertheless comedy/drama. Ford made them as well. Leo McCarey made them. I mean, look at a picture like *Love Affair*, which starts out like a light romantic comedy and turns almost into a tragedy. Hard to imagine that kind of switch being commonplace today. In fact, from my experiences making *Texasville* and showing it to audiences—I mean regular audiences, civilians, as opposed to picture people—audiences are much less prepared for a movie that's funny and sad. It's more difficult to make it work because of the rhythm—it's a particular rhythm and you have to find it. And you have to find the right balance between comedy and drama, and how much comedy and how much drama and how much before you switch again?

H: Was there a quality in the characters of *The Last Picture Show* that as a filmmaker you were able to identify with?

B: Well, I think we can all identify with the characters in *Picture Show*. I think everybody's adolescence touches on some of that no matter where you're from. I mean, you're discovering sex, you're insecure, you're going to school, you're in a strange kind of half-life, not understanding what you're doing, not understanding anything around you. If you're a guy, women are a big mystery; if you're a woman, men are mysterious. It's complicated. So I think the kind of experiences that were in *Picture Show* were in everybody's adolescence. I mean, nothing could have been more different than mine from Larry's. He grew up in a small town in Texas, I grew up in Manhattan on the West Side, and he was with a bunch of not very sophisticated cattle people and I grew up with artists and intellectuals from New York and Europe—very different, yet certain things are the same. I guess what they call the rites of passage are similar, no matter what. It must be, because I've been told by people all over the world that *The Last Picture Show* reminded them of their hometown.

H: What did movies mean to you as a teenager?

B: Well, it was a kind of escape. It was another world where there was hope, adventure, magic and dreams of other times and other places, and I think that's why the title of the book, *The Last Picture Show*, held particular interest for me, because the closing down of that small-time movie theater was kind of a metaphor for the continuing isolation of the world, but specifically America, the closing in of the country, and new ideas.

H: Your former wife, Polly Platt, said that she thought that you two had been a perfect collaborative team back in the early seventies. Would you talk about your working relationship with her?

B: Well, it varied from picture to picture. She was terrific to bounce ideas off, and she had a terrific head for editing scripts, saying, "Maybe you don't need that scene, maybe you do need that one." She had never done a set before *Targets*. She had only done costumes. But I encouraged her so that she would be able to do that. Polly is a great all around kind of person. You could talk to her about any aspect of the film. But she was predominantly dealing with the look of the picture and she had input on the script. I think the two she worked most on in terms of that were *Targets* and *Picture Show*. She had some initial good ideas on *What's Up, Doc?* She made a couple of suggestions early on, but she didn't really work much on the script of that.

H: What did you learn from Roger Corman about making pictures?

B: Oh, I learned a lot about making pictures from Roger, the practical end of it, in terms of shooting on the run, grabbing shots, being prepared, finding ways to do it less expensively. That experience influenced me greatly through the rest of my pictures.

H: During the early 1960s you were a film commentator for *Esquire* magazine in addition to writing a number of books on the work of John Ford, Fritz Lang, Allan Dwan, among others. Consequently, you were able to become friends with many of the directors you admired. How did that affect your own work as a director?

B: It had an incalculable importance in my life and in my work that I was able to ask questions from the people who'd done it, who'd really started pictures. I'll never be able to repay them or express my gratitude for the time they gave me and how much they taught me. Particularly, John Ford and Orson Welles, both of whom had a tremendous influence on *The Last Picture Show*. Welles's use of depth of field in *Citizen Kane* and *The Magnificent Ambersons* was a look that I found very appealing, and the kind of elegiac feeling that the picture tried to convey is something that Ford is famous for.

H: You rose to power during the height of American auteurism in the early 1970s. Were you aware of the kind of power you had at the time?

B: Well, I think the funny thing about success or any experience is until you've had it you don't know what it's like. And because you haven't had it, when it's happening to you, you're not sure that that's what it is. Do you know what I mean? Because you haven't had it, people say, "Gosh, what was it like to be successful?" Well, I didn't really think that I was that successful. I mean, I didn't sit around and say, "Gee, I'm successful." It didn't occur to me that way. I had a picture that came out and did very well. Then I had another picture come out and it did very well. In fact, I had three pictures in a row come out that did very well. I mean, it was pretty unusual. But I didn't sit around thinking this is unusual therefore, I'm very successful, and I have a lot of power and people will do what I ask. I didn't think that way. I remember it made me nervous and apprehensive—the whole situation.

H: Compared to today, do you think that the 1970s were a kind of Golden Age for Hollywood directors?

B: Well, you know audiences have changed and so have movies. That's what they do. The early seventies were a very hopeful time for American pictures. The beginning of the nineties is probably very hopeful economically for the movie business. But as far as the art of the movies, I don't think we've made a tremendous number of great steps forward in the last twenty years.

H: Did Dennis Hopper's film, *Easy Rider*, function as the catalyst for this particular epoch?

B: Certainly *Easy Rider* was one of the first of Hollywood's more radical films to find success, which I think had a very positive effect on mainstream movie making. And, of course, *Easy Rider* was the first Hollywood movie made outside the studios to gross enormous sums of money. It became a real blockbuster, and that impressed everyone, even the most conservative executives at the time. It cost something like seven or eight hundred thousand dollars and made millions. In 1969, that same year, I was under contract at Paramount where they had spent almost a hundred million dollars on five or six movies, and I remember everybody standing around wondering what had happened. So then toward the end of the sixties, everybody started saying this is the way to make pictures. Go out on location with a million dollars, take a script that was a little different to a new director and do it. At the time I remember making a joke saying that the easiest way to make a picture was to not have made one.

H: Some directors, like Orson Welles, are haunted for the rest of their careers by their first picture. Although *The Last Picture Show* was your second film, it was your first major success. Is that something you're constantly reminded of?

B: No, I don't think so. I didn't have that same problem as Orson. I think maybe critically, but not in terms of the public. I think critically, probably, one would never get as good reviews again. And I said that at the time. I said, "I'm never gonna get reviews this good again." Whoever was there when I said that said, "Why?" and I said, "Because you can only be discovered once." But luckily I had a couple of other pictures that the public liked, in fact even more than *Picture Show*, because *What's Up, Doc?* and *Paper Moon* made more money than *The Last Picture Show*. And I can see why, actually, they made more money. If the new version that I recently cut of *The Last Picture Show* [available on laser disc], which is I think seven minutes longer, had been released, I think it would have been a more popular picture. That's odd to say, but I'm now convinced of that, because it's easier to follow. I realize that some of the connections, some of the motivations in *Picture Show* were a little rushed and the audience had to put it together in their minds. I think one of the keys to a popular picture is that the audience doesn't have to think or work very hard, which doesn't mean that it has to be a mindless picture. It's just that it needs a certain kind of rhythm. Personally, I would much prefer the audience to think once the picture is over, mull it over, think about it and have it stay with them. But I don't really want them thinking while the movie's on because thinking about anything else beyond the movie is going to be a distraction.

H: Billy Wilder once said, "If Hollywood has anything in common, it's in its hatred for Peter Bogdanovich." Would you comment on that?

B: Well, Billy was also using that remark to express his own hostility [laughs]. You know, I had three very successful pictures in a row, one after the other, *Picture Show*, *What's Up, Doc?* and *Paper Moon*, and Cybill had two very successful films one after the other, *Picture Show* and *Heartbreak Kid*, and we lived together rather brazenly, openly, without being married and we were doing it on the covers of magazines. I think one headline was "Living Together is Sexier than Marriage," which was calculated to irritate anybody who was married, or not married. Today Ryan O'Neal and Farrah Fawcett not only live together but have a baby together without being married, but in 1971 it really wasn't done with the kind of openness that we did it. So with those successes, and both of us being pretty young, and Cybill being very attractive and a successful model as well, all of that kind of breeds irritation, jealousy, envy, all those wonderful things. And probably we were also about as bad at handling the situation as you can get, so we exacerbated the circumstances. We were not political, we were just stupid really. She was young, she had an excuse. I was not that young, I should have known better. Cary Grant said to me around that time, "Never tell people you're in love, and don't tell people that you're happy. They don't want to hear that." I said, "Why not?" He said, "Because they're not happy and they're not in love." So it wasn't very pleasant, but it was our own fault in a lot of ways. We could have handled it differently.

H: What finally convinced you to make *The Last Picture Show*?

B: I asked my wife at the time, Polly Platt, to read it for me, and a couple of weeks later she said, "Well, I don't know how you'd make it as a picture, but it's a good book, and I think it might interest you." And she felt that it would relate to certain adolescent trau-mas that I'd been through that she knew a little bit about. So after a while I finally read it, having stalled as much as possible. And I had a similar reaction to Polly's, which was that I didn't know how to make it as a picture, but exactly what interested me about it was that I didn't quite know how to do it. It had a lot of characters, sex dealt with in a way that was pretty new in pictures. You know, it was a challenge, a big challenge. At the time I had a contract with Paramount, and when they turned it down I met up with BBS Pro-ductions, and Bert Schneider had seen *Targets* and he liked it and he just said to me, "If you ever have something you want to make, let us know." So a year later, I went back to him and said, "I want to make *The Last Picture Show*."

H: Can you talk about your collaboration with Larry McMurtry on the screenplay of *The Last Picture Show* and then *Texasville*?

B: Well, on *The Last Picture Show* it was whole different story than with *Texasville*. On *The Last Picture Show* Larry and I talked our way through the picture a few times. You know, sequence by sequence. And then Larry would go back home, he'd go back to Washington or Texas, and he would write ten or fifteen pages and send them to me. He'd never written a screenplay before so it was not in screen-play form. He'd just send me basically description and dialogue and then I would rewrite it, fix it up, change it however, and then have it retyped and then send it back to him. And that's how we did it, back and forth. Basically he did the dialogue and I did the construction. And at a certain point, I would say to him, "Well, this scene is good in the book but why don't you give it a shot and try to write another scene?" And he'd send it to me. Invariably the scene would be better in the book. And I would call him and say, "It's better in the book." And he would say slightly irritated, "Then use the book." Larry loses interest in his characters once he's written the novel. And the script for *Picture Show* was being written in 1970, almost five years after he'd written the novel, so he was really bored with the characters. For example, in the book, the scene with the Ben Johnson character, Sam the Lion, out by the tank dam is a completely different monologue. It has to do with urinating off the dam. And I said, "Larry, I don't think this is going to work in a picture." I didn't think that it would be easy to create a romantic mood with somebody urinating off a dam. So then he wrote this speech about the wild young girl and the silver dollar and it was perfect. And those kinds of things we changed. And then Larry came down once while we were shooting. In fact, he only came down once for about two days, and at that time, because the picture was running too long, we realized we had to take out a whole sequence that was going to be shot with the Sonny and Duane characters down in Mexico. So I discussed with Larry how we were going to bridge that and he wrote out a few lines in longhand, and that was it, that was really the collaboration. A lot of the scenes we just took directly from the book. On *Texasville* Larry didn't want to be involved. He was busy writing a novel, and again, he was tired of the characters, so I asked him if he would read a draft when I was ready. And I sent him the first draft and he made comments that were helpful. And I think I sent him one more draft and he read that and made a few comments which basically suggested that I use this or that scene that had been omitted, or drop a scene that I had in there. Then I sent him a third draft and I don't think he read that one. I think he'd had it. And that was it.

H: Were you apprehensive about doing the sequel?

B: Well, to tell you the truth, I wasn't sure if I should do it or not, because it's dangerous to compete with yourself. And a picture like *Picture Show*, which got such big reactions from the press and public, it's hard to go back and do it again, because inevitably it's going to be compared to the first one.

H: Is *Texasville* more a sequel to *Last Picture Show* the film than to the novel? Was McMurtry more influenced by the progression of the lives of the actors from *Picture Show* than he was with the characters?

B: Larry was to a degree influenced by the real actors who had played the characters in *Picture Show*. I think to a degree he was influenced by what they were like. I mean, you have to be, in particular Cybill. He had to have it in his mind to a degree at least that these people might be playing these roles. I never really discussed it with him, but I'm sure Cybill Shepherd had an effect on Jacy, and I know that many of the characters are based on people in his home town, on people that he knew, but I feel confident that some of the spin on the characters was as a result of the actors who had played them.

H: I understand that Polly Platt came down to the set of *Texasville* to visit you?

B: Well, she came down to see us, to see our daughter. She came down for a couple of days. It was nice to have her come down. It was strange. And I think it might have helped heal some of the wounds that are still there. I know Cybill and Polly had been talking before that. I mean they met while Cybill was doing "Moonlighting." They embraced, and having Polly there I think was good for my daughter—to see us there together. There is just so much that goes on between people in a relationship that it's just hard for anybody else to understand. And it's also true that the true principals in a relationship have different memories and different versions of history. It's hard sometimes to know who's right or how it really went down, or what happened. Which is what Jeff is dealing with in *Texasville*—a life that's out of hand. I think we're all dealing with that to a greater or lesser degree.

H: What was it like working with Cybill again?

B: Well, it had its difficult moments. It had its happy times. Basically, I think Cybill and I spent a lot of time like Duane and Jacy, doing the same kind of things that those characters were going through while we were making the picture. I remember we were trying to understand each other, trying to know who we were dealing with, because obviously we were dealing with different people than we had been twenty years before. Of course, that was true with all the actors and me. But with Cybill, of course, because we had such a close relationship, it was more difficult, more complicated. I think we did all right in the long run. She was very, very good in the picture, a very fine performance.

H: In your most recent book, *The Killing of the Unicorn*, you wrote that the eighties were a very difficult time for you. After Dorothy Stratten's murder you said your passion for making films had died in a certain sense.

B: I think part of it was because she had been killed right after we had finished a picture [*They All Laughed*], so you could almost say that she was killed on the picture—I was still cutting it. In some way psychologically I may have blamed the picture, and so I didn't really want to do that as an occupation. A murder is different from somebody just dying—a violent crime of that nature, the shock of it is something I guess you never really get over. Your mind adjusts to it, your body adjusts to it, I even suppose your soul adjusts to it, but some small part of you continues to reverberate. And it was such a cataclysmic event in my life that it made everything else seem unimportant, including whether or not I'd made a few good pictures or not. People said to me, "Well, you made some great pictures," but it just seemed like a lot of talk. It didn't make any difference, it didn't make me feel any better. It didn't make me feel any worse, but it didn't do anything. It had no effect and I really didn't want to work on pictures, I just closed down. I really don't know all the psychological reasons, but I didn't want to work as a director. I was going to produce some pictures, but I wasn't going to direct.

H: Did *Texasville* change that?

B: I think *Texasville* and *Mask* changed that, because I had to go to work. There was a lot of financial pressure and I specifically felt a kind of pressure to do *Mask*, because I thought it had a lot to do with Dorothy—had to do with somebody who was separated from the world by his looks. And whether you're ugly or beautiful as it turns out, the separation is the same. You feel like a freak. And I know Dorothy felt like a freak, she told me she did. Every time she walked down the street people would stop and stare at her, just like they did to Rocky. And so that was really why I did *Mask*. I feel now that I do really want to make pictures. I've regained a kind of equilibrium, and in a way I want to make pictures now more than I did in the early seventies, but I think now it's for different reasons and different motivations.

Filmography

1968   *Targets*
1971   *The Last Picture Show*
1971   *Directed by John Ford*
1972   *What's Up, Doc?*
1973   *Paper Moon*
1974   *Daisy Miller*
1975   *At Long Last Love*
1977   *Nickelodeon*
1979   *Saint Jack*
1981   *They All Laughed*
1985   *Mask*
1987   *Illegally Yours*
1990   *Texasville*
1992   *Noises Off*

DENNIS HOPPER

Art, Acting and the Suicide Chair

Dennis Hopper and I walk through the small gallery in his Frank Gehry-designed studio/loft located in the midst of the graffiti-ridden neighborhoods of Venice Beach. It was here, during the late 1950s and early 1960s, that Hopper enjoyed the vibrant, abstract expressionist beat scene when it began emerging from the back-alley coffee shops off the Venice boardwalk. "I was around taking photographs and trying to paint while guys like Claes Oldenburg, Wallace Berman and Andy Warhol were just starting here and in New York. I bought one of Andy's first soup cans for practically nothing."

Dennis Hopper is a director/actor/painter/photographer who has led many lives. To some he is known as the resilient survivor of the *Rebel Without a Cause* "curse," a phenomenon that has seen all the principal cast members of that film (James Dean, Sal Mineo and Natalie Wood) die in their prime. In fact, Dennis Hopper has repeatedly been physically, artistically and commercially resurrected more times than any other Hollywood figure. From his being blackballed as an actor in the early 1960s, to his being castigated as a director in the 1970s, to his nearly dying from a drug overdose in the early 1980s, Hopper has survived, emerging once again as a reputable artist in the 1990s.

Born in Kansas in 1936, Hopper was raised by his grandparents on a twelve-acre farm about five miles outside Dodge City. At the age of five, his grandmother took him to a movie theater where "It suddenly dawned on me that this is what the rest of the world was like outside of Kansas." As a young boy, when Hopper revealed to his estranged mother, a religious fundamentalist, that he wanted to leave Kansas and become an artist, she discouraged him, saying that such people became degenerates.

Despite his mother's opposition, Hopper pursued acting when his family moved to San Diego, and he was soon awarded a scholarship to the National Shakespeare Festival at San Diego's Old Globe Theater. At the age of nineteen, Hopper was asked to meet with Hollywood mogul Harry Cohn at Columbia Pictures. "He said he thought I was the most naturalistic actor to come along since Montgomery Clift. And I thought this guy's all right. Then he asked me what I had been doing. I said, 'Playing Shakespeare down in San Diego.' He said, 'Not anymore, I hate Shakespeare.' So basically I told him to go fuck himself."

The story circulated around Hollywood so quickly that it took someone like Jack Warner to appreciate Hopper's youthful recalcitrance. A contract with Warner Brothers led the actor to appear in such memorable films as *Rebel Without a Cause* (1955), *Giant* (1956) and *From Hell to Texas* (1958). However, Hopper found himself in trouble once again when he refused to take a line reading from director Henry Hathaway during the filming of *From Hell to Texas*. It wasn't long before no one would hire him.

In the late 1950s, Hopper moved to New York City, where he began acting in television shows, studying with Lee Strasberg, painting, hanging around the art scene and taking photographs, some of which he sold to *Vogue* and *Harper's Bazaar*. Many of these photographs were recently published in a book titled *Out of the Sixties*.

Moving back to Los Angeles in the early sixties, Hopper once more galvanized the Hollywood establishment, this time by marrying into it. His bride was Brooke Hayward, the daughter of actress Margaret Sullavan and producer Leland Hayward, both of whom loathed their son-in-law. Regardless, Hopper again proved his resilience by getting work, and this time in two Henry Hathaway westerns.

With an inkling to direct himself, the actor struggled to finance a script he had written, the first draft of what later would become

The Last Movie (1971). When that fell through, he plunged into a pattern of alcohol and drug abuse, but became hopeful again in 1968 when producer Bert Schneider offered him a chance to direct his first film, a low budget road movie titled *Easy Rider* (1969). "I made it because I wanted to show first that I could direct. I had a good eye. I had been taking lots of photographs and for me directing was it. And I was also confident I could make a film outside the system that could make money. You know, I felt that maybe I could create a type of low-budget, nonstudio film that would establish me. After that I never thought I could be thrown out again."

Grossing millions of dollars, *Easy Rider* proved to be a phenomenal success. "I never thought it would break ground like it did," says Hopper, referring to the slew of successful low budget independent films that were released afterwards. "You know, the success and interest it generated allowed people like Bert Schneider to go on and make films like *The Last Picture Show* (1971) and *Five Easy Pieces* (1971). It became a very special time."

Asked whether he thinks *Easy Rider* acted as a catalyst for a new Hollywood Golden Age, Hopper replies, "Not for me. It was all downhill after *Easy Rider* [laughs]." Based on the success of that film, Hopper made *The Last Movie*, an experimental feature about the medium of film itself. "The movie pissed off so many people that I just said 'fuck it' and got stoned."

Once again the director found himself an outcast. This time he moved to Taos, New Mexico, and began painting and taking drugs. However, through the seventies he continued acting in films, most notably Wim Wender's *The American Friend* (1977) and two extraordinary Vietnam war films, the first to deal seriously with the subject: Henry Jaglom's *Tracks* (1976) and Francis Coppola's *Apocalypse Now* (1979).

In 1980 Hopper was given another chance to work behind the camera when the director of the low budget film he was starring in left the project. But that film, *Out of the Blue* (1980), a dark look at an incestuous relationship between a father and daughter, was released unnoticed, sinking Hopper further into depression. Now indulging in all forms of substance abuse, he reached his nadir in 1984 and was admitted to the psychiatric ward of Cedars-Sinai Hospital in Los Angeles. After his release was secured by friend and former producer Bert Schneider, Hopper once more demonstrated his resilience by working right away. In 1986 he frightened audiences with his lurid portrayal of the obscene, drug-warped Frank Booth in David Lynch's *Blue Velvet*, and the following year he was nominated for an Academy Award for his performance as an alcoholic father in *Hoosiers* (1987). The year after that he was given the opportunity to direct *Colors* (1988), a stirring look at gangs and drug-related violence in south central Los Angeles. Most recently, Hopper has received critical praise for his latest directorial endeavor, *The Hot Spot* (1990), a romantic thriller set in the heat of southern Texas. "I hope I can direct for a while now. It's the only thing I really want to do."

Hopper continues to lead me through his gallery, showing me an abstract graffiti painting he did while in a drug-induced state of mind in Taos. "I call this one 'The Saint Patty's Day Massacre,' " he says, referring to the blotches of bright green paint that seem to float above the sprayed graffiti lines.

HICKENLOOPER: I'd like to go back to when you first began collecting art in the late fifties, before you started painting your-self. You bought Warhol and Lichtenstein and you were aware of Rauschenberg very early on when they were relatively unknown. Then you became involved with the Abstract Expressionists, Wallace Berman, Ed Kienholz. How did you get involved with this movement and what did it mean to you at the time?

HOPPER: When I started out as an actor at the Old Globe Theater in San Diego, I was a kid, thirteen, doing Shakespeare. Then when I became a professional actor at eighteen I went under contract at Warner Brothers. I ran into James Dean and did two films with him, and he gave me a book to read called *Six Lessons in Acting* by Richard Boeslavsky, which was an offspring of Stanislavski.

Also Dean and I discussed the fact that we both wanted to direct, so he said to me that I should start taking still pictures. At least you can learn how to compose that way. So I started running around with a camera and I started going to art galleries. Also at this time I suddenly realized that I was in an interpretive area as an actor. I was doing somebody else's screenplay and there was a director there telling me how to do it. So at best I could call myself an artist, but at best I was still interpreting. Having gone to the galleries—

some people become golf bums, tennis bums, beach bums—I became a gallery bum.

H: At the Ferus Gallery?

DH: Yeah, Ferus Gallery was a big hangout of mine. So I realized I was an interpretive artist. But a fine artist was not an interpretive artist because he was creating something. He was creating a one-of-a-kind thing in his special view. So that's how I got involved in art. And at that time the Americans were Abstract Expressionists. We had always emulated the Europeans before that. We had painted landscapes like the Europeans, but then suddenly with Abstract Expressionism we had an art form of our own where we used paint as paint while trying to formulate the tree or an apple, but we used it as paint. You know, Jackson Pollock, Franz Klein, Adolf Gottlieb, Motherwell, de Kooning. Then there was a third generation of Abstract Expressionists, and after that suddenly everybody was looking at the soup can of Andy Warhol, the Coca-Cola bottle of Jasper Johns, and we had another art form which was totally American. I happened to be at the beginning of that. Then we went into an assemblage period, which was the part I was part of here in Venice, which was Wallace Berman, Ed Kienholz, Llyn Foulkes, George Herms and that group. So that was my involvement in the art scene at that time.

H: Was there any kind of spontaneity to this movement, or were the Abstract Expressionists aware of the movements that preceded them?

DH: Yeah, I think it's all coming out of history. I think you follow history to a certain place as an artist and then that's your stepping stone. You go on to the next step, and generally speaking there are only so many people who make that step and the rest go back to other traditional, easier, ways.

H: I read that in Abstract Expressionism the process of creating art takes on more significance than the objects created. Would one be able to apply this theory to your film *The Last Movie*? Did the making of that film become more important than the end result?

DH: I like your statement, but, I think that statement would apply more to painting. I think the act of an action painting is not the same as the act of making an action movie like *The Last Movie*. *The Last Movie*, I felt, was like an expressionist painting. But the act of making a movie is very tedious. There are so many technical problems. It's not like action painting—taking some paint and throwing it against the canvas and liking the way it hits, the way it drips, and going on to the next painting. That's a different kind of expression than a film, which is a very tedious kind of operation. Even though, I used expressionist terms in *The Last Movie*—where I showed the leader running out or I showed the clap board hitting—to keep saying "This is a film" the same way an Abstract Expressionist says "I'm dealing with paint here, folks. This is not a picture of a tree. This is paint." So I said, "I'm dealing with film." If anybody ever got close to becoming involved in some sort of opiate of "Oh, I'm going to kick back, I'm going to fall into this movie" I kept saying, "No you're not. This is a movie. You're dealing with film."

H: In *The Last Movie*, then, you were trying to make the audience constantly aware of the fact that they were watching a film. Do you think one can successfully critique film with film, or is that an impossibility?

DH: I think it's impossible really. I mean, I like *The Last Movie*. But *The Last Movie* is something that maybe you do once in your life, but most people probably wouldn't [laughs]. It's sort of a one-shot thing, and it's sort of a young idea of dealing with film— you're going to break tradition and you're going to give everybody the artistic finger.

H: You mentioned James Dean. He was said to have taken method acting to an extreme, yet you admire his approach very much. After Dean died you went to New York and studied with Lee Strasberg. How did your studies with Strasberg affect you personally and as an actor?

DH: Dean told me not to go study with Strasberg. He felt that if I just learned how to do things and not how to show them, then I had enough natural talent to get by. But when he died I felt a little

lost and I went immediately to New York and studied with Strasberg. He had a tremendous effect on me. First of all, he never told
you anything really. He'd sit in his class and watch you. And you
learned by just being there. Mostly we did exercises with sense
memory, and eventually if you got through your sense memories
properly in a couple of years, you'd try an emotional memory. But
he was a very quiet guy and we'd do scenes and he would criticize
the scenes. He was a very strange man. I'd get in the elevator with
him every morning for almost five years and say, "Good morning,
Mr. Strasberg." I never got a good morning back from him during
those five years. He'd have his newspaper and he'd clear his throat.
He'd never speak to anyone until class began, then he spoke,
talked, did his thing, but when class was over he was back into
himself. He was a very tough guy. He was strict. I saw three-quar-
ters of the people studying with him taken off the stage in a straitjacket to the booby house or funny farm when they suddenly hit
their emotional memory.

H: As an actor you were perceived as stubborn. There's a famous
story about you and Henry Hathaway on the set of *From Hell to
Texas* when you refused to accept a line reading from him. Consequently, you were blacklisted from Hollywood, yet you still desired
to be truthful to Dean's legacy as an actor, and at some point you
became obsessed with making the performance real.

DH: It was always my obsession to try and make the characters
real, from the time I was very young. I mean, the first two great
performances I saw were all in one week. I saw Montgomery Clift
in *A Place in the Sun* and I saw Marlon Brando in *Viva Zapata*. I had
never seen them act before, and it really twisted my head around.
Before that I had been doing Shakespeare. I had been doing classical theater, so I had been impressed with Orson Welles and John
Barrymore and a very broad kind of acting. And to see Montgomery Clift and Brando, who were so subtle and so real, it just blew
me away. Then to do two films with Dean and see him work, and
then to see Brando from a distance in *Sayonara* when I was at
Warner Brothers, I tried to get closer and closer to that kind of
approach. That's when I got into trouble with Hathaway, and that's
one of the things that forced me then to go to New York and study
with Strasberg, which I did for five years. Then I came back and I

did another film for Hathaway years later, *The Sons of Katie Elder*, and then *True Grit*. Actually, I worked for Hathaway more than I did for any other director.

H: In the eighties there was a backlash against the dark side of the sixties drug movement, the consequences of which you survived. Although you never renounced or regretted having undergone the extremes of those experiences, do you feel now that there was a clear alternative, or were they necessary for your development as an artist?

DH: I would hate to say that people need drugs to create. You know, I used drugs for years under the delusion that it was okay because I was an artist. It was okay for me to drink because I was an artist. You know, those other people were obviously drunks and alcoholics, but I was an artist. But I was a drug addict and an alcoholic. I may have been an artist and that is yet to be seen, but I was definitely a drug addict and an alcoholic, and unfortunately my role models were people who drank and took drugs, from van Gogh to John Barrymore to W.C. Fields, all the great writers and musicians, Edgar Allan Poe, Baudelaire, Charlie Parker. It certainly can't do anything but get in the way. You know, I used to cite van Gogh by saying "Well, van Gogh said he drank for a whole summer to find that yellow." He probably couldn't find the brush for a whole summer!

The great actors generally don't take drugs. You look at Meryl Streep—she has never taken drugs. She's a great actress. You certainly don't need drugs and alcohol to act or to paint or to create, but I can't say that some of us lesser talents don't need those things perhaps to push ourselves over and to give ourselves an edge. That may be possible, but it's the ones without talent like myself who have to do it the hard way. Because anybody with a mind would see that all it does is interfere with your life and make your life unmanageable, make you impossible to work with because you're a Jekyll/Hyde personality that people can't deal with. So it doesn't matter how talented you are. Generally, the only people you hurt are the people who are close to you, who love you. So it's a disastrous kind of life no matter what you're into. It's not a way to go. I'm lucky to be alive.

H: The ethics of the eighties seem to have been a renunciation of everything the sixties were about. Is this regrettable, or is it a lesson of the sixties?

DH: I've always felt in a free society that both extremes are good, that they keep checking and balancing each other; that when we get too conservative there will be a backlash that will come back and do something again, and then there will be the conservatives that will come back, and these things will hopefully go back and forth forever and will keep the checks and balances in line. I think right now in a lot of ways we're a very healthy society, but I don't think we would have necessarily gotten here without the sixties. So I don't regret the sixties, and yet I don't dislike the eighties or nineties. I'm very happy just to be around.

H: During the lowest point during your Taos period in the early eighties, you had a photography exhibit at Rice University. There you announced that you were going to blow yourself up. What lead you to this stunt?

H: Well, actually I did blow myself up. I had this photography exhibit at Rice University, a retrospective, and I did this sort of media show where I refused to appear in front of the people, but I had a closed circuit television video where they could see me in another room. And if they really wanted to see me, they had to be bused—some of my political upbringing—to the Big H Speedway, a racetrack on the outskirts of Houston, Texas, to watch me do the Russian Suicide Chair, which is when you put twenty sticks of dynamite around you and you sit in the middle of a chair and proceed to set the dynamite off [laughs]. With any luck at all you're completely covered in this great nebula of flames, but you're in a vacuum. It's like being in the center of a hurricane.

H: Did you take death into consideration?

DH: [laughs] Yeah, I did actually. But it worked. Dynamite won't blow in on itself. So it creates a vacuum. If three of the sticks of dynamite don't go off on one side of the chair, you'll be sucked out and killed. But if they all go off at once, they create this ball of fire and you sit there and you're okay. So I was out there and it worked [laughs].

H: You once said that you believed in predestination. You felt that something protects the creative person until he reaches his creative potential. Now with *Easy Rider* twenty years behind you, do you think you have reached your creative potential?

DH: I've probably passed it [laughs]. I feel very vulnerable these days. No, that whole idea was sort of shattered for me when James Dean died. Dean had so much talent and had so many things he wanted to do, and certainly he hadn't reached his potential on any level, but then it's strange because when I go into foreign countries, there's no country that I can go into when there aren't three people who are always there. There's Bogart, Monroe and Dean. They're either in the toilet, or in the disco, or on the street in the store windows. They're always present and that's a bizarre kind of phenomenon. So Dean with all his talent is still in there swinging, but I find it unfortunate that he died so young.

H: "Give me the wisdom to accept those things I cannot change." Someone said that to you once and you said, "Fuck that, it's bull-shit." Now that you're working in commercial filmmaking, you're back in the mainstream, do you still believe that you can make changes?

DH: What you're talking about is the Serenity Prayer. I think that you can make changes, but you just have to do it on a day-by-day basis. I mean, you can make changes and there are certain things you can't change. There are certain things you don't want to change because it's sort of like having a canvas and priming the canvas white. You can prime the canvas a different color. You can prime it blue, you can prime it black, you can prime it a lot of different colors, but white seems to be pretty good. So I think there are certain parameters that one should accept. I mean film, a lot of people ask why films have to be an hour and a half to two hours to be commercial. Well, it's very simple, because if it's any longer than that you can't sell the popcorn. I mean you have to take this into consideration, because then your film is not going to be distributed because your commercial people make eighty to ninety percent of their money not off the film. They make it off the people at the concession stand, so if you make a movie that's two hours and twenty minutes long, it cuts out a lot of their business, so they're not going to show your movie. And if you make your movies and you're just going to show them to your friends, then figure out some way to finance them and not bother with commercial films where you're going to go out and try to make commercial films and have people see them and you use the kind of money that it unfortunately costs to make movies. I mean, we're dealing with a lot of money for any kind of business. And at best it's a gamble. It's not like building a building that's going to be there. So there is that kind of responsibility that as filmmakers we have to not only be artists, but to think about the responsibilities we have to people who are putting up that kind of money to make movies.

H: Recently Twelve Trees Press published a book of your photographs that you took when you were between the ages of twenty-five and thirty-one. You have candid photographs of Andy Warhol, Martin Luther King, Jr., and Paul Newman, among many others. When you were taking these photos what was more important to you, the subject matter or the composition?

DH: Probably both. But when I was taking those three people that you were talking about, probably the subject matter was more important than the composition. Generally speaking, I would say the composition is more important than the subject of my photographs.

H: How was photography fundamental in your development as a filmmaker?

DH: Well, I felt that I learned to compose. I shot only in black and white and I think that that's a really good idea, even though we only make films in color. Not to think in color, but to think in what your subject matter is actually. That's how you compose a picture. I did a lot of things which I called abstract reality—walls and things that I shot flat on so they had no depth of field. And I always shot in black and white, so I was never looking for the color—whether there's a red there, a yellow there, a blue there. I was looking to see if the subject matter and the composition would hold, and if it will hold in black and white then the color can only add to it. But I find an awful lot of people seem to be filming just to get the colors. And they don't seem to have enough subject matter. I also never cropped my photographs, because you cannot crop movie film—you can, but it's really expensive. You have to learn to compose in a full frame. I also played with various lenses.

H: When you came to direct *Colors*, it had been a number of years since you had played "auteur."

DH: Since *Out of the Blue* in 1980, I think. About eight years, yeah.

H: Were you nervous about going back to it?

DH: No, I'd been ready for a long time, and in point of fact I'd been very close on a number of occasions. But you know that old story.

H: How did *Colors* finally happen?

DH: Well, Sean Penn asked the studio that I direct it. I had met him through his brother Chris while I was starring in *Rumble Fish*. We had a mutual liking for Charles Bukowski, and later when Sean was asked to star in *Barfly*, he asked that I direct it. When I wasn't allowed to, he dropped out of the project. So when *Colors* came up he asked that I direct that too, and Orion, which knew my work from *Hoosiers*, agreed. In fact, that counted more than my having directed *Easy Rider*. Most of them probably hadn't even seen it.

H: I understand that after your first meeting with Orion they were outraged because you wanted to change the script.

DH: Well, their original concept was stupid. It was about a couple of cops in Chicago who try to bust a gang for selling a narcotic used in cough syrup. I said, "This is idiotic, man. Why don't you guys make this real. Make it cocaine, make it crack, make it about gangs in L.A. Make it real." They got nervous because Hollywood doesn't like movies about drugs. I think *Easy Rider* may have been one of the few exceptions. But anyway, Sean got another writer and we changed it.

H: On your first day of shooting, were you ever thinking about *Easy Rider*?

DH: No no no. *Easy Rider* was a much less complex film. It was all straight cuts. *Colors* was a lot more complicated—the logistics, the people, the special effects. It was a much bigger budget than *Easy Rider*, and a lot more complicated. *Easy Rider* was as easy as a motorcycle trip. But what a trip it was [laughs].

Filmography (as director)

1969	*Easy Rider*
1971	*The Last Movie*
1980	*Out of the Blue*
1988	*Colors*
1989	*Back Track*
1990	*The Hot Spot*

MICHAEL CIMINO
A Final Word

After nine years of self-imposed exile from the media, Michael Cimino agreed to meet me for lunch on a humid June afternoon on New York's upper East Side to discuss *Heaven's Gate* (1980), the most controversial film of his career, perhaps even in the history of motion pictures.

Born in 1943, Cimino has led a very private existence, once confessing, "I have no personal life outside of my work." After graduating from Yale University with an MFA and a passion for architecture, he jumped into the frenzied world of Madison Avenue advertising and emerged a star director of television commercials. This led to a number of shared movie writing assignments: *Silent Running* (1972), a highly acclaimed science-fiction thriller about environmental preservation, and the Clint Eastwood vehicle, *Magnum Force* (1973). He also did some uncredited writing on Bette Midler's *The Rose* (1979) in addition to having Norman Jewison produce his screenplay for *The Dogs of War* (1980).

In 1974 Cimino made his directorial debut in one of Clint Eastwood's earliest motion picture successes, *Thunderbolt and Lightfoot*. Cimino, however, did not attract recognition as a director until four years later when he scripted and directed his most acclaimed work, and the first major Hollywood film to seriously portray the Vietnam War, *The Deer Hunter* (1978). Winning Academy Awards for Best Picture and Best Director and also the New

York Film Critics Award, *The Deer Hunter* overcame the movie industry's longstanding timidity toward the taboo subject of Vietnam. Though the film drew controversy over its depiction of the Viet Cong, the story, in addition to the highly charged performances of Robert De Niro, Christopher Walken and John Savage, worked to create a powerful indictment of war, establishing the director as a major new talent.

When Cimino arrives for lunch he is accompanied by Joann Carelli, his friend and associate of almost twenty years. Having graduated from associate producer on *The Deer Hunter* to producer on *Heaven's Gate*, Carelli is regarded as an unpretentious businesswoman. Immediately, I am reminded of Steven Bach's book *Final Cut*. An immensely popular bestseller, this controversial account of the making of *Heaven's Gate* chronicles the former United Artists executive's working relationship with Cimino and Carelli during the production of one of the American cinema's most scrutinized and reviled films. According to Bach, the director had almost every major studio wooing his talents after finishing *The Deer Hunter*. Finally, he chose United Artists to embark on the third directorial effort of his career, *Heaven's Gate*. Approved by the new executive regime that included Bach, Cimino's film went into production in the spring of 1978. Within the first few weeks of shooting tensions grew between the director and studio. Cimino, a supposed Randian perfectionist, required more money and time to capture his vision on celluloid. A year behind schedule, the film's budget soared from twelve to forty million dollars, at that time the most costly film in history, drawing considerable media fire from newspapers around the world. Following its disastrous first run in New York, the film, according to Bach, was directly responsible for the demise of United Artists and a number of careers.

Despite the negative press that followed *Heaven's Gate* well into the middle of the eighties, the film slowly built up a popular following abroad. French and British critics have recently revived it, calling it an unrecognized American masterpiece and comparing Cimino to such underappreciated geniuses as Orson Welles. But why was *Heaven's Gate* such a failure in the United States? Were American audiences unable to cope with its unusual dramatic pace? Was the film ahead of its time? Was the film just bad? Or did the advance negative press destroy *Heaven's Gate* before it had a chance? Bach himself admits to the possibility of some of these factors, noting that several of the major film critics revised their negative opinions when a truncated version of the movie was distributed nationwide following the studio's withdrawal of the original three-and-a-half-hour epic from its New York engagement.

HICKENLOOPER: Lets first go back to a much earlier time in your life. I understand you received an MFA from Yale. Was it then you decided to become a filmmaker?

CIMINO: I'm not sure, but it was probably during the last two years at Yale. Precisely when or how I don't recall.

H: I read that you were a painter.

C: Well, I very much wanted to be an architect and I had painted and I had been studying art history. And then somehow the idea of making movies took hold.

H: When did you first get into the business?

C: I made my first picture in '73. Prior to that I had worked on a couple of screenplays, which I began to do in order to make movies. I had no real desire to be a screenwriter, but at that time that was a way of beginning.

H: Was that in New York or L.A.?

C: I think the first screenplay that I wrote was in Fordville, North Dakota.

H: Was that *The Fountainhead?*

C: It was a picture which hasn't been made. The *Fountainhead* was actually done between *Thunderbolt and Lightfoot* and *The Deer Hunter.* Had that been made I would never have done *The Deer Hunter.*

H: Is that a project you would still like to do?

C: Very much. I've gone to see it [the original film] a couple of times in a commercial cinema, and it's always been completely sold out. A very interesting crowd—every age range, men and women. It's enormously popular. As you probably know, the book has been in continuous publication throughout the world since 1943. The movie was made in 1948. I think it's even more interesting today.

H: Is that because of Ayn Rand's philosophy?

C: I don't know if it's that so much as the notion of what, perhaps, is inexplicably tied to her philosophy—the notion of this character Roark who stands for a certain kind of excellence and pride in work. And that's something that has largely gone out of this country. It's one of the reasons we make such dreadful automobiles, and we have to go to another country to learn to make something we once made better than anyone else. We had to go to Japan or Europe. It's clear Americans don't want American automobiles.

H: What do you think causes that cynicism or lack of excellence?

C: I don't know. At one point we really were a country of craftsmen. I think there was a general pride in work, across the board. And I don't think it mattered much if you were making farm implements or houses or movies or automobiles or whatever. There was a satisfaction in doing the job better than anyone else could do it. I don't know if people derive as much satisfaction from their work as they used to. I think doing a job well was a reward unto itself at one time, quite apart from any compensation or rewards that were received.

H: Does the same apply to Hollywood?

C: It's difficult to say. I'm not the kind of person who jumps to easy conclusions about Hollywood. Hollywood moves in cycles. Whether we'll ever see a year like 1939 again is hard to say. That was the most incredible year in the history of the movies. John Ford made three movies and Victor Fleming made *Gone With the Wind* and *The Wizard of Oz*. It was absolutely astonishing. The commitment to excellence in every department is so apparent. Every-thing, the writing, the casting, the props, the horsemanship. It's professional filmmaking at its best.

H: Getting back to your writing—when you're working on a script, what is your average day like?

C: Basically, it's seven days a week, and if I'm working on a screenplay myself, then I tend to start work very early. I like to start before the sun is up, so I'll start around five in the morning. I try to set a general quota of so many pages a day, which you end up not sticking to, because some days you do more than you think and some days you do zero, but it averages out. It's exhausting, but in many ways it's also very pleasant.

H: Where do you start?

C: I kind of plunge ahead and let the characters take me through the story, through the process. With something like *Heaven's Gate* there's a considerable amount of research as well. Once the char-acters start working, once they're really on their feet, it can get to be downright fun. There are times when I find myself laughing at things that they do. It seems that they're doing these things in spite of you, that they have this life of their own. You're constantly sur-prised at what they're capable of.

H: Early in your career you were a successful screenwriter. How do you think your talent as a screenwriter influences your directing?

C: I never really thought of myself as a writer to begin with, and in many ways I still don't. It was something that was necessary in order to make movies, and then ten or twelve years later you find you've written ten or twenty screenplays. But certainly it has an effect when you're making a picture. It's easier, for one thing. If you've written the screenplay, worked on the screenplay, co-writ-ten the screenplay with someone, it's just easier to make the movie. You have that much more of it in your head. And you don't have that whole period of time where you have to acclimate yourself into the process of making a picture. You go in very easy stages from the writing to the casting to the physical stages of the picture.

The foundation for the building is already laid.

H: Do you improvise or change dialogue much?

C: You really have to qualify what you mean by improvisation. Do you mean improvising lines? Improvising the structure of the scene? Improvising the structure of the story? Changing what you have or putting in what you don't have? A lot of people approach shooting with an unfinished screenplay. You come to a place in the screenplay where it says, "Now you come to the biggest, best, most exciting swordfight in the history of the movies." Obviously what you put on screen would be something you either improvise on the day of shooting or something that you planned on the day before shooting in each case. It's no longer an improvisation. What does one really mean by improvisation?

H: Do you rehearse with your actors?

C: Yes. There are so many different ways that people approach the work. Some people work with very carefully planned story-boards, where every frame is predetermined. All that remains is to fit the living images into what has been drawn out in the two-dimensional storyboard. That's become very common. Some people need to know in advance of creating the image what the image needs to be or wants to be, and it's a perfectly valid way of making movies. There are also other approaches.

H: What was your approach to *Heaven's Gate?*

C: What I try to do is spend a great deal of time finding locations, and that's probably one of the more enjoyable aspects of making movies. You're free of the daily pressure of shooting, and yet you have quite a lot to accomplish and you're free to explore. If you're simultaneously working on the screenplay, then that work of preparation has a way of helping the screenplay. Once one has selected the locations and determined what sets one is building and what the physical movie is going to look like, then I like to work with floorplans, rather than storyboards. And after we rehearse the scene, and we block the scene in a rehearsal, based on how the space in the hall came to approximate the real location, that's when I begin to lay out my shots and make my shot list, based on catching the choreography of movement that happens in the rehearsal process. If we have a battle scene or a scene that involves dancing, some kind of physical action, my tendency is to try and work those things out so that they happen in real time. For example, the waltz or the roller-skating sequences in *Heaven's Gate*, they are choreographed to happen in the amount of time that is on the screen. There's a minute and half of "The Blue Danube" at the beginning, and if you had only one camera, a videotape camera, and you were a newsman, you could cover that scene as if it were a real event. It then allowed the actors and the music to play from beginning to end. All that dialogue and all that action would happen within that minute and a half or two minutes. It gives me the opportunity to cover the same event in an almost documentary manner. You can combine the large, formal compositions with a very free, very loose second component of cameras, so you have these very formal grand shots combined with very free, almost improvised activity.

H: Why do you like [scenes to play out in] real time? Why did you do that in the graduation scene of *Heaven's Gate*?

C: It's probably due to my lack of formal training in movies. If I knew better I'd probably do it the other way. What it does do, however, is allow the local people to participate in the real event, such as the wedding in *Deer Hunter* or the roller-skating in *Heaven's Gate*. It's a less theatrical enterprise for them. It's a real roller-skating party, it's a real wedding. They feel less like they're performing. They don't feel quite such a heavy burden to act, because they are performing real tasks in real time.

H: The graduation scene bothered a lot of critics. Stanley Kauffman said you could have done in five minutes what you did in twenty. As a whole, how is that graduation scene related to the rest of the film?

C: What do you think it is?

H: Theoretically, it might allow one to sympathize more with the Kristofferson character. He's a blue blood from Harvard yet he goes off to help the immigrants. He appears to be philanthropic.

C: Would you like the movie as much without it?

H: I don't know. I haven't seen the film without it. However, aesthetically I like it. It's like looking at a painting for an extended length of time.

C: Personally, I wouldn't have liked the film without it. If people say something works or it doesn't work, you have to ask what they mean. Something is being said, clearly, or it wouldn't be in the movie. There are speeches of quite some length that are saying something. You might listen to the dialogue and say, "I don't agree with it, or it's unnecessary, or it's untrue or it's not effective dramatically," or whatever. But to simply say it doesn't work, that isn't sufficient. The country was still in what one would call the post–Civil War period, and there was a certain sentiment in the eastern establishment about what the future of America was to be, about class responsibility. Those speeches were derived largely from actual commencement speeches that were made at that time, and they expressed attitudes which people genuinely felt at that time. You can say that what those people felt had no merit—

H: Maybe to Americans, because European critics really loved that scene.

C: Maybe it has to do with the fact that people would rather watch than listen, or listen and watch. One thing is clear, and that is that the real history of the American West, which is so incredibly rich, has barely been scratched by the movies. The greatest stories about the West have yet to be told in film. And the amount of information available is astonishing. In every historian's files are tens of thousands of pictures of the West as it actually was, and so few movies have approximated that reality. One can say it's entirely unnecessary . . .

H: Is *Heaven's Gate* a Western?

C: It's certainly more that than anything else. There was a great attempt to reflect the reality of that time as documented by hundreds of photographers—the social reality of the time, the political reality of the time—in a story about three people. And whether or not a speech can be made in thirty seconds as opposed to a minute and a half is debatable. When we talk of the West we often act as if the West sprang intact from so many Westerns as we've seen it. But actually the West was something that occurred because of a migration from the East.

H: You were praised for your visual accuracy, but you were criticized for taking liberty with history. The Averill character wasn't actually a sheriff, he was a postmaster.

C: On the one hand people are saying we don't like what you've done because there's too much accuracy, then at the same time they're saying there's not enough accuracy. Which is it? In point of fact there was this army of mercenaries—they posed for a photograph which you can find in the Wyoming Historical Society. You can find a copy of the telegram that Canton got, you can find all the information about the death list and how much the mercenaries were paid. It's all there for anybody to check if they care to take the time to do it. We made *Year of the Dragon* and they talked about the improbability of these vast armies in the middle of Burma or the jungles of Thailand. Well, in fact we know now, they've finally admitted that they do exist. And what we talked about three or four years ago, they're now proclaiming that it's new news. Well, it's not new news, it's old news, and there are quite a few people who knew this long ago. It's a question of scholarship.

Even with Lean, who's as meticulous a filmmaker as can be, he's taken certain liberties with the life of T.E. Lawrence to make it work in screen terms. There are many Englishmen who take great exception to the film version of *Lawrence of Arabia*, saying, "He wasn't like that" or, "I don't agree with it." And surely one always takes a certain amount of dramatic license with any film subject, but for the most part there's an accurate informing spirit. And I think if a journalist wants to talk about that aspect of the movie, I think surely a work which has involved so many people's effort over so many years deserves at least a commensurate amount of scholarship for no other reason than to double-check the facts. To say, "Okay, they got all the facts right, I don't agree with how they've used them, I don't agree with what they did dramatically, but they certainly did their homework, they know what happened at this time. I don't like the way they put it together but it is accurate." I think that should be the least that's required of a criticism that moves in that direction. Certainly you're not obligated to do that, but if you choose that as the territory you're going to deal with, then you have a natural obligation.

H: How did you first learn about the Johnson County War?

C: We were researching the history of barbed wire, the development of barbed wire in the West, which is a fascinating story in itself, and lo and behold there was the Johnson County war in the middle of this saga about barbed wire.

H: What particularly attracted you to that story and that period?

C: Well, I think for one thing the fact that there was a decision taken to wipe out an entire group of people. That there was a death list, people's names were on it, and mercenaries were hired and paid to execute these people. They had the sanction of certain elements of the government, both state and federal. That's astonishing. It's something one thinks about perhaps in connection with Latin America or the drug wars now. But we don't think of that kind of activity with respect to this country, and the fact that class difference did play a part in it. The membership of the Wyoming Cattleman's Association is surprising. And once you look it up and see who was a member of this club, it's really rather fascinating. And who was on the other side. It's just an astonishing moment in American history. Whether it's a major or minor turning point is arguable, but it is a turning point. And something surely worth having a movie made about it.

H: It's been said that *Heaven's Gate* was dark, and that it showed America was not a land which welcomed the dispossessed and the unfortunate, as opposed to *The Deer Hunter*, which implied that America's idealistic qualities can revitalize the war-weary.

C: What do you think was the difference?

H: *Heaven's Gate* said America is a very avaricious nation, and that there's no hope for the poor.

C: Is *The Searchers*—because Ethan loses everything in the end—
a movie which has a bleak outlook for America? I don't think so.
One doesn't look at *The Searchers* and come away with a bitter taste
about the country. Even though this man suffered the loss of everything that he loved. In fact the door is shut on him at the end and
everything goes black. But we don't use his personal tragedy to
characterize Ford's view about America. One has to distinguish
between a loving view of a country, and what specific characters
represent. If one thinks about it, most of Ford's films have a very
bleak ending, most of the characters end up losing, whether its
They Were Expendable, The Informer, whatever. I don't think that you
can infer, from what happens to one character, what somebody's
attitude is.

H: Can you tell me something about your collaboration with
cinematographer Vilmos Zsigmond. What kind of mood or look
were you trying to achieve?

C: We really wanted to give people a picture of the West that
they had never seen. We wanted to give them the same kind of
vitality that was in all the pictures we looked through of the real
West, because they were so astonishingly different from what we
had seen in movies. We wanted to communicate a richness of imagery that one rarely sees in Westerns. One is used to very bleak
landscapes and sparsely peopled towns, and the photographs of
the period communicate such a different image. We wanted this
incredible bustling activity and this explosion of energy, and a
sense of something about to be born. And a different landscape
entirely.

H: *Heaven's Gate* has been called a poetic film rich with symbolism. One writer spoke of your obsession with circular shapes. Is
symbolism something you're conscious of while directing?

C: I don't think it's something that one is so consciously aware
of. I think certain inner necessities compel you to make certain
decisions. And after the fact you find a kind of a pattern. But then
again, as the Plains Indians said, life is a circle. I think it's really an
after-the-fact process that takes place. I think you do what you do
because of what you feel is the dramatic necessity of the story,

telling a story about people and being as true as you can to that story and those characters.

H: *Heaven's Gate* may be one of the most controversial films in the history of movies. While American critics said it was incoherent, many European critics thought it was one of the greatest films of all time. How does this affect you, and how does it help you gauge the value of your own work?

C: Whether it's painting, architecture, music, filmmaking, it takes a tough spirit to weather the critical storms, and to weather both praise and criticism. It's easy to by undone by both. The answer is, it's a hard job to steer a middle course, and to do your best and not to be unduly influenced by either extreme. It's a discipline you have to work at.

H: Pauline Kael came to your defense to some degree and wrote that when *Heaven's Gate* was released the press was ready to ambush you because of your success with *The Deer Hunter*. Do you think that's true?

C: I don't really know. I'm still really puzzled by the passion of the response. I don't really understand it.

H: Some criticized United Artists for the financial failure of the movie, saying they didn't publicize it enough. What do you think?

C: I think any studio can have an enormous influence on a movie by just sticking with it. The advance word always comes from within the studio. I think there's a big difference in public perception of a movie (and I include the critics in this) if the studio is behind a picture. *Full Metal Jacket* is an example of that; Warners stayed by it and it made a tremendous difference. *Reds* is another example—Paramount stayed behind it.

H: Did you feel responsible for the demise of United Artists?

C: If you're referring to the Bach book, I found that account of my film sensationalistic and inaccurate. I made *Heaven's Gate* the best way I knew how. It cost what it cost because that was what was needed to make the film. Now forty million dollars is considered standard.

H: Do you think the failure of the film made it difficult for other directors to retain creative control with the same kind of free rein they had in the seventies?

C: It certainly made it difficult for me.

D: Do you have any particular influences? Filmmakers, painters, architects?

C: I think that among them, Ford and Visconti and Kurosawa have achieved some pretty sublime heights.

H: Is there a film you look at over and over again?

C: Certainly Ford's *They Were Expendable*. I think it's one of the best films ever made about World War II. I think Visconti's *The Leopard* is exquisite in every way. And I think that in this country, certainly, Frank Lloyd Wright and Louis Sullivan—it would be impossible to be in the visual arts and not be influenced by those giants. I think they're major forces in American life. They embody a uniquely American point of view.

H: What do you think is the difference between American audiences and European audiences? Do you think European audiences appreciate a film's aesthetics more? American audiences seem obsessed by story.

C: I don't think so. I think that Americans are quite capable of appreciating anything Europeans are capable of appreciating. I think that perhaps we are a bit more easily led in our opinions. I think we are a bit more swayed because we have such a massive media apparatus. I think that given the chance, there is no reason that American audiences can't appreciate anything a European audience can appreciate. With movies all over the world you can see the same reaction to scenes in a dozen different languages. I don't think it's a question of different sensibilities. I think it's a question of allowing the audience to come to something as open as possible, to letting the audience make up its own mind.

H: Some filmmakers blame the studios for underestimating the audience, aiming for the lowest common denominator.

C: I don't think that people go the movies seeking out the lowest common denominator. I think they go to be entertained, to see something that's interesting. They certainly are not a mob in search of the lowest common denominator. They're in search of unique experience.

H: It's kind of a vicious circle. The audience doesn't appreciate quality entertainment because the studio won't give it to them, and the studio won't give it to them because they don't appreciate it.

C: Well, we keep trying. Or as Strother Martin said in Sam [Peckinpah]'s movie [*The Wild Bunch*], "We'll do better next time."

Filmography (as director)

1974   *Thunderbolt and Lightfoot*
1978   *The Deer Hunter*
1980   *Heaven's Gate*
1985   *Year of the Dragon*
1988   *The Sicilian*
1990   *The Desperate Hours*

DAVID LYNCH
The Film Spirit

David Lynch sits down with me in Musso & Frank's Grill in Hollywood. He orders a Swiss cheese sandwich ("Real Swiss, please") on white bread with the hungry exuberance of a teenager. I am immediately struck by his friendly, nextdoor neighbor-like openness, and how incongruous it seems to a body of work that is psychologically extraordinary, and that includes such critically acclaimed films as *Eraserhead* (1976), *The Elephant Man* (1980), *Dune* (1984), *Blue Velvet* (1987), *Wild at Heart* (1990) and one of television's most talked about series, "Twin Peaks" (1990–1991).

David Lynch is not like any nextdoor neighbor you'll ever meet. Attending the Pennsylvania Academy of Fine Arts in the mid-1960s, he made his first film, a one-minute 16mm short continuously projected from one reel onto a two-dimensional screen. "I started making films out of curiosity," he says. "It was neat to see stuff move on a two-dimensional surface." One of his films, a four-minute mixture of live action and animation titled *The Alphabet* (1970), won him a grant from the American Film Institute. During his first year at AFI he made *The Grandmother* (1972), a grotesque family comedy about an introverted boy who creates himself a grandmother out of primordial ooze. His next project, *Eraserhead*, became an ambitious five-year venture that culminated in one of the most fantastically bizarre films ever made. "It was just a dream of dark, troubling things," says Lynch.

Given *Eraserhead*, Lynch might have seemed an unlikely candidate to direct mainstream Hollywood films, but fortunately a series of projects came along for which he was perfectly suited. In the late seventies, after *Eraserhead* became a cult hit on the midnight movie circuit, Lynch was suggested to Mel Brooks to direct his company's first project, *The Elephant Man*. The film, about the horribly deformed John Merrick's life in Victorian London, went on to be nominated for eight Academy Awards, including Best Direction and Best Screenplay.

"I think it was the best thing I could have possibly worked on after *Eraserhead*. I was able to find my way into the mainstream and at the same time not compromise. I don't ever want to compromise again like I did on *Dune*." In 1982, Dino De Laurentiis hired Lynch to direct *Dune* after the phenomenal critical success of *The Elephant Man*. Based on Frank Herbert's classic science fiction novel, the film had several false starts. "The whole experience was a disaster. I was lying to myself the whole way through." A sixty-million-dollar box office bust, *Dune* was Lynch's first critical failure and one that causes him great pain even today.

Two years later De Laurentiis let Lynch direct a small-budget film based on his own original screenplay. The result was *Blue Velvet*, a disturbing black-comedic melodrama starring Dennis Hopper and Kyle MacLachlan. After the failure of *Dune*, *Blue Velvet* restored Lynch's credibility with critics and at the box office. In 1990 Lynch went on to win the Cannes Film Festival's highest award, the Palm d'Or, for *Wild at Heart*, a contemporary, surreal drama about a young couple whose obsession leads them down a dangerous path of sexual self-destruction. That same year Lynch collaborated with "Hill Street Blues" writer Mark Frost on network television's strangest series, "Twin Peaks."

After just a few minutes with Lynch, one gets the impression that there is something different about him that you can't quite pinpoint. There is an elusive quality to him, perhaps in the way he articulates his ideas. One moment his thoughts will be concise and simple, then next he will start using abstractions, running off on wild tangents that at first confuse you, but then, like a collage, these different ideas create a balance that begins to make perfect sense. The way he speaks may even provide some insight into the way this highly celebrated man thinks, writes down his ideas on paper, shoots them on film, or applies them to a canvas with a brush.

HICKENLOOPER: You're on the cover of *Time* this week. What is that like?

LYNCH: Yeah, it is something. It is kind of weird too. Like my agent says, it's all downhill from here.

H: Do you feel like your image is becoming too mainstream?

L: Well, these things are all out of our control. And they do have a way of building you up and tearing you down. And it's sort of happening simultaneously for me now. Some people are kind of turning on me and others are not, so it's just a weird thing.

H: *The New York Times* wrote that "Twin Peaks" was becoming absurd for absurdity's sake, that it had reached its limits. Do you think now that you've done some impressive work, the critics are ready to tear you down?

L: Well, I'm sure it has something to do with human nature. Critics are not why you work. It's a bummer. I don't know who they are. With some I can appreciate the fact that they like my stuff and others I can see instantly why they don't. Like I said, it has nothing to do with what you're supposed to be thinking about.

H: Which is working?

L: Right.

H: I want to go back a little bit. You said in an interview that you grew up with white picket fences, beautiful trees and dreamy after-noons, but at the same time you felt frightened by something unknown.

L: I didn't feel frightened. I felt that there were mysterious things happening, but I liked that feeling very much. Mysteries are so exciting—they catch you and excite you when going forward.

H: Mysteries in life or fiction?

L: Mysteries anywhere. You know, some mysteries in fiction can sidetrack you from mysteries in life, and they are just as beguiling and wonderful. Mysteries, in general, I really love.

H: You read a book that you said was inspirational, *The Art Spirit* by Robert Henri. Would you talk a little about the book?

L: Well, somehow I got caught on this idea that, number one, it was the ultimate thing to be an artist, you know, because you were outside of a lot of things. It was a romantic sort of thing, and it was just beautiful. I started creating the art life, which was the kind of life where one would be free to work. When I was in art school, you had to drink coffee and you had to smoke cigarettes and you had to paint, that was it. If women entered the picture they were danger, because the art life is bad for marriage. Anyway, that's the art life from the art school standpoint. I know it's not so simple as all this, but it was like a beautifully romantic thing and it was conjured up from that book. It's just an inspiring book, and it just makes you love the life of a painter, which is the ultimate sort of thing.

H: You started out as a painter. What particularly appealed to you about painting?

L: Oh, everything. It's a complete world and all the ingredients are important and not one is more important than the other. They all have their balance and their way of being. When you talk to painters, you can hardly talk to them anyway, because I don't think that it's necessarily a gift with words they have. It's far away from words, but it's a certain kind of communication. At the same time they all understand the things about painting, and it's an abstraction, and that's just the world of painting.

H: Did you ever feel limited by painting? Is that why you went into film?

L: I might have at the time. Then, painting wasn't limiting at all, it was just number one! You could paint forever and never paint the perfect painting and fall in love with a new thing every week and there's no end to it, your painting is never going to die. I reached a point where I wanted to have sound and I wanted things to move, and they weren't doing that, so I got involved with film, and then with animation. Once that happened, then I fell in love with just film.

H: Once you were asked how you conceived of an idea, and you replied that you didn't think it but you felt it. Could you explain what you meant?

L: Well, I don't really know what I'm talking about, but I think there's instinct, and then there's intellectual thinking, and then there's a combination of the two which they call intuition, where you use two different things, feeling and thinking, at the same time. I think a lot of things are intuitively felt and that's just the way ideas seem to come about. You're thinking and you're feeling and all of a sudden the next thing comes along.

H: Critics say your work is rich in symbolism. Are you conscious of putting symbolic images in your work?

L: No, you're on a sort of automatic pilot. Sometimes you can do things that are smarter than you actually are and you'll capture a bigger picture than you really are perceiving, and that's the beautiful thing about intuition.

H: In *Eraserhead* how did you convey the images in your mind to the people you were working with so that they could render them on film? Was that difficult?

L: No. I must have a strange way of communicating. When I was just coming out of painting, I really couldn't talk. I did an interview once where I was unable to speak and they were shooting film of me and I froze up. The guy's questions were, I thought at the time, really dumb. He asked me all the questions before the actual interview, and I wasn't hip to the fact that he was trying to allow me to think about these things he was going to ask me again. I kind of felt that I had already answered him, so I couldn't answer him again, because that would mean I would have to be an actor. And I could hardly talk anyway. I had a very bad time communicating with people, but actors are really great because everybody's sort of the same. With actors you can communicate using only four or five words because pretty soon the words stop mattering. You kind of get into a thing where you know you're getting something across and they are nodding their heads like you're nodding your head and you do the next thing and you talk about that, and little by little the thing takes shape. It's nice to sit down and intellectually, with beautiful words, explain precisely, but it's still a process—you don't know a hundred percent what you want. You have a feeling about it and you start working and you see the things that aren't working and the ones that are and you learn from each rehearsal and it's a beautiful process.

H: Was *Eraserhead* a parody in your mind?

L: No. No way. What could it be a parody of?

H: It could be, well, a very subtle parody of lower-middle-class existence in an industrial city. Some of it is very humorous—for instance, at the dinner table when the father says, "Just cut it like a regular chicken, Henry." Stuff like that.

L: I didn't really know what a parody was when I made *Eraserhead* so it couldn't have been that. It just was *Eraserhead*, that's it.

H: You once said that you know you're onto a good idea because it seems exciting, it feels exciting, but that there has to be this coherent line holding it together. Would you elucidate?

L: It's sort of common sense. Again, if you get an idea that's exciting, it's thrilling to the soul. But then if you start falling in love with the story, it can all go bad and get rotten. But as long as you're in love with it and it's exciting, it's pulling you forward and it's helping you attract new ideas. The new ideas can add to it or can suddenly start leading you to a place that becomes less exciting and it eventually dies. It's all trials through the unknown that can end in beautiful things or end in disaster, as you know.

H: You once said something wonderfully quotable. You said that you felt ideas were broadcast and that we were antennas that picked up on ideas, which to me sounded something like Jung's idea of the collective unconscious.

L: Well, yeah. I think that ideas exist outside of ourselves. I think somewhere we're all connected off in some very abstract land. But somewhere between there and here ideas exist. And I think the mind isn't conscious enough to go all the way to where we're connected, but it's conscious of a certain amount of that territory. And when these ideas fly into the conscious part, then you can capture them. But if they're outside of the conscious part, you don't even know about them. So you just hope that you can make the conscious part of your mind bigger or that these ideas will fly into your airspace, so you can shoot them down and grab them and take them home. So that's all you try to do.

H: Do you sit in a room to get your ideas?

L: Yes, I sit quietly in a chair. That's what I find is the best thing.

H: In a room by yourself?

L: Yes. But sometimes an idea will strike you while you're standing. Sometimes music will also help you. If I thought I could just sit still in a quiet place and get ideas, I would do that all the time, but sometimes nothing happens. Just the other day I got an idea, kind of a complete and perfect idea for a certain thing—why it flew into my head at the time it did I will never know. I was with lots of other people in the middle of a mix for "Twin Peaks" and a completely unrelated idea flew into my head, so there's no rhyme or reason to it.

H: Do you write them down?

L: Yes, you've got to write them down right away. I forget so many things. Then if I forget it and try to remember it, my whole day is ruined because I can't remember and I feel horrible. And I imagine that it was one of the all-time great ideas. And it probably wasn't. I'm sure it wasn't. Anyway, whatever it was, it's gone.

H: Is mood and atmosphere more important to you than narrative?

L: Everything's important. Mood and atmosphere are superimportant, but if you don't have a story, then you got diddily.

H: Is it hard for Hollywood to understand something abstract unless it ties into a conventional narrative?

L: It's impossible.

H: How far along do you think the evolution of storytelling has come in narrative filmmaking?

L: Well, I don't know. A great story is always another beautiful thing. It doesn't have to be told in a new way, really, if it's just solid, a great story. But then there are stories that are not so great, but they're told in such an interesting way that makes them special too. There are all different ways of doing things, but the thing I was saying about Hollywood is a general statement—they like a certain kind of thing that's easy to understand by masses of people. If anything isn't understood in a script by the twenty executives in the room, or however many people are needed to okay it, then it gets thrown out or changed or made to be understood so everybody understands everything. And that's not the way life is, so it makes the film seem completely uninteresting to me, because I love mysteries. I love not knowing about certain things because in the mystery I feel more than what would be there if it was explained to me. Once you start explaining something so twenty people understand it, there's no magic to it anymore. It's a small light bulb—it's not like a big bunch of light. It's a dim light bulb.

H: Do you think stories need to be told in Aristotelian terms, with a beginning, middle and end?

L: Well, it works real good if you start in the middle, then go to the beginning then get to the end. It could work, like a flashback— they do it all kinds of different ways. A great story should hold your interest and you should be dying to know the next step. It's really tricky to do. It's so tricky. But I think the story is the most important thing.

H: Is it true that you will only direct a film if you have final say in the script and cut?

L: Yes.

H: So it must be more frustrating for you to direct films than to paint?

L: In what sense?

H: With painting you only have to buy the brush and canvas, but in film you have to raise the money, other people's money, so there's always that outside pressure.

L: Yes, with painting you're on your own and nobody's telling you what to do. In film it's different. But I do think you should always be open to suggestions and ideas, and they can come from the people you're working with—somebody who's helping you outside or with something you see. If you're not open to ideas to make the thing better, you're really stupid. But what I'm saying is, if you don't have the final say on what goes into the film, it's not your film. It's the film of the person who has the final say. They're the ones who are in total control. I can't see how that would be a workable thing for me. And I've been really lucky that even when I didn't have it in the contract to have final cut, I worked with people who gave it to me anyway, except in *Dune*, which is definitely my least favorite film that I've made because of that.

H: But you said that you liked the film when it came out.

L: I said that I did. I convinced myself that I did. But I was a very sick person at the time. I was dying inside. And I didn't realize how much I'd fooled myself during that whole process. It was a terrible, terrible thing.

H: Would it have worked if it had been longer? Does the footage exist to make a longer version of it?

L: The footage exists to make a longer version of it for sure. Whether it's a better version or a satisfactory version, I don't know. But it would definitely be better than what's out now.

H: *Elephant Man* was your first film after *Eraserhead,* and it was a far more conventional one. What interested you in doing that film?

L: A lot of things. It was black and white, had to do with the Industrial Revolution, and had to do with distorted flesh in the middle of industry. It's so romantic, so sad, so emotional. To me it had a fairy-tale quality. And I had an opportunity to do some abstractions within a real solid story. It had many things going for it. To me it was like a little gold mine.

H: What was it like to suddenly find yourself working with one of the world's greatest classically trained actors, Sir John Gielgud?

L: Luckily I thought about it more in the morning when I got up. If I started thinking about it the night before I worked with Sir John Gielgud, I don't think I could have slept. It struck me in the morning when I was putting on my underwear. I said, "Here I am putting on my underwear and I'm going off to direct maybe the top guy in the world." And I was thinking what a joke it was, that he's going to listen to me. It turned out real nice though. I was always very polite with him and I would hardly ever say anything, and when I did say something I would always apologize to him. And he really dug it. He was super. And he wrote me a letter afterwards. In it he said, "David, you never told me what you thought about my performance." He says, "I hope you think it was satisfactory for you and I hope that you feel that I did a good enough job." So I quickly wrote him a letter back to tell him how great I thought he was. But it just goes to show you, no matter how big you get, you want that feedback. You're only big in other people's eyes. He's just himself.

H: Would you tell me how you conceived of the idea for *Blue Velvet?*

L: I guess one day long ago I listened to Bobby Vinton singing "Blue Velvet." Then one day I wanted to sneak into a girl's room and observe her through the night. And then I imagined being in this room and I would see something, but I wouldn't understand it. I'd be in the middle of a murder mystery and I'd see a piece of evidence which, if the police had it, would instantly give the an-swer. But I didn't know what the police knew, and the police didn't know what I knew, so everyone was in darkness. They each had a piece of the puzzle, but didn't know it, so that kind of got me going. And then one day I thought of finding an ear in a field, and that this ear would be the thing that would get the person finding it involved in this. It would have to take them to the police. And from there it kind of got going with the policeman's daughter. It was not like a thing that came to me all at once at all. It never came together. And the only time a dream ever helped me with an idea was with *Blue Velvet*. I had a dream one night that I saw a yellow man standing, but he was dead. Actually, I already had that, but it was a dream of the thing I already had, but in the dream I saw a police radio in his pocket. In a dream you can see through some-thing and I saw that he had a gun. Obviously he had a gun, he was a policeman. And so those two things would help me finish the script. I didn't dream that Jeffery tricked Frank Booth by going to the back bedroom and putting the gun under the bed and going to the closet. But all that sort of got me going on that idea.

H: You once complained that audiences didn't know how to take *Blue Velvet*'s affirmative love theme, that audiences were more un-comfortable with the corniest virtues than they were with violence.

L: Yes. I have a theory. There is such a thing as embarrassment. And with audiences, because many people are in a room together, they do funny things that they wouldn't do if they were on their own. It's like a gang. And sometimes love things, things that have become sort of cornball in today's world, make the temperature of the audience's body rise and sweat begins to come out of their foreheads and they start to make small giggling sounds. But I'm really interested in embarrassing moments on film. I think there should be something embarrassing in every film.

H: So, was the naïveté of the dialogue in *Blue Velvet* deliberate?

L: Well, yeah. I've got a naive streak in me. The characters in *Blue Velvet* needed to talk about certain things in their own way, and Sandy particularly is kind of a dreamy girl next-door, and I always figured you say, strange, goofball, cornball type things when you're alone with your girlfriend in a car. And if anybody recorded what we say, it would make us get that hot, sweat-filled feeling. So it's sort of that kind of thing.

H: What would you like your films to do for people?

L: I don't try to do anything for people. I try to do something for myself. Like everything else, they strike people in different ways depending on how the person is. And some people get violently ill and some people go into a euphoria. You never know what it's going to do. You can't try to do something to people. With *Wild at Heart* I learned a little bit through test screening certain things. And it's sort of manipulating yourself. If you are interested and you are happy and things seem to be working for you, that's as good as it gets. You can't be guaranteed of satisfying anybody else.

H: When it comes to violence, such as in *Wild at Heart*, it really seems that you don't have any inhibitions. Did you ever pull back when it came to those more shocking elements?

L: Well, sort of, but I think a lot of it may be because I was coming off "Twin Peaks" where I couldn't be violent. And when I started reading *Wild at Heart*, which is not a violent book at all, in my mind the world was totally filled with violence. I just got into it. The thing about the world is that it changes real fast. And it just hit me, that was a very weird summer for movies. If the atmosphere had been different, *Wild at Heart* could have been a lot more successful. It had turned funny. Same thing happened on *Dune*. If I had snapped my fingers and it could have come out when I first decided to make it, instead of three and a half years later, maybe it still wouldn't have been a great film, but it would have done better. You know, the world changes.

H: But also the world knows your work better now, too. You've created a new appetite for a new, offbeat, surreal way of telling stories. But do you ever feel that you're pushing things too far?

L: Oh, yes. If I do, then I stop, but then again, I don't stop too soon, so I'm somewhere in the middle.

H: You adapted *Dune* and *Wild at Heart* from books. What was that process of adaptation like versus writing an original script like *Blue Velvet?*

L: When you write an original script, number one, you never know when it's going to be finished. It could take forever. You know, half a story isn't good enough. You can't start a film unless you have a story. So it's a little bit frustrating if you want to be working. Unless you're lucky and ideas just come to you complete. They don't seem to do that for me. So I like the idea, and if I can find something that I fall in love with, and adapt it to film, it's okay. I like the process of changing it into film. Same way with *Blue Velvet*—the ideas came from me but it was still the same process, once it was a script, to change it into film. Like I said, I love that part of it. I like writing too, I really love it, but like I say, usually I write things that are completely absurd and it scares me because I would just be relegating myself to the back lot instantly.

H: Would you talk about your shooting style. It seems like you enjoy going with longer takes, your work has a certain mise-en-scène quality to it. Do you resist getting in too close?

L: I don't know how it all happens. Cutting, you know, is a real art form. And I work with I think the greatest editor in the world, Duane Donnem, and even though I don't give Duane a whole lot to work with, he manages to create a good pace for the thing. I do like things to look like they're on a stage sometimes, and I don't know if it's just something you think. But it feels right. Again, the scene tells you how it's supposed to be, sort of, and in rehearsals you learn the final things.

H: In many ways television has accelerated the pacing of films. It seems that less information can be absorbed by the viewer.

L: Yeah, in a way *Wild at Heart* was sort of like that. I'm trying to get more things into one film. That's sort of what I'm interested in now. There's kind of a thing about getting information from so many places now and fragments of it. But it's okay. It's like a collage of things that make a total strange feeling. And that's an interesting thing, too. I don't know. I think that pacing is extremely important. Like Duane says about pacing, "It shouldn't be boring, but fast pacing doesn't make interesting or good." It may jar you, but it's the feeling of the story that you want and it wants to be told in a certain way and pull you. And a certain slowness, not boring, but a certain slowness contrasted with something fast is very important. It's like music. If music was all just fast it would be a bummer. But symphonies and stuff are built on slow and fast and high and low, and it thrills your soul. And film is the same way. There are certain rules. For a whole piece to work it has to obey certain rules. And if people don't want to obey the rules, then the piece isn't going to go to the max.

H: In November of 1989 you were part of a music ensemble piece called "Industrial Symphony No. 1" at the Brooklyn Academy of Music. What was all that about?

L: It was done very fast. In that context it's pretty cool. It's the first time I ever did anything on stage. And Angelo [Badalamenti] and I for three weeks put all this stuff together. And he wrote some new stuff and there are some things that we did from this album we did together, and little Mike, who was in "Twin Peaks" and who worked with me before, was in it.

H: There's a rumor that you once tried to see a therapist . . .

L: I sort of promised someone I would talk to a therapist. It was like a circle. I kept doing the same things in my life and so I figured that if I could break this circle it could help a certain aspect of my life. So I got the name of this psychiatrist, and it was kind of weird because I always said that phrase, "People who go to a psychiatrist ought to have their head examined." Anyway, I found myself going. And he was a real good guy. So I found myself talking to him in his office and I asked him halfway through the hour if he felt, in his professional opinion, that if I continued in therapy it could affect my creativity. And he said, "Well, quite frankly, David, I have to honestly say that it could." And so I told him, "Thank you very much." And I left the room.

H: I guess that kind of falls under Freud's idea that artists sublimate a lot of their energies and anxieties into their work.

L: Yeah, if you start fiddling with it, it's trouble. There are all kinds of different theories. I heard anyway that Woody Allen or somebody could get a lot of ideas by going to a therapist. So the opposite could happen. It could enhance creativity by talking about all these strange neuroses. But for me, I didn't want to really fiddle with it.

H: Do ideas always come to you, or do you ever feel blocked?

L: It's like sex. If you start worrying about stuff . . . it's the wrong approach [laughs].

Filmography

1970   *The Alphabet* (short)
1972   *The Grandmother* (short)
1976   *Eraserhead*
1980   *The Elephant Man*
1984   *Dune*
1987   *Blue Velvet*
1990   *Wild at Heart*
1990-   "Twin Peaks"

II

Politics and Aesthetics in American Film

COSTA-GAVRAS

State of Mind

During the last twenty-five years, Constantin Costa-Gavras has emerged as one of the cinema's most revered political filmmakers. Perhaps not since the revolutionary work of Russian master Sergei Eisenstein has a director been able to balance the fine line between politics and aesthetics as conscientiously and artfully as Costa-Gavras.

Born in Athens, the filmmaker received a strict orthodox education before leaving for Paris at the age of eighteen. There he received a degree in literature from the Sorbonne and then moved on to study filmmaking at I.D.H.E.C. (Institute de Hautes Etudes Cinématographiques). After a brief apprenticeship with René Clair, Marcel Ophuls and Jacques Demy he made an auspicious directorial debut with *The Sleeping Car Murders* (1965), a commercially successful suspense thriller starring Simone Signoret and Yves Montand.

For the past two decades Costa-Gavras's work has explored a variety of controversial issues, from racial bigotry in the United States—*Betrayed* (1988)—to his most popular film about political assassination and civil war in Greece—*Z* (1969). In 1973 Costa-Gavras began work on one of his most provocative films, *State of Siege*, a powerful and contentious look at United States foreign policy toward Latin America. But first, Costa-Gavras wants to talk about his most recent film, *Music Box* (1989), a story about the

United States government having given sanctuary to Nazi war criminals in its cold war against the communists.

"What interested me most about the script was that it was a personal thriller, a daughter's discovery of her father's sordid past, the fact that he collaborated with the fascists," he says. "None of us really know about our parents' lives, we can't imagine them making love, we can't really envision them in their youth, we can't picture them doing wrong. The story is quite visceral. There are elements of thriller in all human relationships."

When I ask him if the thriller is a genre he feels comfortable working in, he laughs. "The thriller is as natural to me as the Greek tragedy. I was born in Greece and raised on Hollywood movies, so what could be a better combination for learning to work in the genre? If you look at my films, you will see that they are all thrillers to a varying degree."

HICKENLOOPER: You're most often labeled a political filmmaker, yet you've called this a simplification of terms, simple in the sense that you believe all filmmakers are political. How is that?

COSTA-GAVRAS: I think every film carries the ideology and philosophy of its authors. When I was younger I saw movies with Esther Williams which showed a kind of extraordinary life in the United States—a kind of paradise. Those films gave me a completely different vision of what society was really like in this country. So you see, every movie, each in its different way, carries a certain kind of political message, whether it's about foreign policy or bathing beauties.

H: So to you all films are political, no matter how apolitical the content?

CG: I think when you make a stupid movie which says nothing it is also a political movie because it doesn't make people think. When I was a kid and saw all those innocuous westerns, all of my friends and I were in agreement that the American Indians should be wiped out. And I got this from those cowboy movies during my childhood. It really affected me. I consider those political films because they evoked a blood reaction against a certain group of people. So, yes, every film is political.

H: *Clair de Femme* was a film you made about an intense romantic relationship between two middle-aged people. How was that film political?

CG: I think human relationships are political. A relationship between a man and a woman is political. If you simplify politics to "vote for this man or that man," then it's a big mistake. Politics is the way you work, the choices you make in running your house, your family, your kids, the kind of education you give them, and the authority you exercise over them—though these decisions are at the simplest level, they are still political. To be a communist or not to be a communist, to be a democrat or not be a democrat is not the only form of politics.

H: Some critics have called your films more propagandistic than political. For you, what is the difference?

CG: The difference is obvious. In a propaganda film you try to explain to the people, to convince them how the false idea is a good idea, just like in a Nazi propaganda film, for instance, Leni Riefenstahl's *Triumph of the Will*. In that film she very successfully evoked strong feelings with powerful images that misled the German people, did not tell them the truth about Nazism. This is why when I make my films I try to present everything, every character, every incident with as much historical accuracy as possible. I'm trying to make a movie based on a real story so the important thing is to try to be as close as possible to the truth. It's so easy to manipulate—with a line, a face, an angle, a look. It's quite terrifying how easy it is sometimes. I try to stay as close to the truth as possible with my films. I don't believe in the concept of bad guys and good guys, cowboys versus Indians. It's all relative. For the bad guys, there is always some justification for their actions, which is something you rarely see in movies. So I try to see why and explore that. I did it with *Z*, with *Missing*, with *State of Siege*, with all my so-called political movies. And if I distort the facts, every journalist, everyone, will know. And if they find that it is not true, I have to answer for it.

H: You emphasize that it's important for films to raise questions in people's minds. What role do you think entertainment should play, and how would you define entertainment?

CG: Raising questions is entertaining. The Greek tragedy, Shakespeare, Molière was political theater, yet it was entertaining at the same time. There is no contradiction there. Must entertainment be limited to making people laugh, like Johnny Carson? Just a couple of jokes and that's all? But even he is political, yes? I remember after the Tripoli bombing in '86, he dressed up in a beret and made fun of the French government's refusal to grant the United States air space. There, you see, everything is political, even if it's stupid.

H: But entertainment in the traditional Hollywood sense is escapism. Films that raise questions tend to be commercially unpopular in Hollywood. How do you deal with that kind of mentality?

CG: Escapism means what? That we are living in a prison? This society is a prison? People feel as though they need to escape from this prison? No, I don't think that this society is a prison. I think this society is one of the best in terms of change, where people can freely discuss anything they like, see anything they like, or write anything they like without fear of being censored or oppressed. Why would you want to escape from that? Is freedom too tedious to bear?

H: As a filmmaker do you feel compelled to become involved in the politics you render, or does your responsibility end as a director?

CG: No, a director is a human being living in society just like anybody else, so he has, as an individual, a political responsibility to that society. So all I can do is my best. No one can ever say that the director or writer must do this or that. Everybody must follow his conscience, or the freedom he has or doesn't have. What else is he to do?

H: At what point in your filmmaking do politics and aesthetics meet?

CG: There is no doubt that there is a problem in the relationship between content and form. Every story imposes its form in a certain way. Eisenstein in particular did an extraordinary amount of research on aesthetics. But since the thirties, aesthetics altogether have shifted much more from form to content. The balance of the two is a permanent problem. For me it's a permanent problem, there is no doubt. One has to make choices. I often think that the best way to use form is so that it's more understandable to a large audience. It is more democratic that way. Political movies should try to reach a mass audience, otherwise they are limited to a few intellectuals and that's not fair. Of course, you can be more specific, more experimental, but in the end I like them to be entertainment in the same sense as we discussed before. I enjoy comparing the cinema to the ancient Greek dramas which were truly popular theater. But it's definitely a constant problem. Every movie is different. Every movie has its own right form.

H: Your first major success as a director was *Z*. How did that project get initiated?

CG: Back in 1967 my brother, who is a lawyer in Greece, gave me the book, which a friend of his had written. A few days later the coup happened and I felt helpless living in Paris. I wanted to do something. So I decided to make a film about it, but I had difficulty finding a money source—someone who would be willing to produce this subject. I went to nearly all the producers and distributors, American and French, but I couldn't get anywhere. Finally, I found some Algerians who would give me the money. Algeria was an unusual choice, but we needed a military town. It turned out very well. They paid for all the hotels and transportation, which was close to half the cost of the movie. The actors weren't paid, I wasn't paid, but we still made the movie.

H: The film was a success?

CG: Yes, but I made the mistake of letting the Italians distribute the film. They paid us only $60,000, and over the past few years they have made millions.

H: Did you succeed in doing what you set out to do in making *Z*?

CG: I was happy with it. I thought I had to make something, an action against the Greek colonels. Some people make bombs. I'm against bombs because they kill people. I prefer to make movies. So I made *Z* against them, to show how things were in Greece. So on that level, yes, I think I accomplished that.

H: The film gave you a lot of exposure . . .

CG: Yes, it was very fortunate. Then I started getting offers from American companies.

H: I understand that Paramount offered you *The Godfather*.

CG: First I was offered the script to *Deliverance*. Then Paramount offered me a tremendous amount of money to direct *The Godfather*. Now I had problems with *The Godfather* because I thought it was a pro-Mafia movie. Those characters were portrayed very sympathetically, very romantically, and the fact that Corleone was eventually played by an important actor like Brando made them even more likable. So I went to the studio head and asked them if they would let me make the story about the Mafia and their control of drugs. I felt that this would give them another dimension. They said no, so I said I couldn't do it. And now look what's happened. The Mafia gets glorified in movie after movie.

H: *State of Siege* deals with political and social corruption in Uruguay in 1968. What initially drew you to making a film about Latin America?

CG: I originally wanted to make a movie about the American ambassador who was in Greece just after the civil war. He was a big technician in the State Department. There is a great deal of doubt concerning his position as a diplomat, so let's just say *technician*, for lack of a better word. He established himself in the Greek government during the civil war and was responsible for the direct intervention of the United States in that war. After Greece he went to Guatemala in '56 when the country was going through a very difficult time. He went there when it was a very democratic but unstable country and then they established one of the worst regimes in Latin America. Now there are killings every year. So I was trying to find material on this and I went to Brazil, Mexico and Guatemala to learn what historians and writers had to say. Little by little I discovered that a whole new generation of technicians had succeeded him and were put to work all over Latin America, much like the Metrione character in my film.

H: How did you balance historical fact with the fictional elements you needed to create an effective story?

CG: You know, a movie is two hours. This story went on for weeks, so it would have been impossible to present all the facts in all the right contexts. The important thing was to try to understand what both sides were thinking. I wanted to stay close to the essential elements because I think every human action has a kind of spine, so if you succeed in staying next to this essential thing, then it would be safe to say that it is as close to the truth as you can get.

H: Was *State of Siege* made for an American audience?

CG: In a certain way, yes. Probably the movie could be made in English and with American actors—the idea was there. If it had been done in English, it would still be the same movie. With an American actor or actress it might be easier for an American audience to follow, but it would also be more expensive to make. The American studios have a much different way of financing movies, and at the time, I didn't know how much I was ready to fight or not fight, which means to change the content and make it commercially acceptable.

H: How did American audiences respond to the film?

CG: As far as I can remember, quite well. It also caused quite a bit of controversy. Even after fifteen years, people come up to me and speak very favorably about the movie. When I show the film at a university and have a discussion afterwards, it's fascinating to see how the audience thinks that the film is about Latin America today.

H: After making *State of Siege* you drew a comparison between the American Revolution and the situation in Uruguay where a small band of guerrillas were fighting to free themselves from an oppressive system. Today, how would you treat another revolution in Latin America—for example, in Nicaragua where the Contras are fighting to overthrow the Sandinistas?

CG: At the time I was not making a direct comparison between the American Revolution and Uruguay. I said that the American officials, the government, not the people, are against the kind of revolutions out of which this country was born. The American government sees revolutions today as a form of terrorism, which seems to me a kind of historical double standard. I mean, this country was made through revolution. Sometimes it's necessary to go through revolution to find the identity and freedom. So whatever the revolutions are, communist or Christian or anything you like, essentially the movement is to create a new situation, to free themselves from the high pressure and extraordinary misery imposed on them by an oppressive system. I think today I would still make the comparison. Let's take the example of Nicaragua. For thirty years Somoza was there. Nobody said a word against him. Somoza had the worst government one can imagine—thieves, dictators, killers, everything—and they were friends of the United States. Now the new government is a communist government. I'm not saying it's a right government. I think there are many wrong things going on there. There is certainly not enough freedom, but I do think the Sandinistas are trying to do something different, and, of course, something better, so I tend to sympathize with them. It's like Cuba. The situation is much better there today than it was under Batista. Starving people want to be fed before they think about political ideology. Castro gave them food. Now that hunger is no longer a problem, it is time to talk about political freedom. You see, there will never be a kind of perfect revolution that will bring instant paradise. Anytime you have human beings involved in a struggle, whether communist or capitalist, there will be mistakes.

H: *State of Siege*, you once said, was not to praise the revolutionary movement in Uruguay but to draw a distinction between two kinds of violence. What were those two kinds of violence?

CG: You're referring to official "legal" violence versus revolutionary "subversive" violence. As a director I try to make no preference in the movie. I think the audience has to make a choice between the two, if there even *is* a right kind of violence. I don't think so. In some cases violence may be right. For example, in a fascist regime where there are absolutely no democratic options available. In those instances violence is the only solution.

H: I understand that while you were researching the film you met with the guerrilla leaders in Uruguay, the Tupamaros.

CG: I met them and discussed with them, and they offered to participate directly, but I refused them. I said, "No, you give me the information I ask for, but that's all. I will do the movie the way I would like to do it—as fairly and objectively as possible."

H: Did you sympathize at all with their ideology or methods?

CG: Their methods, no; some of their ideology, yes. But their methods, no, because at the time of filming in 1972 they were living in a democratic country. Democracy in Uruguay at that time was probably one of the best in Latin America next to Salvador Allende's Chile. They could express their ideas to the press through unions, by creating new parties, through everything. So the violence, at that time, was not really necessary.

H: How do you know for certain that the United States had Don Metrione involved in torture?

CG: In my research I came upon documents which told me that he had been part of a police academy in Washington, D.C. The academy had foolishly published a brochure which contained photographs of all the technicians who were training various Latin American police forces in effective methods of dealing with dissident groups. This brochure was given to me by an Uruguayan policeman who was so disgusted with the torturing that he had established a clandestine relationship with the Tupamaros. So I went back to the United States and verified Metrione's background.

H: That must have been during the Nixon Administration. Did you have any difficulty finding more information in Washington?

CG: Not really, because one of the wonderful things about the United States is that you can find almost anything you want to know in the Library of Congress. All the budgets and monies allocated to Metrione were right there. It was incredible. When the movie opened, a senator asked me where I had found my information, and you can imagine his surprise when I said I had discovered it in Washington.

H: Your film *Missing* seems to share the same theme as *State of Siege*, in so far as Washington's turning its back on an American, allowing him to be abducted without any protest.

CG: I am not convinced that the American government knew what happened with regard to the Horman case. The father seems to think they did. I think that perhaps some down there knew and others covered it up. I also believe that responsibility goes much deeper. The responsibility was in helping the Chilean military overthrow Allende. When you accept that kind of coup, you know they will kill 50,000 people. So by helping Pinochet I think that, yes, the American government accepts 50,000 murders and turns its back if it interferes with the political or economic interests of the parties involved.

H: Would you elucidate?

CG: This gets back to the interests of the larger, industrialized nations. American interests are the most important thing all over the world. If something happens in a country anywhere in the world, the American president will have a say in it, and everybody follows. The U.S. has become the father for everybody because everyone will obey the man who has the money, who puts the bread on the table. It's completely insane. Your country interferes with everybody.

H: How do you react when someone refers to you as an anti-American director?

CG: It's not true, I like America. In fact, I think that it's unfortunate the world doesn't appreciate the more positive things about American democracy. Because these are the things that can allow society to grow and change. Of course I am against many of the things your government does. But to say I'm anti-American is to say I'm an anti-Russian director, an anti-Czechoslovakian and an anti-French director. You have to take apart every one of my movies to see what's inside. They are specifically against many things.

H: For instance?

CG: See my films—intervention into foreign countries, assisting Pinochet in Chile, the United States's involvement in Nicaragua and El Salvador. Soon your country's government may create an unnecessary war just like what happened in Vietnam. During the Vietnam peace talks in Paris, people said to me, "You are anti-American." Later on, most Americans agreed that the war in Vietnam must be stopped. So we weren't anti-American anymore. We had only spoken out earlier. It's simplistic to say I'm anti-American.

H: But your film *State of Siege* is very critical of U.S. foreign policy in Latin America.

CG: No, the movie only portrays a small part of American foreign policy. The aspect of it that I deal with really only started under the Kennedy Administration. His government created organizations like the Peace Corps, not necessarily military organizations, but nevertheless groups that could have some kind of relationship with countries in the Third World. And then the next two administrations, especially Nixon, switched all of their movements and brought in the CIA. It was frightening to see what was going on down there, especially in the Peace Corps, which became a kind of front for interfering in the politics of the Third World, particularly Latin America. So we cannot say that American foreign policy has always been all bad, but we must not forget the Nixon period, the CIA and Vietnam and all that has stemmed from the Cold War. This hysteria about the domino theory and saving the world from the communists is a bit archaic and unflattering to the American people, don't you think? You lost Vietnam—so what? I don't see all of Asia becoming communist. In fact, I see communism around the world slowly breaking apart.

H: Some critics thought that your film *Betrayed* treated the FBI too well. After being so hard on other U.S. agencies and departments in the past, some felt that you were trying to make a gesture by presenting the FBI favorably.

CG: That's simply rhetoric from an extreme left. First of all, the film is not about the FBI. Secondly, what I do show of the FBI is presented with some ambiguity. The FBI does some awful things; at the same time I'm sure there are some decent people who work there. It would be a foolish position to go entirely one way are the other.

H: You said the film isn't about the FBI. From whose point of view is the story told?

CG: My films always have a point of view, otherwise they would be empty. *Betrayed* is about the old American cowboy myth that God is on the side of the white man. It is about the resurgence of racism in the U.S. and around the world. In the sixties, during the civil rights campaign, right-wing elements in the United States had to remain silent. Then you had Reagan. He goes to Bitberg, the Nazi cemetery, and lays a wreath. So in a sense, he legitimizes the Third Reich. So all the fascist elements now assume that it's okay to speak their mind again. Soon their rhetoric leads to action and the reemergence of racism. On a more subtle level, just look at what's going on in your Supreme Court. Civil rights case after civil rights case is being overturned by Reagan's legacies. In Europe the scapegoat is no longer the Jew but the Arab. The crimes against the Jews were so horrible and are so well known that people find it difficult to admit they are anti-Jewish. But they can speak against the Arabs. They can still be anti-Semitic. That is what my film is about. Not just America, not just the FBI, but the world.

H: What was your political view regarding *Music Box*?

CG: Well, with respect to the Holocaust, it's important that people's memories are refreshed because we too often tend to forget. Frequently, we choose to forget because of economic or political interests. For example, I researched Allan M. Ryan's book *Quiet Neighbors* and learned that 10,000 Nazi war criminals were given sanctuary in the United States in exchange for cooperating against the Russian communists. And it still goes on today—for instance, Reagan's 1984 trip to Bitberg, where the SS officers are buried, or when the chiefs of state from all over the world went to Hirohito's funeral, a man who was considered a war criminal less than forty years ago. But economic interests in Japan obliged all those leaders to forget.

H: May I ask you a more technical question? Would you tell me something about your rehearsal process?

CG: Well, with the cast of *Music Box*, we had three long sessions over a weekend at Jessica Lange's home in Virginia, where we discussed every line of the script. I wanted to emphasize the importance of playing down the script, not to have them underline certain key lines so that they wouldn't give away whether or not the father had committed these crimes. I also felt that it was critical to discuss with them the historical background. I gave them all copies of my research, which offered some unbelievable information regarding the U.S.'s position toward Nazi war criminals. We then had several rehearsals with Jessica, especially the scene with her father in the end. We had to work on that scene a lot, rehearsing it just for the movement, because I wanted that scene to be filmed in one shot. I am more of an improvisational director. I never storyboard like many American directors. I find that that can be a problem if you've blocked the action before you see the actors perform it. The actors also don't like it because it restricts their movement before they can really bring life to the scene. You know, filming a scene can be like writing a story. If you want to get certain rhythms, you must select the words you want to use, perhaps certain adjectives. In filmmaking, this is replaced by camera angles or movements, so I find that it's better if I rehearse with the actors on the set, at which point I can decide how to photograph it.

H: Do you think your films can invoke change? Do they make an impression on your audience?

CG: What's frightening is that a few people have told me that my films have changed their lives. I would hope that it would take more than a film to change a person's life. But perhaps on a smaller, more realistic level I hope that my films can at least provoke discussion. With respect to *Betrayed*, if the audience can discuss the film and see the racism from the outside, then maybe it will occur to them how ugly it is. A film is like a short moment, just a thought, like a song or a speech, so I don't think a movie can change the world or country or something. If you believe that, then you're misguided. You see, change is a long cultural process, and the cinema, art or literature can only contribute to that process, not be responsible for it.

Filmography

1965	*The Sleeping Car Murders*
1967	*Shock Troops*
1968	*Z*
1970	*The Confession*
1972	*State of Siege*
1975	*Special Section*
1979	*Clair de Femme*
1982	*Missing*
1983	*Hannah K*
1986	*Family Business*
1988	*Betrayed*
1990	*Music Box*

OLIVER STONE
Homeric Patriot

Unlike the image I had conjured up of him, that of rough, cynical Vietnam vet turned angry and rebellious filmmaker, I found Oliver Stone to be articulate and soft-spoken. Answering a question, he pauses to assess a thought before replying with the acumen of a scholar. However, under the surface of his equanimity, one gets the impression that there survives the angry fervor of the sixties, now partially dissembled by Stone's Cheshire cat smile.

"Somebody once wrote, 'Hell is the impossibility of reason,' " a character in his film, *Platoon* (1986), writes in a letter from the war in Vietnam. A semi-autobiographical account of Stone's experience as a soldier in Southeast Asia, the film reflects his two years spent in combat where, he now says, he was trying to rationalize his own existence. Stone was born into a privileged background. His father was a successful Wall Street financier who was enthusiastic about his son attending his alma mater, Yale University. "It was too much of a conformist place," Stone says. "I had to get out." Much to the dismay of his parents, he dropped out of school and threw himself into the political and moral chaos of Vietnam, taking with him his refined background and his interest in classical literature. "Vietnam was my *Iliad*, and my life up until the making of *Platoon* was a kind of *Odyssey*."

Stone's *Platoon* screenplay became a ten-year journey of rejection for the author before he was able to find a home for it with an independent studio in 1985. "There had been no realistic Vietnam War movies, and I felt it was important to remember the way it was . . . I wanted to fix it in the memory for those who were there, and to remind the younger generations that it had happened, so it could never happen again." Winning four Academy Awards, including Best Picture and Best Director, the film offered a compelling, visceral account of the Vietnam experience.

Upon meeting Stone at his Santa Monica editing facility, I recount my first viewing of *Platoon* in a Times Square theater, waiting in line with a rowdy crowd who were fired up to see a Rambo-esque version of the war. At the end of the movie, the lights came up and that same audience was now dead silent, as if shell-shocked by the graphic realism of the film. "Some people accuse me of not being subtle enough," Stone says with a large grin. "It was simply my experience."

Pummeling his audience with overwhelming images that illustrate his own personal passion plays, Stone's films hit hard for gut-level reactions that can leave the viewer feeling emotionally fatigued, as though he had just walked off the battlefield. And like *Platoon*, his other films, *Salvador* (1986), *Wall Street* (1987) and *Talk Radio* (1988), deal with characters who are taking journeys into their own hearts and minds. "My characters are truth-seekers. And they are willing to experience hell if that's what it takes to discover who they are."

In 1989 the director again decided to tackle the subject of Vietnam, but this time the protagonist was a man returning home. "*Born on the Fourth of July* is not a sequel, it's more of a companion piece to *Platoon*," Stone says of this film, which for the second time brought him an Oscar for Best Director. Based on the 1976 autobiography of Ron Kovic, the film retells the heroic story of a veteran who comes home to an unsympathetic world while trying to cope with his paraplegic condition. "Making *Born* and *Platoon* was cathartic to me. I felt an obligation to do them . . . My story and that of the other vets is subsumed by Ron's," says Stone. "He is very special to me. I wasn't able to deal with talking to another vet until I met Ron in 1978. And that was almost ten years after I'd come home."

Returning from Vietnam in 1968, Stone tried to find solace back in the "civilized" world of New York City. Enrolling at NYU film school where he was taught by another young director at the time, Martin Scorsese, Stone discovered in himself a passion for writing and directing films. While trying to cope with a drug problem, he spent much of his time writing the screenplays which, by the end of the 1970s, became his calling card to Hollywood. Alan Parker's *Midnight Express* (1978), John Milius's *Conan the Barbarian* (1982), Brian De Palma's *Scarface* (1983) and Michael Cimino's *The Year of the Dragon* (1985) were all penned entirely or partially by Stone. After one unsuccessful attempt at directing in 1973 with *Seizure* and then another in 1981 with *The Hand*, Stone burst onto the scene with an audacious look at the war in Central America in *Salvador* (1981). "*Salvador* was a new beginning for me after my detour into mainstream movies," says the director, leaning far back in his chair.

Stone and I sit next to his editing table, where he is piecing together his newest film, *The Doors* (1991), a biographical film of rock legend Jim Morrison.

HICKENLOOPER: You've said that you've read Lewis, Conrad, Kazantzakis and have studied the screenplays of Paddy Chayefsky. Has literature been a major influence in your own screenwriting?

STONE: Oh, sure. It goes all the way back to school. When I did some earlier interviews, I was talking about *Lord Jim*. It had a lot of influence in my life and moved me out to Asia when I was young. And Dickens certainly, Kazantzakis's *Zorba* . . . I read very eclecti-cally. It had no pattern to it. But Conrad had a real influence on my life at seventeen when I left college and went to Southeast Asia.

H: Steven Spielberg said after receiving the Irving Thalberg Award that film should rely more on the written word. Do you agree? Do you think American film should be more literary than it is?

S: I'm of the opinion that American film should be both literary and visual. I think there's something to be said of the films of Chayefsky, which have wonderful dialogue. You can also do a cer-tain kind of film without any dialogue. *2001* is an excellent exam-ple. Some other films that flash in my mind are those of Joel and

Ethan Coen [*Blood Simple, Miller's Crossing*]. They seem to be on the nonverbal end. I think ideally you should do a combination of both. I don't think that one should block the other. Why should you have limitations?

H: Traditionally, film narrative has been modeled dramatically more after the stage play than not. Do you think there's new ground to be broken with respect to the film narrative as a visual medium rather than as a three-act play in the Aristotelian sense?

S: I think that's what keeps a lot of people going. There's that feeling that we're in the first century of development of a new form, like in medicine. There're new avenues to explore all the time. But ultimately there are classical truths that seem to come to bear which go back to the *Odyssey* and *Iliad*, through Shakespeare, Dante and Dickens. I mean, there are certain things that interest people. I think people identify with other people. You can't quite get away from that. I hope we'll always need actors. I can see eventually having computer models, claymation type figures. We'll have stills of Harrison Ford which we'll be able to animate into all kinds of pictures.

H: *Apocalypse Now* and *The Deer Hunter* were two outstanding examples of Vietnam films made in the seventies. Do you think the fact that it took you ten years to make *Platoon* was an indication that Vietnam was a subject Hollywood preferred to avoid?

S: Of course [laughs]. Are you serious? Yes, there was . . . I liked both films. I liked both enormously as films. They were powerful pictures made by great filmmakers, but they really didn't have anything to do with the struggle that I saw or experienced, or what many of the other vets I talked to felt in Vietnam.

H: Those films were box-office successes. In light of their success, why do you think the studios had such a hard time giving you the go ahead for *Platoon*?

S: There was a feeling among executives that Vietnam had run its course. You couldn't do much better than get a Best Picture with *The Deer Hunter*, which even with its Oscar victories, only made twenty-five, thirty million dollars gross at the box office. I don't think *Apocalypse Now* did that well because it cost a lot of money. They weren't sufficient successes to warrant more films on Vietnam. They were not considered a great revolutionary thing like, I suppose, *Platoon* was eight years later when it unexpectedly took off. So there was a feeling that it had been done, which I think was frustrating for me because I always felt that the Vietnam story had never been told. A lot of fighting and grief, and even civil war had taken place, but they were never addressed. And certain moral issues had not been addressed with respect to what we had done over there.

I still feel that the Vietnam War was fought in a very immoral fashion by the United States. Not only in its objectives but the way it was fought. I still think that the oppression is going on around the world. America has been pursuing a policy, like the Roman Empire, of American imperialism. It's pushing its foreign policy and intervening in countries in Central America, in Asia, in Europe and the Middle East. I'm really against that. I would like my work in some way to reflect that rebellion against a policy that's been in existence since the dawn of the cold war and now after the cold war. I'd like to see our country move into a more pluralistic and humanistic world society. I have no illusions that movies are going to help, but they might in a little way.

H: Do you think there's room for political filmmaking in Hollywood?

S: I'd like to believe so. Judging from the results of *Salvador*, it's hard to say yes to that question.

H: Do you think you have the freedom now to pursue any subject you'd like?

S: Not any one. I think within reason. I think that there are still taboos that are hard to break. I am pursuing a couple. I can't tell you what they are because I'm a little sensitive about announcing something too far in advance, but I have a couple of humdingers in the works that are really going to piss off a lot of people. I'm doing them independently and abroad with foreign financing, and I'm only seeking an American distribution deal. I'm not going to make it with an American studio. They're going to burn the shit out of some people who are very important in this country. And I have my ongoing crusade against the foreign policy of this country, and that's out of the bag with *Salvador*, but I'm still working on the Central America thing.

H: How do you think the post-cold-war world will affect Latin America?

S: Not at all. If anything, America is just keeping up the same old party line in Central America, at least in covert action. When you don't hear about us down there, that's when they're succeeding. You know, the CIA was probably involved with the killing of the six Jesuits, and they are now probably heavily involved in Guatemala, and Guatemala is having a lot of fucking violence. But you don't hear about it because it's done. They keep the media away. And the media is too scared to go in there and ferret out the story. I can't blame them. It's pretty scary. The same thing goes on in Honduras. We militarized the region successfully. I think it's a really ugly score. I don't see a change unless we get a Democrat into office courageous enough to make sweeping changes. Dukakis would have been very good. He spoke Spanish. He understood these people very well. He was a Peace Corps guy down there. I talked to him about it. He really understood, so does Chris Dodd. But they don't have the power to do anything. The American people are backing Bush and Vernon Walter's school of thought, which is gunboat diplomacy essentially.

H: It was interesting in the news lately about Bush's decision to start opening talks with Vietnam.

S: But only about Cambodia, not about Vietnam. I was in Cambodia last year, and I must tell you that everybody I spoke to, whatever age, who'd been in one of the camps or relocated, told me straight in the eye that their lives wouldn't have lasted another year unless the Vietnamese had come in and saved them from the Khmer Rouge. They looked on the Vietnamese as having been their saviors. Yes, it was time maybe for the army to get out, but they're all terrified of the Khmer Rouge, which is a Nazi horror show. For America to support the Khmer Rouge just shows the madness of its China politics. I think we should take a counter position to the Chinese and use Hanoi as leverage because Vietnam is a very strong country with a thousand years of effective opposition to China. We should have a very strong relationship with Vietnam which wants one with us, so that we could leverage the Chinese. It's just common sense. It's national interest. George Washington would do it.

H: Why do you think someone like Goering or Eichmann can be brought to justice for war crimes against humanity, while Pol Pot who murdered three to four million gets swept under the rug and is allowed to continue flourishing in Cambodia?

S: It's the covert era, you know. Things are much more ambiguous than they were in World War II. That was the good guy/bad guy era analogy. Hitler was so black that not even William Morris could represent him. With the new guys it's much more difficult. You know, after World War II, we brought into this country so many war criminals to run our military operations, to run our intelligence, to run some of our churches, and to run a lot of political groups. They're here you know, by the hundreds. So we never made a pact against Nazism. We made a pact against communism. And we were willing to embrace the Nazis, to use the Nazis in a covert form to fight the communists.

H: It seems like the entire world is in a tumult—Europe, the Middle East, China—while the United States just sits around stagnating. What are your feelings about what's going in this country in light of the end of the cold war?

S: Well, we wasted a lot of money on the military. There's just no question about that. It's too bad. I think our biggest problem right now is education. When you go to Europe and Asia you notice the difference right away. The standard of education is just so much better. They don't have these fucking violence problems. Now part of that is in the American character, which is incredible. We're still living in the Wild West, you know. It is free. And I'm not all for having our kids like French school children, because they have a tendency to be too conformist. It would just be nice to get a little balance between the two. I'm concerned about the quality of the teacher, what they've got to go through, how much they're underpaid.

H: Despite the fact that *Platoon* won Best Picture, it was criticized for some of its characterizations. Some critics felt that the characters of Willem Dafoe [Sergeant Elias] and Tom Berenger [Sergeant Barnes] were too pat to seem real. Were these characters based on real soldiers you knew, or were they used in the extreme for dramatic reasons?

S: It's funny you ask that, because actually Barnes and Elias were based on real people. I was in three different combat units and Sergeant Barnes—he wasn't called Barnes but something similar—had in fact been shot in the head and had that same scar tissue network over his face. It was like a seventh or eighth wound. He was sent to Japan and brought back after a year and I had to carry his radio for two months. He was one of the most frightening people I had ever met in my life. And in some ways he was a very good soldier, but he had a very racist outlook on "gooks." So Barnes was very much based on a real person. I was also taken with another sort of mythic figure I met over there, Sergeant Elias, who was in a long-range recon unit with me. He was an Indian from Arizona, a Spanish Indian. His name's on the wall. If you look under Elias, you'll see it . . . Jose Jan Miguel Elias. And he was a hippie kind of soldier. I couldn't find an Indian. That's why I went with Willem [Dafoe]. Willem, you know, is Scandinavian, but I could not find an Indian who could do it the way I wanted it done, so I changed ethnicity, but essentially Elias was that soldier. He was very loved, and he was killed by one of his own grenades on a recon in May of '68. So I thought for dramatic story-telling purposes that it would be interesting to put these two guys in the same unit. I was moved around because I was wounded several times, so I put them in the same unit for the sake of the story. They're actually based on real people. It's funny that people thought they were too pat. Maybe life is too pat.

H: You were praised for your recreation of jungle warfare. Was this based on your own experience in combat?

S: Yes, most of it was.

H: There's one sequence where an American soldier brutally kills an Asian civilian. Were you witness to this kind of brutality?

S: Quite a bit.

H: How did you prepare your actors for such an emotionally charged film?

S: I think they took it seriously to begin with because they were all kids, babies, when the war was being fought, so they all had this sort of mythic reverence for it, I suppose. They know about it from books and documentaries. We sent them through a training period of two weeks in the jungle. Taught them what it means to be infantry and to respect what they were doing. We wanted to give them a dirty look, a real look of smelling and looking like they lived in the jungle—unlike most war pictures where they always look like they go home at night. We kept them out there in the bush.

H: I was interested in your choice of Tom Cruise for the role of Ron Kovic in *Born on the Fourth of July*. Would you talk a little bit about your rehersals?

S: Well, rehearsal is just killing off my urge to get deeper into the onion. I do a lot of rehearsal during auditions for the actors. I like to hear a lot of the dialogue back through many different mouths. Sometimes you'll hear an actor you thought was good for one role much better in another. So you want to hear it again and again. You're also writing during this whole period. You're discussing. Then we do a formal two-week rehearsal with the final cast where we read, discuss and block out scenes. Then often during the last week of rehearsal I'll try to get down to the locations and rehearse there. That way we get a little closer to it. And I find that that helps because it could be eight weeks later when we actually shoot the scene, and by then a lot of it is forgotten. But it sort of remains in the subconscious. And sometimes you do things in rehearsal that I find interesting. When you try a scene one way, no matter how good it is, it generally never goes that way again. It goes another way. But it's a necessary step. I think you can over-rehearse. I agree with John Ford there. And I try not to rehearse the more emotional scenes. I'd rather be on the set and have the camera there so I don't lose the spontaneity of the actor's performance. I'd say that I'm more actor-oriented in terms of getting it down on film.

H: Did you actively include Kovic in the rehearsal process?

S: Parts, not all. No, it was usually just me with the actors, and then Ron would come in on occasion for a special thing, you know.

H: What was it like introducing someone of a younger generation into that part of your life?

S: Well, I'd done it with Charlie [Sheen], and that was interesting. So I did sort of the same thing with Tom. And it was really fascinating to see that, you know. Tom cares about it, and he is obviously motivated to teach his own generation and younger people some of the truths that he found out—to make people question their government is certainly the duty of the patriot. It's a great line I've sustained from Edward Abbey, "The true patriot is the one who defends his country against government."

H: You once said in an interview that after you left Yale, you were very gung ho about going to Vietnam. What were your feelings about the peace movement in 1966 as to opposed to when you returned in 1969?

S: At that time I was very prowar. And I stayed that way even when I returned. It wasn't really until the '70–'74 period that I really changed my outlook.

H: Do you think there's an irony involved with the fact that many of the fatalities in Vietnam were suffered by young American men who didn't go to college, or whose environment wasn't conducive to going to college, versus the antiwar movement whose main participants were from upper-middle-class backgrounds and had parents who could afford to send their kids to college?

S: Well, I'm glad if they stayed home with a college deferment. At least those that protested the war were saying something. They were following to some degree a doctrine of civil disobedience. I think people like [Dan] Quayle, who supported the war and yet hid out in the National Guard or got psychiatric discharges, which were easy to get, or who had trick knees, which were also easy to get if you had a family doctor . . . those people are hypocrites. I think Johnson made a huge mistake. I think it's against all basis of a democracy to fight a war and to send only the underclass. Yes, I think that's a huge mistake. It undercuts the basis of democracy. When you fight a war, you have to send everybody. And if we had sent everybody in 1965, including the businessmen's sons, the senators' sons, the war would have ended in 1966 because, believe me, senators and businessmen don't like to lose their sons in a war that has no practical purpose or objective. They would have ended the war, and as a result democracy would have really worked better, wouldn't it?

H: I got a sense in *Born on the Fourth of July*, when Kovic returns home and all the demonstrations are going on, that you were perhaps parodying the demonstrators in a very subtle way.

S: Would you be more specific?

H: Yes, when Kovic's girlfriend runs off with the bandwagon, leaving him speechless, his character doesn't respond to it. It seemed to me like a silent laugh, that maybe you were parodying the conformity that was going on with the antiwar movement.

S: To a degree, perhaps. That movement did, in fact, become a kind of fashion of the times. But on the other hand, I do think that the girl, Donna, was very important to him, because she provided the seismic change. She was the first manifest symbol for him that would later work on his mind. She was a good person doing a good thing, and it was okay to be against the war. Ron was not too bright in that sense. This is where the critics always had that problem with the working-class kid. They think that he's going to read something and turn against the war. Well, it's not going to happen that way. Ron turned against the war for visceral reasons. He turned against the war because he had been in the wheelchair. Why not admit it? It had a lot to do with that motivation. I'm defending my point. He was from a different class of people and that was the way he thought. He was simpler, perhaps, than some of the critics of the picture. You know what I'm trying to say? The truth is too simple for the intellectuals.

H: So like Kovic, you were at first opposed to the antiwar movement?

S: No, it was more like I was removed from it. I was the more typical Vietnam vet in the sense that I was still fighting the war in my head. I just stayed away from the protests. I didn't take either side. I felt like I had many doubts about the protests because it took me awhile to deal with what I'd been through. I was in shell shock I'd guess you'd say—alienation and shell shock—so it took some time. I'm not going to tell you that I came back from the war and knew it was wrong. No, it took me a long time to deal with that. You see, when I went to the war, I was a believer in govern-ment, the great Greek tradition of democracy. I just didn't realize that our particular government lied a lot. That took me some time to figure out. In retrospect I think that the demonstrations were a very heroic thing, and I think they were right and I was wrong. I think they were doing something that was very good for this country.

H: Did you have problems readjusting when you returned from combat?

S: Tremendous problems, yes. I was in jail for marijuana smug-gling when I got back.

H: You said your experience was subsumed by Ron Kovic in the sense that his experience epitomized all veterans' experiences.

S: Well, it was more dramatic and more radical. My return home was more idiosyncratic and specific, and I felt like his story was really, frankly, a better story. More people can relate to it. And I was as passionate about his story as I was about my own, to be honest. You know, he had a far worse experience than I ever did. His story evoked in me great passions, great feelings. My heart goes out to Ron for what he went through.

H: Will *Born on the Fourth of July* preclude your other film you were going to do, *Second Life*, about returning home after the war.

S: How did you know about *Second Life*? Jesus Christ! I told you that?

H: No, I read it somewhere.

S: Yes? That's pretty sharp. You're a detective, one of the bright ones. I can't believe this. I've left pieces of *Second Life* all over the place, all over the years, you know. It's never come together yet.

H: Then it might make up the last part of your Vietnam trilogy?

S: It's unofficial. I can't say though. I do have another Vietnam film I plan to do. *Second Life* may not be it, but I have played with it in the back of my mind as something I'd like to do. It's very personal. It's about me and my dad. I got a piece of that relationship into *Wall Street* with Marty [Sheen] and Charlie [Sheen] and the Hal Holbrook character.

H: That's interesting. You're father seems to come up in a lot of the other interviews I've read.

S: No, it's a question people always ask me. My mom is just as interesting, but nobody asks me about her.

H: Well, didn't you once say that you saw a lot of Evita in your mother? Would you talk a little bit about her?

S: [laughs] She was very glamorous. She used to go out a lot, a very well dressed lady—French, New York, fifties, sixties—very sophisticated. She traveled and had a good time, lived her life like a French courtesan.

H: What did she think about your . . .

S: Mom, forgive me.

H: What did she think about your going to Vietnam?

S: She was obviously terrified. She thought I was crazy. But she couldn't do anything to stop me, because in part I was running away from her too. I didn't want anything to do with either of them anymore.

H: And your father was "one of them" too?

S: He couldn't stop me. At eighteen in this country you can enlist, you know.

H: Your father passed away recently.

S: 1985.

H: How do you think he would have responded to *Wall Street* had he seen it brought to fruition?

S: He probably would have said to me what he used to say when we saw films together when I was a kid, "He could have done it better."

H: Were you writing about your father?

S: To a degree, yes. As I said, Marty and Hal Holbrook's characters were sort of two parts of my father. In Marty's care for his son where you see his love, I think there was my father. And in Hal's taking an interest in the kid and saying, "Stand for something. Don't listen to what's going on in the street. Be out of fashion, be old fashioned." My dad was very straight. He had integrity. He was scared in a lot of ways. I mean, I can't say he was, you know, Franklin Delano Roosevelt, or anyone like that, whom he hated, but he had a lot of integrity. He gave me a great education.

H: You've recently finished production on *The Doors*, a film about rock legend Jim Morrison. Would you talk about your fascination with him?

S: I guess because a piece of me is in him. I very much sympathized with him and identified with him at the time, in his sense of struggle. One sensed that he was a tormented person, and that he was not your conventional rock star. He was not in it for fame or bliss. He enjoyed it, but he seemed to want to go elsewhere. I think he grew a beard and got heavy because he went on a Hemingway trip, a writer trip, and I think he even had aspirations to direct. He was a man of many shapes, and always questing, always looking. I think that's the ultimate identification, the quester. I look at him also as a kind of Dionysian figure, a poet, a philosopher.

H: Do you think it took his death and the deaths of people like Jimi Hendrix and Janis Joplin to make their music endure the way that it has?

S: No, I think the music was good and solid, but you know, no doubt we would not have made a movie about him if he were still alive. I don't think so, no. I think that that is part of the mythology he created, a Rimbaud figure, a poet who arrived at a place and time, had a very strong impact and left. He lived for his death in a sense. I think that he was half in love with death. All of his poetry is a metaphor of death. We mention the word death twenty-five times in the movie, because that's where he was. He talked about it. Castaneda has an expression about death being always on the left shoulder. You walk with death all your days. You could be intimate with it. You could be a friend. So we tried to explore that aspect of being in touch with your death on a daily basis. You know Jim lived a bit like Achilles. If you remember the line, "To glory in the day of your death." Death was important to the Greeks. It's something I think they stored up a lot of energy for. To die nobly, gloriously, was the greatest thing of all. To die in shame was to go to hell.

H: You and Morrison are part of the same generation . . .

S: Yes, but I was a little younger too.

H: But you both became adults in the sixties, except that he stayed in the country and sang, and you went to Vietnam. You both took very different paths. Do you think that you and he were able to accomplish anything by the different choices you made?

S: Yes, but they were entirely different approaches. I had to go to Vietnam for reasons I explained in *Platoon*—an authenticity of feeling. I had the feeling when I was a young man that I was leading a fake life, so I had to go and seek other realities. I wanted to go to the bottom of the barrel where everybody goes, you know, hell, war. That's what gave me a sense of reality and dreams, both mixed. Jim did not go to Vietnam. He was in more of an advanced soul. And he wrestled with death from a very young age. He had such an imagination that he could create, in effect, Vietnam in his head without having to go. I mean, he didn't need a physical reality. He seemed to live in his mind so intensely that he trusted his imagination to do the work for him. He did "Unknown Soldier" about Nam and that cost him heavy. Several people told me that he was very upset and in some ways spiritually wounded. In '67 when "Unknown Soldier" was banned from the airwaves by all the radio jocks, he went into a deep depression.

H: In *Platoon* you dealt with that Vietnam experience, and in some degree also in *Born on the Fourth of July*. But what about those kids who didn't directly participate in the Vietnam conflict? What is it about their experience that you're trying to share with the audience in *The Doors*? What specifically is it about that era here in the United States that you're trying to render?

S: My feeling is that I'm groping, too. I know there's something there. And I know I have a lot of different things to say. I could not lay it out for you in a sentence. There are many layers in this story that I'm just becoming aware of in the editing of this film. It's not simple. You've got music, you've got behavior, you've got sexuality, you have rebelliousness, social change. You have breaking the law. Jim was a man who went up against limits, and he always tested the limits. And I think that legally, chemically, sexually, he pushed. I think the fame was a limit, and it bored him after a while. And it would bore any intelligent person. And I think at the end of the day he was bored with life. And I think that death became a new limit. I think he was a man who was trapped in a sort of a prison of his own device.

H: Do you find your own fame boring?

S: No, it gets me good tables in restaurants, and some wonderful people come up to you and tell you things, share things. It gives you access to people which, in the Capra-esque tradition of democracy, is a good thing. It's boring in its limitations and categorizations. It's boring when people write the most mundane things about your life or those around you. Morrison had a lot of that. You know, "Oh, he's the rock God, the sex creature, the Barbie doll—all that shit bored him. Then eventually he had to go around the country, and he had to give these shows where the crowds where so huge and so demanding. I'm sure that became boring. They had this image of him—complete licentiousness, misbehavior, and I'm sure he felt compelled to live up to it. He could not give a sane concert. The bigger the auditorium, the smaller his figure, the wilder he had to be. And I think he played to that. And I think he loved the audience up to one point, but then started to hate them. They became "the beast of hell," "the mouth of hell." That's the way we try to show it in the movie—that the audience changes for him, as did the late sixties too when everything became taken over by drugs. The Haight-Ashbury scene went sleazy. Free sex led to a lot of complications. Its innocence changed. You got the Manson murders. So Morrison consciously had to deal with that shit in his music. His lyrics began to change. And that is what I was trying to say earlier. The perception that we're trying to wrestle with . . . this is not your question.

H: It's interesting, what you're saying . . .

S: The perception of Morrison in the tabloid version of his life is that he was successful. So he became a slave to that image, but he failed because he drank and drugged and became no good, you know. That's what everybody believed, that's why he flopped in his later albums. But I strongly disagree. I believe that his work became much more interesting. He did not become the standard rock-and-roll cliché. What happened was that his work got better toward the end. He was writing great poetry. And he was doing some of his best musical work in "L.A. Woman," which is his last album, and in "American Prayer," which is his collection of poems he put on audio shortly before going to Paris. So out of this he began to live, you know, the Blake line, "The palace of excess leads to the palace of wisdom." That does apply to Jim, but in this age it's very difficult to understand. Sometimes excess can lead to spirituality.

H: The Romans certainly thought so.

S: And that's the point. "Roman wilderness," remember that line he did?

H: But excess can lead to insecurity as well.

S: Excess can lead to a lot of things. And that's the theme that should be embraced and not shirked or hidden from.

Filmography (as director)

1973	*Seizure*
1981	*The Hand*
1986	*Salvador*
1986	*Platoon*
1987	*Wall Street*
1988	*Talk Radio*
1989	*Born on the Fourth of July*
1990	*The Doors*
1992	*J.F.K.*

NATIONAL SEARCH

ACCEPTING SUBMISSIONS FOR THE

CITY PLAYHOUSE ANNUAL TEN-MINUTE PLAY COMPETITION

City Playhouse is accepting submissions for its annual *Ten-Minute Play* competition. Once a year, City Playhouse in association with the Theatre Academy will be producing an original play festival of Ten-Minute Plays. All submissions will be considered and those selected will receive a fully mounted production of their play at the Caminito Theatre, an established 99 Seat Plan in Hollywood.

Winners will work with theatre professionals, including actors, designers, and directors. Some plays will be nurtured for full-length status, to receive a slot in the Theatre Academy's season of plays, therefore eligible for consideration for competition in the Kennedy Center/American College Theater Festival.

This is a national search for new material to be produced in the heart of the entertainment industry at no cost to the playwright beyond a registration fee of $15.00. Deadline for submissions is June 1, 1996. Production of plays will be produced in the following winter slot.

Entrants may submit as many plays as they would like. There is a $15.00 registration fee for each submission. Send plays and check ($15.00 for each submission) payable to "City Playhouse" to:

CITY PLAYHOUSE TEN-MINUTE PLAYS
L.A.C.C. Theatre Academy
855 N. Vermont Avenue
Los Angeles, CA 90029

For further information: (213) 953-4336

Los Angeles City College & its Theatre Academy Awarded Upward Bound Grant

As a result of a proposal submitted by the Theatre Academy last December, Los Angeles City College has recently been awarded a four-year, $900,000 federal Upward Bound grant which will provide academic enrichment sessions and workshops for local high school students.

Beginning this November, 50 high school students will attend Saturday sessions at the college throughout the school year and participate in an intensive academic and conservatory program during the summer. The Saturday sessions will cover math, language arts, speech and introduction to theatre and film. During its six-week summer session, the students will also take additional courses in lab science, computer technology and also be involved in various courses that focus on theatre in a conservatory environment.

The students selected for this very special program will be drawn from LAUSD high schools including Manual Arts, Jefferson, Locke, Dorsey, Fairfax and Fremont High Schools.

LACC's Upward Bound program, being administered by the Theatre Academy, is geared to providing enrichment activities for college bound high school students from disadvantaged backgrounds. The targeted students are high academic achievers who will be the first in their families to enroll in college.

In addition to the enrichment courses, students will be provided with field trips to museums and theatrical performances. Guest speakers from business, government, medicine, law, the arts, government, and various support agencies will also be brought in to provide motivation for the students and to talk to them about professional career opportunities.

The Theatre Academy has been recognized as one of the leading professional theatre training academies in the country. It is proud to be associated with the Upward Bound program and is excited about sharing its work with high school students from the greater Los Angeles area.

BARRY LEVINSON
Baltimore Son

Barry Levinson wears his background on his sleeve. He's so much a part of the chrome-trimmed diners and row-house neighbor-hoods of his native Baltimore that as soon as you meet him you've forgotten having spent the last thirty minutes finding his palatial home neatly tucked in the rolling hills of Bel Air.

Levinson is one of the more interesting directors to have em-erged in the early 1980s. He first gained recognition for *Diner* (1982), his meat-and-potatoes examination of "The Boys," a group of wisecracking guys in their early twenties who spend much of their time shooting the breeze on the right side of Baltimore's Hill-top Diner. Loaded with snappy dialogue and authentic minutiae that captures the mood and look of 1959, the film is a semiautobio-graphical account of Levinson's youth.

Five years later the director returned to the same part of Balti-more to direct *Tin Men* (1987), a movie about a group of middle-aged businessmen who were also regulars at the Hilltop. Sharing their breakfasts and lunches together, the tin men would boast or grumble about the trials of selling aluminum siding to unwanting customers. "My friends and I would hang out in the right-hand side of the diner and the tin men would eat on the left side," says Levinson. "They were all real Runyonesque characters—colorful, carefree and wild. Big hustlers and gamblers. We all found them very exciting."

In 1990 the director wrapped up a third chapter in his series of feature films set in Baltimore. Unlike *Diner* and *Tin Men, Avalon* spans three generations of Eastern European immigrants assimilating into American culture. Loosely based on Levinson's own pedigree (from 1914 to 1968), the film chronicles the life of the fictional Krichinsky family. To write the screenplay, the director interviewed relatives whom he hadn't seen in years. "They're full of so many wonderful stories," says Levinson. "Every time I shoot in Baltimore, I get the urge to shoot something else," he continues. "But the most important thing for me is not to be nostalgic. I'm not interested in nostalgia. What excites me is investigating periods in our lives, in terms of what they meant, what they represented, and how they were affected by the times."

Born April 6, 1942, in Baltimore, Maryland, Levinson was raised in the predominantly Jewish neighborhood of Forest Park, where his parents, grandparents and other relatives had immigrated from Eastern Europe in the earlier part of this century. After graduating from high school, he attended junior college and worked as a salesman hustling encyclopedias and used cars. Moving on to Washington, D.C., he eventually attended American University while working part-time at a local Washington television station. "I didn't know what to do with my life," says Levinson, reminiscing about his move to California in the late 1960s. "I enrolled in an acting class and started writing and performing skits." After some of his work was broadcast by a local television station, the producers of "The Tim Conway Show" hired him as a writer in the early 1970s. Based on his success there, he went on to enjoy a prosperous stint on "The Carol Burnett Show," ultimately winning three Emmy Awards for his writing.

During the mid-1970s, Ron Clark, a screenwriter working closely with Mel Brooks, suggested Levinson to co-write Brooks's voiceless slapstick comedy, *Silent Movie* (1976), and later his Alfred Hitchcock parody, *High Anxiety* (1977). "Mel taught me every aspect of the business," Levinson says fondly of his mentor. "He was the best film school I could have ever attended." It was Brooks who also suggested that the Baltimore native write a screenplay about his youthful memories of the Hilltop Diner. "Mel thought 'The Boys' might make a funny movie, so I wrote the script and MGM let me do it."

From *Diner* Levinson went on to direct a diversified body of work, including *The Natural* (1984), *Good Morning, Vietnam* (1987) and Steven Spielberg's adventure-mystery *Young Sherlock Holmes* (1985). In 1988 Levinson won Academy Awards for Best Director and Best Picture for *Rain Man.* "Boy, all the guys back in Baltimore got a kick out of that," says Levinson.

HICKENLOOPER: Peter Bogdanovich said that he thought directors reached their prominence, in terms of their studio clout, in the seventies with Martin Scorsese and Francis Coppola, and now some people, like Roger Ebert, believe that the power has shifted back to the studio/agent/actor—the package deal—and away from the director. You rode to prominence in the eighties— do you have any thoughts on this?

LEVINSON: I'm not sure that I would agree. I think what he's saying is valid in terms of a group of directors that came up in the seventies. There's a new group of directors who've come up in the past five, ten years and they're beginning to dominate more. I don't know that the balance has shifted. I think what he says is partially true. If you say give me Arnold Schwarzenegger, give me Sylvester Stallone, give me this thing or that thing and let them do this vehicle, yes, okay, that is the package deal. But that is coexisting with a *Raging Bull* or an *Unbearable Lightness of Being* or a *sex, lies and videotape*. But look at the movies of the seventies. Does that negate *The Sting*, which had big stars and George Roy Hill and all that kind of stuff? You could say that was a package movie. It was good entertainment. But that was in the seventies. If I were to point to anything today, I think movies are threatened in the sense that everything is about a thirty-second spot. If you have a movie that translates well into a thirty-second spot, you can sell tickets on opening weekend. Some movies can never be done in a thirty-second spot, therefore you cannot sell them, therefore you cannot have a first weekend that is extremely big, and then it's going to rely on whether or not the movie is good enough to exist in that marketplace. So films that do not work and cannot be distilled that easily are going to be in shorter supply.

H: Do you ever feel a need stylistically to make your films move faster in order to keep the audience's attention?

L: Well, yeah. I'll tell you something that I bet no one would probably ever be aware of. I generally have people talk much faster in movies than they may normally do. It looks kind of laid back, casual, because there is something about film speed that I've never quite understood. But things that look at the right speed when you watch them are slower when you watch them on film. It's strange. All I basically do is to try to deal with the things and ideas I have in a way that I find interesting. And hopefully it's interesting to someone else. There would be nothing more threatening to me than to make a movie that I didn't believe in, to make a movie because I think that it would do well with an hordes. I've been lucky that I've been able to pursue what I find interesting and not have to pander to the hordes. You know, with *Rain Man* the studio took it to some sneak preview audiences who wrote on their cards that they didn't like the fact that the film had an unhappy ending. Well, of course nobody's going to be thrilled about an unhappy ending, but I couldn't listen to all that crap because I believed in that ending. And I was fortunate. The film did well.

H: *Diner* and *Tin Men* have very distinct styles from your other work. Are these two films quintessentially Barry Levinson pictures more than, let's say, *Rain Man, Young Sherlock Holmes* or *Good Morning, Vietnam?*

L: Well, I'd say *Diner* and *Tin Men* are certainly more Barry Levinson films than *Sherlock*, which is to me kind of playing around. I wanted to do something radically outside of what I was used to because there's a point when you need to expand as a filmmaker. I thought I may get a real education here, and I'm going to play with the things that I like, particularly the elements concerning Victorian England schoolboys. That really appealed to me. I think *Rain Man* in its own crazy way has a lot of stuff that would almost be compatible with *Tin Men* and *Diner*. Though the story itself is not something that would come from my own experiences, like *Diner* and *Tin Men*, there's work in it that's very much of what I enjoy playing with. And I think *Good Morning, Vietnam* would apply to that as well. When I made *Diner* there were those who would have loved me to keep doing just that film, you know, exploring average people in a city growing up and their various life experiences. But what I found interesting is that I'm always fascinated by other things, so I love the idea that I can do a *Diner* and I can do a *Natural* and then I can do a *Tin Men*. You know, and I can do a *Rain Man*, and I can do an *Avalon*. And then I can go do whatever, so that some of the work is of one type and some of the work is all over the place, and we can find the things that may interconnect. I like having two different types of work, because I think my interests jump around. Sometimes you can get a little stale by working in a certain area.

H: *Diner* was based on your experiences with "The Boys" you used to hang out with in Baltimore. How did they feel about being portrayed in a movie?

L: I think at the beginning they found it kind of confusing, be- cause they'd say, "Wait a minute! Shreegie didn't do so-and-so, and Corky did—whatever, but he didn't do—." It wasn't one hundred percent all of what anyone did, so they were baffled by it initially. Now, they can celebrate it. But it took awhile. The best comment was from my cousin Eddie (who the character Eddie is based on), who did give his wife a football test, just like the script had it, except in a slightly different situation. He said, "I saw the movie four times, and after the fourth time I realized how stupid it was to give my wife a football test." I said, "Really think so?" He said, "Yeah, you know about two weeks after we're married she forgot all the fuckin' answers! So, it was a waste of time." He didn't think it was a stupid idea in the beginning, it was only that the result was not worthwhile.

H: When you were living in Baltimore in '59 or '60, was there anything in the back of your mind saying, boy, maybe I could use this someday?

L: No, I never had any aspirations to write or direct, so it wasn't stuff like, gee, I should keep this in mind. It never entered my mind that any of this, which was truly considered a giant waste of time, would ultimately have some validity.

H: Would you talk a little bit about casting *Diner*? I understand you wanted to go with unknowns at the time.

L: Yes.

H: Was it difficult trying to cast your friends?

L: Not really. I just wanted to find a group that I could picture as a group. You know, although we're different types, there was something casual about our relationship to one another that was the hardest thing to put together. There's nothing I hate worse in a movie when everybody's friends and they talk about friendship. You know? When they say good-bye they're not always hugging one another. I prefer, "Yeah, I'll see ya!" There's a shorthand to a very good, strong relationship that is much more real.

H: Would you talk about your rehearsal process on *Diner*? What kind of leeway did you give your actors with the material?

L: I don't do much rehearsing. I don't work on the scenes. All I really want to do is let everybody be familiar enough with the work. But I'm not that interested in rehearsal.

H: Were any of the conversations in *Diner* ever taken verbatim from something that actually happened?

L: I don't know verbatim, but the conversations, like Mac talking about Frank Sinatra, were the kind of conversations that would have gone on. Those things were based on what I remember, how close is hard to know.

H: What was the origin of *Tin Men* and what was your writing process like on that film versus *Diner*?

L: Well, the writing process was a little different. *Tin Men* is based on the tin men who, post World War II, when aluminum siding started, used to hang out in the diner. And there used to be a sign sometimes in there, "No tin men allowed." The diner people wanted to keep them out during busy hours. I was fascinated by them. So it was in the back of my head when I was shooting *Diner* that maybe I would get to them. That's what I would look at, the guys that hung out at the tracks, the hustlers and wheelers and dealers, this criminal element that was part of the other thing. I've always thought one of the most crazy comments was in Pauline Kael's review of *Tin Men*. It was sent to me by someone from Baltimore who said, "Is this crazy?" because Kael called them shinglemen. She says they were shinglemen, not tin men. And that was like saying, "Then I don't know what they're called in my own hometown. I don't know why I saw signs that said tin men when they were shinglemen!" But they put up tin. They sold tin. You know, aluminum. But it was tin, not shingles. So she wrote this giant piece about these shinglemen and I found it extraordinarily egocentric, because it is like saying, "This is what I know; therefore, it is." I suppose I could say maybe that is true of the New York area, it's not true in Baltimore. I didn't invent it. I didn't make up the word. That was the word. And a friend of mine from Baltimore said, "Oh, is this what I was? I thought I was a tin man." They were in Baltimore. They came out of Pittsburgh and down through Maryland, and you know, there are those who could trace the whole ancestry of the development of the aluminum-siding business. I liked those guys. They could make the money, and they lived for a quick buck. And I found that to be a fascinating character to deal with in the second half of the twentieth century.

H: *Diner* and *Tin Men* deal with male characters who find it difficult to communicate with women. What are your observations about relationships between the sexes, then versus now? Have they changed?

L: I feel that men still have an enormous lack of understanding about women. We were segregated from them for so many years in the sense that the guys were with the guys, and the girls were off with the girls. So we didn't interact enough in a way other than as hunt sport, for sex. There's real poor understanding of their sensibilities, which *Diner* is dealing with, how little we know, and how naive men are. I think it has to be changing, but how quickly we improve is debatable.

H: In *Tin Men* why did you decide to cast name stars, as opposed to *Diner*, where you went with unknowns?

L: When you're doing movies about guys in their early twenties, there are going to be a very few stars. Those who are unknown are going to get discovered, like a lot did after *Diner*. When you get people who are supposed to be in their late thirties and forties who are totally unknown, it's very hard, because if they're unknown, there may be a reason why they're unknown.

H: You've just completed *Avalon*. Some people have referred to it as the last panel of your Baltimore triptych. When you started *Diner* and *Tin Men* were you aware of the fact that you were going to do a trilogy of films about your past in Baltimore?

L: I don't know that it's a trilogy. There are now three, but maybe there'll be more. I don't think this concludes anything. When I first did *Diner* I never thought I would do anything beyond it, but as I was doing *Diner* and achieving it, then I realized there was *Tin Men*. And then I think doing *Tin Men* was when I started thinking that there was something else. I wasn't sure, but as I shot in my old neighborhood, in front of my old house, I thought about what eventually became *Avalon*. There are a couple of others that I have in mind now, in fact, that are interesting, but I just don't have the compulsion to do it yet.

H: How does *Avalon* differ from *Diner* and *Tin Men*?

L: Well, it's much larger because it's generational, dealing from 1914 to 1968. Its structure is very different, its design is much different. It keeps going backwards and forward in time. Some things are—I wouldn't say they're surrealistic—but they are less than realistic at times, so there are stylistic things that differ very much from *Diner* and *Tin Men*, which tend to be much more of a straightforward reality.

H: Are these moments surreal for the audience or the characters?

L: The question is, if you begin to tell stories is what you tell real? How much of it's supposed to be real? What is the image that we get from what you tell? And how much of it has been distorted by what you tell? So when we hear the grandfather telling stories in the beginning of the movie to the children, as the great storyteller, one of the motifs to the piece is that he was a storyteller. At the end of the movie he would start to tell the story, but the child just turns away to watch the TV.

H: That's very depressing.

L: But it's real and television is one of the things I'm trying to deal with in *Avalon*. I think the impact of it has been phenomenal in our society. I mean, I could spend hours talking about it, but for the sake of this interview, I'll just say that it's replaced our need, particularly in the family, to communicate with one another. It's been extremely threatening to that. It affects the way we think, dress, act, and it's probably affecting us in ways that haven't even been evaluated yet. Look, Americans watch eight hours of television per day on the average, that's approximately two hours of commercials, divided up into thirty-second spots, telling us how much we need all this crap which we really don't need. It affects us in enormous ways. You know, there was a time when the family name meant something, when people were proud of their heritage, when there were certain codes of behavior that weren't acceptable, but now television has confused all that. It's giving us images of who we should be, of whose family we should be a part of, "The Hogan Family," "The Partridge Family," "The Brady Bunch," the Beaver, any family but your own, who you've stopped talking to because you want to park it in front of the television. It's saying violence is okay, it's fun, so then some kids go out stab some guy to death and then go dancing, *GO DANCING!* Where's the guilt? Where's the remorse? No, it's okay, I saw it on TV. The impact of television is not only breaking down the nuclear family, but society. People are getting very confused about what they know. So in *Avalon*, why should the little girl want to listen to the grandfather when she's got television.

H: So the grandfather is the narrator?

L: He's one of the narrators in the piece—if there is a narrator. It doesn't work in pure narrative, but the movie begins with him telling about when he came to America. He says at one point— they keep saying we've heard that story, we've heard that story—he says, "If you don't keep remembering, you might forget." And he tells this story through the movie. He's in a home and he's telling stories to his great-grandchild, the great-grandchild doesn't understand him, finds the way he speaks too peculiar. The television set with the parade is more interesting than what the old man might say.

H: *Avalon* takes place over such an extended period of time. It must have been quite a challenge dealing with the different chronologies and structures. Usually you just dictate scripts, but is *Avalon* something you had to structure on paper first?

L: No, I still dictate all my scripts. I enjoy writing out loud.

H: You wrote for television for a while, and you have very strong feelings about television now. Did you have them when you were writing for TV back then?

L: I think more so as time has gone on. I mean, I watch it all the time. I got a satellite dish or whatever. I'm hooked on trying to find good television. I now have a hundred and sixty stations, and am still trying to find something interesting other than the news. But there are things that come up periodically. There are those great documentaries that come up a lot. There are a few things that I find fascinating.

H: How did the experience of writing for television affect your own writing?

L: I don't know, I guess it made me write. Writing is writing and the more you do the more you write.

H: Is it more of a challenge for you to direct material that's autobiographical than stuff that's written by other people?

L: Well, sometimes. There's a different kind of challenge to each kind of work. What I find interesting about movies that I haven't written is that I am generally going to be in environments I would not necessarily think of, and in places that I wouldn't necessarily write about. I'm dealing with characters that I might not necessarily address in the work that I write. So I love stepping into that. I love suddenly being in Thailand and trying to make sense out of that piece and suddenly working with the Asian actors and so forth, and trying to make something seem credible to me.

H: Before you directed *Rain Man* there were a lot of other directors slated to direct the film, Sidney Pollack and Steven Spielberg, for example. And I read that they turned it down because they felt

there wasn't enough plot, not enough story. But that wasn't a problem for you?

L: Well, I always think most movies have fake plots. You just
invent plots so everybody says, "Oh yeah, that's got a real plot!"
You know, the film *Ghost* is thick in this kind of plot, because Patrick Swayze's character is dead, but he hasn't gone because he's a
ghost hanging around to tell the girl that someone wants to kill
her. And there's your plot and everything works off of that, so you
can say "There's your plot! You get to be a box-office hit." I don't
think you have to always have events that are feeding the plot. If
you can find situations about people that are somehow intriguing,
revealing and keep us involved, then that is fine. I hate contriv-
ance. That's why there are so many goddamn cop movies being
made. Movies invent these ridiculous fake plots that reduce the
characters to cardboard. It's the characters that need to move your
piece. I know a lot of times critics complain that there's not
enough of this.

H: What ultimately interested you in *Good Morning, Vietnam?*

L: Well, I liked the script. I liked the idea of the piece, because if
you say Vietnam, we always think of soldiers fighting in the jungle.
And here it says Saigon, the city, before the shit hit the fan. A disc
jockey and Vietnamese who go to school and work in shops, that's
what was interesting to me. I was interested in the city aspect of
the Vietnam War before it really escalated. And the idea of radio
appealed to me because I started out in radio.

H: Do you feel the need to direct bigger movies like *Rain Man*
and *Good Morning, Vietnam* in order to do the films that are really
close to you like *Tin Men* and *Diner?*

L: I don't think I look at it like "I've got to do that in order to do
this." I enjoyed *Rain Man* and *Good Morning, Vietnam*. I had a great
time with that kind of work, so I'm not trying to do that so I can get
the cachet to do the other. There are two sides of my personality—
I like to work both sides of whatever the hell I'm about.

H: Is there something that you do to keep yourself grounded?

L: I think my success could only overwhelm me if I were to sit around and celebrate my celebrity status. I think if you love the work, you are grounded, because that's what's going to motivate you, that's what drives you. That's what I'm getting fed by and that's why I love to work often. I don't want to work every four or five years. There's an excitement to each thing you try, and the only way of ever getting better is by working at it. You know, all modern directors are at an enormous disadvantage because we never had the sixty to seventy movies under our belts that John Ford and some of those guys had. We're talking about a dozen movies or something like that—nothing compared to what they used to direct. And you see how much they had to learn. But they learned, they solved other things, they saw another way to work it. You could only learn by working. And that's what excites me, not all the other nonsense like Hollywood parties or whatever.

Filmography

1982   *Diner*
1984   *The Natural*
1985   *Young Sherlock Holmes*
1987   *Tin Men*
1987   *Good Morning, Vietnam*
1988   *Rain Man*
1990   *Avalon*
1991   *Bugsy Siegel*

STANLEY KRAMER
Policy of Truth

I met Stanley Kramer as he was moving into his Beverly Hills office after a half-decade respite from Hollywood. "It's good to be back. It's interesting," says Kramer who spent most of the 1980s in Seattle, Washington, where he lectured at a university, wrote a column for the *Seattle Times* and hosted his own television show. "I needed to leave. I began to stagnate in Hollywood," he says, remembering the late 1970s when he felt disillusioned by the major studios' lack of interest in serious filmmaking. "I couldn't picture myself directing a space movie, so I went up to the Pacific Northwest hoping to find some answers to questions that I couldn't get in Southern California."

The director of such classics as *The Defiant Ones* (1958), *Guess Who's Coming to Dinner* (1967), *On the Beach* (1959), *Inherit the Wind* (1960), *Judgment at Nuremberg* (1961), *Ship of Fools* (1965) and *Bless the Beasts and Children* (1971), Kramer came to the height of his powers in the mid 1960s. Known for his socially conscious themes that have drawn praise from critics, the director has also been condemned by organizations and religious groups, from the National Rifle Association to Christian fundamentalists. Consequently Kramer has been placed in the ranks of filmmakers who have had to ardently struggle to make the movies they thought were important. "Now I'm back to give it another shot," says Kramer, referring to a screenplay about Polish Solidarity which he hopes to direct

151

within the year. "If I can't make it in Hollywood, then I'll do it on my own."

Stanley Kramer became an independent producer, working outside the big Hollywood studios long before anyone thought it could be done or was worth the effort. Following his service in the Army Signal Corps at the end of World War II, Kramer formed an independent motion picture company, Screen Plays, Inc., where as producer he oversaw a series of highly acclaimed yet modestly budgeted films that were noticed for their seriousness. *Home of the Brave* (1949), *The Men* (1950), *Cyrano de Bergerac* (1950), *Death of a Salesman* (1951), *High Noon* (1951), *The Wild One* (1954) and *The Caine Mutiny* (1954) were just some of the films that preceded his reputation as a dedicated filmmaker.

As a director Kramer is also known for his candor and introspection. Unlike many directors who are stylists, and whose work grosses large sums of money at the box office, Kramer is an auteur who sometimes doesn't score well with mass audiences. He is constantly searching for his own voice and unfolding the story and characters in a way that is truthful and real. By fighting the forces of commerce that often work against filmmakers with a unique perspective, Kramer has succeeded in giving us a provocative body of work.

HICKENLOOPER: Often you're writer, director, and producer all on the same picture. Do you find that you run into the problem of not having enough outside opinion, or are you open to the opinions of others?

KRAMER: Well, that's an all-embracing question. First of all, this is an arrogant profession. To direct a film, particularly in Hollywood, you must do what pleases you first, and it must please you before it pleases other people. It's your dream. Therefore, that has with it an arrogance and a detriment, or a set procedure, which is that you don't listen to anybody. However, because of the fact that we're human and we know the necessity of encompassing the opinions of other people, many of whom have great ideas, you create a climate for their being able to contribute ideas. But it is a profession and a procedure where one man runs the show. That's the way it goes.

H: You've said that you rehearse your actors extensively. What is your rehearsal process like?

K: Well, my rehearsals begin a couple of weeks before I begin shooting. After I assemble the cast, we'll go through the entire script from page one. I also have the cinematographer, the production designer and the composer there so that they can come to know the story the way the actors do.

H: Do you physically block out scenes?

K: Yes, and we'll frequently make script changes depending on what works and what doesn't.

H: How do you deal with actors who may have two entirely antithetical approaches to acting if they're in the same scene?

K: Some people like to rehearse, some people don't. In *Ship of Fools* Oskar Werner was a rehearser, Simone Signoret was not. She liked to do it off the cuff. That's a problem for the director. You have to create a climate in which everyone gives. Hopefully, they will be flexible enough to give for the other person's needs. You create the climate through contact and relationship. My own feelings I share with Spencer Tracy who always said, "Improvisation is perspiration." And I think we've perspired most of it out in preparation. Some actors will want the cameras to roll and just let it happen. Well, I don't believe it just happens on film. First of all, there are extra elements like the camera. If the camera doesn't get it, it isn't there. So I like to be prepared for that. And I think that a close-up is a God given privilege. When you look at someone, you can see the soul in their eyes. Tracy proved that to me many times. At any rate, I believe in being very well prepared.

H: You've worked with Marlon Brando. How do you feel about actors who subscribe to the "Method"?

K: Well, I don't feel anything. That's their method. As I say, they have to finally fit what is my pattern, the atmosphere I create, which is loose and helps cultivate good performances. As long as we've talked it out, and we know what we're driving toward, then there may be many ways to reach it. What difference does it make if you pause for a moment in the doorway and then cross to the table or enter the door and immediately cross to the table? I mean, does it accomplish what the overall purpose is?

H: How closely do you work with your writer?

K: Page for page. I mean, I try not to be the writer. I contribute. But I work very closely because the writer's concept and mine must be in agreement. If I don't know the concept, as the director, I could change the whole tone of the story. I don't want to do that. We worked too hard on the dream and the fine texture of the scene, or the character's motivation, to have a misunderstanding that could ruin the film. When I get to the set, I'm representing the writer and myself together. Now, occasionally there are changes, if an actor does something unique that is not in the script but which works for the character, we will make changes on the set—not necessarily improvisational at all. It is merely some concept he has which he now expresses that turns out to be more powerful, better, more striking, more dramatic, more something than what we had, so I have to make a judgment.

H: Do you ever shoot a scene two ways?

K: No, there is only one right way to shoot a scene. You diminish it if you become unfocused on two different ways of doing it, then consequently you only come up with two bad versions of one scene.

H: How closely do you work with your editor?

K: I edit the film myself, frame for frame, and I mean it.

H: You once said that editing was more directing than actually being on the set.

K: Sometimes. After all, where you cut, how long you hold a close-up and whether you create a succession of cuts, all of this has to do with the total impact, and you control that in the editing room. But obviously, you have to get it on film first. That's the job of the director.

H: With respect to adapting material for the screen from a novel you said that there is no satisfactory way for a filmmaker to please himself and the novelist simultaneously. How can a director or a screenwriter capture the essence of a novel, or should they try to be faithful at all?

K: You can't be faithful. That's a ridiculous word in this instance. When a novelist sells a book, he sells it to people who read. When a writer adapts a novel, he has to sell it to a movie audience. He has to put it in film language which sometimes may be impossible to translate in visual terms. You hope that the spirit is true and remains solid, but he settles for an adaptation. Also, if you were to do it directly as a novel, you would have a four- or five-hour film, and unfortunately they're not in fashion. Distributors won't stand for that. No novelist is completely satisfied with the adaptation, because there've been cuts and you resent them—just as a film-maker resents cuts which somebody else makes, and that's usually the distributor.

H: I suppose you don't think it's fair for a critic to compare a film to its original source material?

K: Sure, I think it's fair. I mean, if somebody wrote a book called *On the Beach*, and I make the film, and the spirit of *On the Beach* was antinuclear in base, and pointed out the dangers of an all-out nuclear war, which would be the destruction of all humanity, if the film fails to say that, then I think it fails. If it's not true to the book, then the script isn't an adaptation but something else. When I made *On the Beach*, I may have been naive in other ways. It never satisfied critics who felt that I was again coming to bat to save the world with one film. But really, I think they're ridiculous because I saw a screening of *On the Beach* at a retrospective twenty-five years after I made it, and I was overjoyed. When Fred Astaire's character of the scientist says, "Don't you understand? We have finally managed to come up with a weapon which, if used, will destroy ourselves," there was a great burst of audience applause and that made me feel better than anything else, because that's the truth.

H: What initially got you involved in *On the Beach*?

K: I was interested because I grew up during Franklin Roosevelt's change in society. It was a big change. I was in college when it happened, graduating soon after. He and Eleanor Roosevelt both had an influence on me. I was particularly moved when she stood to support Marian Anderson, the black singer who was forbidden to sing in Washington before the Daughters of the American Revolution. Eleanor also had a great awareness over the dangers of the bomb. When Nevil Shute wrote the novel, I read it and wanted it badly because it dealt with an issue that became important to me. I tried to do my best by it. It probably didn't satisfy him either.

H: At the time did you know that you were dealing with a subject that was a political hot potato?

K: Oh, of course. I had terrible, terrible pressures. The scientists were divided. Linus Pauling and Oppenheimer were all for the project. Pauling and Harrison Brown were two of the technical advisors. Dr. Teller thought that it would be ridiculous that through the atmosphere radioactive dust could proceed to destroy the world. Well, it wasn't until the recent volcanic eruption at Mount St. Helens, that they realized that the ash, or any particles, could travel through the atmosphere as far as Europe. Then I realized that I really had told the truth, because a nuclear exchange would be much more powerful.

H: You said you had certain pressures. Did you have any difficulty getting the film made?

K: All films are difficult to get made. However, there were pickets against the film. After its release I was called unpatriotic and against strong defense. Of course, there was much support from the antinuclear groups who felt very strongly about it too. It was a highly volatile subject. And I didn't look for that. I never looked for that in the films I made. Everybody assumed that's what I looked for, but it's simply not true. I just simply believed in *On the Beach*. I believed the danger exists that the world could be wiped out in a nuclear conflict.

H: Was there an official government reaction to the film?

K: They didn't want to give me their cooperation by giving me the use of a nuclear sub. The submarine *Sardo* was in Hawaii at the time, and I wanted to use it. They gave me the equipment to do the interiors, but wouldn't let me use an actual submarine. The submarine used in *On the Beach*, the one that Gregory Peck commanded, which is supposed to be a nuclear submarine, was not. It was a transformed British submarine made to look like one. I could never photograph at full tilt, because a nuclear submarine doesn't have the wake that a normal submarine has.

H: I understand Oppenheimer was a consultant on the film. That was at the time when he was speaking out against the bomb while being accused of his past communist affiliation.

K: Certainly, but it didn't affect the film too much. He was just another consultant. But I certainly did support him. He was much more patriotic than many of the hard-line conservatives who were condemning him.

H: Some of your greatest works—*On the Beach, The Defiant Ones, Guess Who's Coming to Dinner, Bless the Beasts and Children*—have been politically very controversial. Do you think that these films, the issues they cover, are still important to audiences today?

K: Well, certainly all of them are relevant to today, because they are human in scope. In other words, they are about human beings and the things human beings do. You didn't mention some of the really controversial films that I did like *Inherit the Wind*. That film became a real political football out of its religious base. It was about the Scopes trial and it was letter for letter true. And what really appealed to me about the story was the Clarence Darrow character played by Spencer Tracy. When he says, "The Bible is a book—it's a good book—but it's not the only book," I got such negative reaction from the fundamentalists that they picketed the film with intense religious fervor. They tried to black it out. Ironically, I think more people went to see it than would have if they hadn't said anything. Because the film opened in eighty cities, the fanatical reaction to the film was much more widespread.

H: How did you respond to the criticism from the fundamentalists?

K: Violently. I quoted everything from my right to do what I believe, the right to make a film, the right to publish facts about film, the right to expose a situation, and not necessarily asked to be agreed with, but merely present it as I saw it.

H: *The Last Temptation of Christ* was recently the subject of much controversy. Many fundamentalists and Catholics lobbied hard to prevent Universal from releasing the film. Was there ever any pressure on the studio not to distribute *Inherit the Wind?*

K: There's always been pressure. My goodness, when I did *Bless the Beasts and Children,* I don't know what pressure the National Rifle Association exercised, but I found plenty of it when I got out in the field in Kansas City and Denver. I was doing television interviews to publicize the film. It had no stars. And I would get these calls in which people would call me a Bambiist. I thought it was bizarre using a strange term like that more than once, you know. Well, it turned out that that's the gun magazine's appellation for anybody who doesn't want to shoot animals, because they look too cute, like Bambi. They call them Bambiists, if you can believe it. Well, you know, I was furious, so I ended hurting that picture a lot by going on national television with two fellows with funny hats to argue about gun control. That's not what the picture was about. I didn't intend it to be about that. I believe in gun control, but it wasn't about that. I do, however, believe in gun control more now than ever before, too.

H: Eric Segal wrote the screenplay for your film *R.P.M.,* which you made in 1970. Was the film based on the Kent State incident, the Harvard student strike, or Yale President Kingman Brewster's defense of the Black Panther Party?

K: It was based on the times in which we lived. I wanted the audience to identify with the Anthony Quinn character who played the acting dean. He was a teacher who supported the student demonstrations, but then when he was appointed dean, he discovered that he was responsible for the library which they threatened to burn down. It becomes a real dilemma for him because he doesn't believe in burning down the library. So he takes a stand that becomes very unpopular and he gets booed and shouted down. Then the school board asks the question: "What is it that these students want? What are they after?" So Quinn expresses the idea that they want to be heard, they want to express their feelings and opinions. Well, that was really what those times were about. They were very confused times. Where do you begin and where do you end? I identified very heavily with that. Unfortunately, I don't think the picture brought it off very well, myself. But then that happens. That's the story of the attempt to do drama. Sometimes you fall too short.

H: Obviously many of your films have dealt with important political issues. Did you ever consider yourself ahead of your time?

K: Well, as a matter of fact, I thought I was a half a step behind the times. That's why I'm back in Hollywood after being away for five years. I came back into action because I was itching to. I found my newest project about Lech Walesa and was intrigued by how an electrician could become a Nobel Prize winner. It's a great personal story, one like which I was unable to make for a long time. So I left Hollywood to find the answers to a lot of questions. I didn't find any of the answers. All I found were many more questions. But, I summed it up by saying somewhere in this vortex there's a place for me between Sylvester Stallone and space movies.

H: What were you looking for, specifically, when you moved to Seattle?

K: I was looking for answers, answers to what it is that people believe. Do they believe in this violence? Do they believe in the kind of silly movies that they're gravitating toward? Why aren't they more active on the important things? I didn't find the answers to that. It's not a question of being ahead of your time, it's just a question of reading the time that you're in.

H: Were you bitter?

K: No, I just needed to get the sense of what do I do now? What do I do next? What interests me? I had no burning desire at the time to make any other kind of film in Hollywood because Hollywood didn't seem to be interested in my kind of filmmaking. So I went up to Seattle, taught at the university, hosted a television show and wrote a column for the *Seattle Times*. I guess, I wanted to get a reaction from people, I wanted to be in an atmosphere where people discussed ideas and politics. I just wasn't getting any of that in Los Angeles. But, of course, I never found any answers up there either.

H: Your films seem very political, yet you've adamantly denied the label political filmmaker. How do you explain that?

K: Because in all the films I've been associated with, their political content has been dubbed by the critics, not me. I've never regarded them as having political content. I regarded them as the drama of human beings in varying situations, in which the conclusions took on political implications. I mean, if a black man is chained to a white man all through a film [*The Defiant Ones*], and they find that they need each other, feeling as antipathetic as they do at the start, that has some political and social significance. I was dealing with the fact that I believed the black man and white man did need each other before they started, just as we all need each other now. That's a broad statement, of course, but I believe it. If I made *Judgment at Nuremberg* about German guilt I thought it was world guilt and tried to point that out. Nuclear danger is as great today from these plants as it was from dropping the bomb before the end of the cold war. I don't know, there are so many pictures of so-called content. In *Ship of Fools* I just took a slice of the human variety, put them all on a ship, as Katherine Anne Porter did, and said, "Look at you! You're all fools!" My point is that you can come across looking silly if you take yourself too seriously. So I don't try to pretend that I'm a political filmmaker.

H: Costa-Gavras said that he felt all films were political, no matter how frivolous or simple their content, and I know that your film *It's a Mad Mad Mad Mad World* was called by some critics, most notably Russian critics, a wonderful commentary on capitalism.

K: Well, that's because greed is always a great base for comedy. That's what it was about, so they thought it was a message picture.

H: You've said that you hate labels, yet conservatives have tried to pigeonhole your work as being far to the left, and leftist groups have praised your work for being an accurate critique of the right. Do you find your work ever being used by the right or the left?

K: I don't pay too much attention to it to tell you the truth. Those labels are horrible things, particularly in an art form. This is an art form, despite the efforts of many people to make it other-wise. It's the expression of an individual creative talent who may be impeded or not impeded by outside sources, everything from colorization to editing. But the thing is that it's an individual ef-fort, something that is part of a dream, something that you start with, and you say, "fade in" and a hundred and thirty pages later you say "fade out." Now that represents your dream if you've got control of it up to that point. Therefore, I never think of it as left, right or middle. I don't think I've been accused very often in politi-cal days by the left as being too conservative . . . and by the right as being completely progressive, liberal, leftist, pinko, whatever you want. I've been picketed on both terms. I don't know, I think we all search for the truth, don't we? I mean, there is no such thing as total truth in a complex society. There's part of the truth, and that's what you usually come up with. And knowing only part of the truth can be very dangerous, because on part of the truth you can build the biggest lie ever. Your own truth is the only impor-tant thing. It's defensible. It's what you believe. You can be wrong. You can be partly wrong or right, but it's your truth.

H: It's known that you like to show your work to students and younger audiences. In 1967 you went on a university tour showing your film *Guess Who's Coming to Dinner*. At the time you were quoted as saying, "My best audience is under the age of twenty." What are audiences under the age of twenty like today as opposed to twenty years ago?

K: I really don't know. I tour the college circuits just as much as I ever did, mostly with *Judgment at Nuremberg*, because I find out that even on the college level there's a high percentage who don't believe the Holocaust ever really took place, not to the extent that it's been reported. They say, "How can they kill six million Jews?" So for that reason, I like to tour with the film and say, "Yes, it happened. I lived through that period." But I don't know what a young audience thinks, and I don't try to create or work toward a young audience. So I don't know. I'm sorry to lose everybody under twenty if that's the case.

H: How has Hollywood changed since the time when you started?

K: Different management now, there are a lot more younger people. Incidentally, they disappear as quickly as they appear.

H: You took some flack for being a white director making a film dealing with some important black issues. For instances, there was some criticism of your portrayal of Sidney Poitier and his character in *Guess Who's Coming to Dinner*.

K: That was one of the biggest errors in critical comment in the history of show business. Look, the point of *Guess Who's Coming to Dinner* was a black man who has everything, who didn't need anything, was educated and had money and had a career, meets a white girl. Now he says to the family, "Look, if it in any way disagrees with what you believe, I don't want it. Forget it." Now, the big point was that Sidney Poitier was cast in that part because there could be only one reason for their objection to the marriage, if there were any objection, and that was that he was black. That was the point of the film. They missed it completely.

H: How do you feel black issues are dealt with today in Hollywood?

K: Well, they're being dealt with, at least—sometimes well, sometimes badly. It depends upon what the film is and how it's met, and whether you're lucky enough to create it as a piece of work that is worthwhile. It's like any other issue that's been going on a long time. I think strides have been made. I come from a generation where Poitier stood alone. He was the only black star, the only black person who could work in mainstream films. That's changed, but it's gradual.

H: Has an audience ever disliked a film that you, personally, liked very much?

K: Sure. One of the lowest grossing films in the world was *Inherit the Wind*. Nobody went to see it and I went all over the world with it. It had great reviews, and nobody went to see the film, so they must not have liked it. Word of mouth was not good until it came of age on television, and then it got a whole brand-new audience. There were others too. I liked Marlon Brando's first film, *The Men*, about paraplegic war veterans. Nobody else did. It did nothing at the box office. We did business on *The Wild One*, which was about motorcycles, and that was maybe ahead of its time. I don't know, it never did the kind of business I thought it'd do, or could do today. *The Secret of Santa Vittoria* was another one I thought should have done more business.

H: You've said that the critics have loved and hated your work unduly. Are there any critics who you like or read regularly? Perhaps there are some that you loathe?

K: I have no favorite critics. I don't have any enemies among critics. I just say that there's no such thing as "they." There are no critics who react the same way. Sarris may differ from Pauline Kael on a picture just like those two fellas on television from Chicago.

H: Roger Ebert and Gene Siskel.

K: Sometimes they totally disagree. Now what are you going to do with that? I mean, they diametrically disagree, so they're like people in the creative business itself.

H: When you were on the board of the Director's Guild you said that you resented film being referred to as a director's medium. I take it you don't have much faith in the auteur theory?

K: I don't believe in the auteur theory because I believe it is the responsibility of the auteur to bring together all the creative elements in music, design, editing, writing, everything—bring them all together under one roof, under his supervision. Now that may be a colossal ego, I don't know. But nevertheless, that's the way I operate and that's what I feel.

H: You received the prestigious Irving Thalberg Award for your outstanding contribution to Hollywood filmmaking, yet Orson Welles condemned Irving Thalberg as being the first man to destroy the creative freedom of the director in Hollywood. I was wondering, as both a producer and director, to what extent do you feel a producer or studio executive has the right to influence the aesthetics of a film?

K: Well, that's too aesthetic a question, because you see, after all, when you talk about films, somebody puts up the money. It's a very expensive thing to do. Now if somebody puts up ten million dollars for a film, you can figure that the producer, or the studio, is going to have a foot in the door. How strong a director, how much you know the business, how much you can cope often prevails in the end, but you have to come to expect interference from the outside. It won't just go away because you're an artist. Now, I was a producer before I was a director and learned a great deal. I was on the set all the time. I couldn't stand what I did as a producer if it happened to me! I was there every minute, making sure every penny was being spent correctly. So I was there every single moment watching it as creatively as I could. And unfortunately for the director, I was also the one who had the last word. If Orson Welles were alive today and had all the money in the world, then he could dictate the whole thing. You just have to learn to live with it.

Filmography (as director)

1955   *Not as a Stranger*
1957   *The Pride and the Passion*
1958   *The Defiant Ones*
1959   *On the Beach*
1960   *Inherit the Wind*
1961   *Judgment at Nuremberg*
1963   *It's a Mad Mad Mad Mad World*
1965   *Ship of Fools*
1967   *Guess Who's Coming to Dinner*
1969   *The Secret of Santa Vittoria*
1970   *R.P.M.*
1971   *Bless the Beasts and Children*

1973   *Oklahoma Crude*
1977   *The Domino Principle*
1979   *The Runner Stumbles*

ROBERT WISE
Gentle Maverick

Robert Wise's humility is one of the first things that strikes me upon meeting the seventy-six-year-old director. He greets me at the door of his modest Beverly Hills office, and we sit down as I pause to think of what first to ask the filmmaker who's directed thirty-nine films spanning the last forty years. The breadth of his work is far reaching and eclectic: from his musical triumphs, *West Side Story* (1961) and *The Sound of Music* (1965), to the powerfully moving dramas *I Want to Live* (1958) and *The Sand Pebbles* (1966), to science fiction and horror classics *The Day the Earth Stood Still* (1951), *The Curse of the Cat People* (1944) and *The Haunting* (1963). In addition to his accolades as a director, Wise has also been celebrated for his achievements as a film editor, most notably for his powerfully innovative work on Orson Welles's *Citizen Kane* (1941), and most notoriously for editorial changes he made in Welles's *The Magnificent Ambersons* (1942).

In an unassuming, almost grandfatherly way, Wise suggests that we start by talking about his latest film, *Rooftops* (1988), a contemporary drama he made after a ten-year hiatus from directing, a period which found him serving three consecutive terms as the President of the Academy of Motion Picture Arts and Sciences.

"*Rooftops* came after I got the itch to make movies again," says the director. "Well, I suppose I had the bug all along. Ten years is a long time to not work, but I just found myself too busy to do it," he adds tapping his wire-framed spectacles. Shot on location in New York City, *Rooftops* follows the lives of a young couple in love in a tough part of Manhattan's West Side. "I was very unhappy with the critical comparisons that were made with *West Side Story*," he says leaning back in his chair. "It wasn't a musical. It was sort of a drama with music in it, but it was not a musical. Nobody got up and sang in it." Though the film didn't fare well at the box office, Wise is generally happy with it. "Some of my best work never does well at the box office," chortles the white-haired director who has often been noted for his gentle but liberal views on politics and filmmaking.

Born on September 10, 1914, in Winchester, Indiana, Wise was forced to quit college as the country sank deeper into the Depression. At the age of nineteen he found work at RKO Pictures, where his brother David worked in the accounting department. Starting out as an assistant cutter, within six years Wise worked his way up to the position of film editor, sharing credit with William Hamilton on a number of noteworthy films, including *The Hunchback of Notre Dame* (1939) and *The Story of Vernon and Irene Castle* (1939). In addition to his own work on two of Orson Welles's great masterpieces, he cut *All That Money Can Buy* and *The Fallen Sparrow*. In 1943 Wise suddenly found himself at the helm as director when Gunther von Fritz failed to meet the production schedule on his production of *Curse of the Cat People*. "It's not unduly common that editors move on to directing," he adds. "But every so often there's an editor who's meant to move up. I think it's a fairly natural step because you've already been exposed to so many facets and elements of making a film." Sent in to finish the picture, Wise completed the film within ten days. It went on to become a horror classic, subsequently launching Wise into a prolific and highly commended career.

HICKENLOOPER: I watched *The Sand Pebbles* last night. I hadn't seen it in a long time, and it really moved me. It's such a timeless film. I couldn't believe it was made in the 1960s. It even seems ahead of its time today.

WISE: Well, I made it in 1966 and I think in a sense it was meant to be an indictment of the Vietnam War, though we were not heavily involved with that conflict at the time I made it. But I had visited Saigon just a few years before when we had something like 10,000 American "advisors." And I saw all these American sailors and soldiers in uniform, and I saw tanks and Air Force bombers, so none of it had a good feeling to me. And so when *The Sand Pebbles* came along I started seeing how that particular situation back in China seemed very close to what I saw going on in Vietnam. And I've always had an interest in China although I'd never been there, but I thought that this story would give me a chance to remind the American public that the phrase "Yankee Go Home" was not something just born in World War II. It had been going on much of this century around different parts of the world, and *The Sand Pebbles* was a perfect way to show this with a fascinating story. And I thought it was time that we were reminded that we had strung our flag up around the world a lot. And I thought the whole process was very questionable.

H: The film has one of the most disturbing scenes of any picture of that era: when the character of Mako is being tortured by the Chinese peasants and Steve McQueen shoots him out of mercy. At the time, how did audiences respond to that?

W: Well, it knocked the audiences out. As a matter of fact, after previews we had to trim that scene down a little bit, because in the first cut, it was actually a lot longer. It was a real full-blown sequence. But it was just too much for the audience; however, it did have tremendous impact. And that scene, by the way, is right out of the history books. It's not something we dreamed up.

H: In your eyes was it an antiwar film?

W: I would say it's an antimilitary film.

H: In one of the closing moments of the film the character of the missionary berates the American naval officer with a speech about how the whole concept of nation and state is obsolete, and how it only invites blind pride and bloodshed. Was this your view?

W: Well, I sort of agree with him. The smaller the world gets, the less need we have for these barriers and different flags. And I think in a small way that's happening in Europe. The barriers are coming down.

H: As a director, are you happy with the fact that you're most recognized for having directed two very popular musicals, *The Sound of Music* and *West Side Story?*

W: Well, I am very pleased with those films, but of course, it's always a pleasure to me when people know some of my other films. But the musicals are films of mine that are equally good in their own way.

H: How is directing a musical different from directing a drama?

W: Well, technically it is a very different path in the sense that there is a lot of preproduction work to be done. Preproduction is very important in any film. But above and beyond the normal preproduction, you have to plan on your dance rehearsals and your prescoring and all of that business, getting your playbacks made and rehearsing your singers and all that. All the musical end has to be done, as much as you can, before you start shooting. The main thing is the scheduling, organizing, rehearsing, and planning and doing of the musical end of it. Otherwise, it's not appreciably different from shooting a drama.

H: What about stylistically? Do you consciously give your musicals a look that is very distinctive from your dramas?

W: Well, it all depends. You see, you approach each project in terms of what you feel your best cinematic treatment is. The cinematic treatment of *West Side Story* is considerably different from *Sound of Music* if you were to look at the two together. The poetry and tone of *Sound of Music* and the realistic feeling the film gives competes quite differently with the unrealistic elements of *West Side Story*. So you approach each one in terms of whether it's the difference in two musicals or whether it's from war or whether it's a western or whatever. If you notice, I rarely have the same cinematographer all the time. I don't think I've ever used the same cinematographer in over two films. That's why I spend a lot of time carefully selecting a cinematographer that I think will be best suited for that film.

H: Can we talk a little about *I Want to Live,* your film account of the famous execution of Barbara Graham. I understand you literally witnessed a state execution while preparing the film?

W: Well, I was given an article that had been written about this woman in San Francisco who was about to be executed. And I thought it was a real life horror story. Barbara Graham was a real tragic figure who got caught up with the wrong crowd, and in a sense was being condemned not just by society but by the press for her lifestyle. And in any film you do, you must do the research. You have to find out about the subject matter you're dealing with, the realities of it, and how things actually happen and work. If you do a film or a period piece like *The Sand Pebbles,* you read the books and see the pictures and study whatever. Well, I had to do this about the execution of Barbara Graham and it was current, so I went up to San Quentin to see the death row, and I felt I had to see an execution. I felt as much as I hated the idea of having to watch that, I felt that I needed to put it on the screen the way it really was. I didn't want the critics to be able to say, "Well, that's a Hollywood screenwriter's version of how it is to go to the gas chamber." I wanted to be able to say that's it. This is a truthful version of how it happens. So I went to the warden at San Quentin, feeling like a ghoul to have to ask this, and said, "Warden, I'd like to observe an execution." And I gave him my reasons. And he said, "Mr. Wise, I understand where you're coming from. I know exactly. Capital punishment is the law in the state of California, and I think it's good for the citizens to see just how it functions." So I went back to L.A., and he called me a couple weeks later and told me there was going to be an execution the coming Friday. So I came up Thursday, and arrangements were made to let me in. There was a dividing space between the chamber and outside where the witnesses, the warden and the doctor are. So I was there with the warden and the doctor and the man who operated it. The man being executed had killed a couple of women in Oakland a few years before and this was the end. I didn't know what to expect, whether there would be hysterics or less emotion. It was very quiet and he was very, very calm. There was nothing—no hysterics at all. And I didn't know whether I'd be able to watch it or have to turn away and get sick or what. But because it was quiet and there were no emotional, hysterical outbursts, I was able to force myself to watch the whole proceedings. And I tell you, it's a pretty awful thing to watch, because after they drop the cyanide pellets it's a good seven or eight minutes before he's pronounced dead, and that body is strapped in just writhing and twisting away all over the place, and the body functions just don't stop automatically. It must have been that long before the doctor who had a stethoscope attached to the heart pronounced him dead. So I had seen that, and I had been through the place, and I had my production de-signer with me, and he photographed what he could, because we didn't know whether or not they would allow us to shoot up there. And then I had an idea, why not talk to the priest whom Barbara Graham spoke to just before her execution? He had left the prison and was now a parish priest in San Rafael nearby, so I went out to meet him, during which time I incidentally tried to get him to divulge what her last words were, which of course he wasn't about to do, so I asked him why he left the prison. And he said, "Well, Mr. Wise, I don't suppose you have any idea of the awful, dreadful, depressing atmosphere that descends on a prison the night before the day of an execution—when the whole prison knows that all the preparations are being made to take a human life." Then it struck me, in order for it to affect the audience the way a real execution does, they have to not only see the execution, but witness the prep-aration. So I went right back over to San Quentin and had the guards show me everything they do when they prepare the gas chamber.

H: It was meticulously detailed and very powerful.

W: That's just the way it was. Just the way it was. And it's all a matter of record, and those last-minute stays of hers and every-thing, that's all right on the record, and all done right to the min-ute. It was terrible for her to have gone through all that. Real torture.

H: Did you show these in order to create suspense rather than to evoke empathy for her character?

W: Yes, part of it was, of course, to capitalize on the awful grue-someness of the suspense of it, naturally. But also to say this is the way it is. This is what happens. This is what goes on.

H: How did the public respond to the film?

W: Even though a lot of the people thought that the film was tough, I think it was moderately successful commercially. It was not a big blockbuster, but I think it did well. It was criticized, of course, by the law enforcement people, by the D.A.'s office here, and the police who said we slanted the film when we suggested an innocent woman had gone to the gas chamber. I suppose the fact that we had Susan [Hayward] playing the part and that we were telling her story, Barbara Graham's story, that the sympathy was that way. We didn't literally say that. We kept raising questions about it. You know, I think that toward the end, half the guards were saying, "What the hell was she doing shacked up with those bums anyway?" You know, at heart she was a good person. But really, our feeling about it was sort of expressed in the editorials the day after her execution. They read, "No matter what a person's innocence or guilt, nobody should ever have to be put through the kind of torture that Mrs. Graham was put through yesterday at San Quentin, and we should change our laws so that could never happen again." That was really what we were trying to say. As to her innocence or guilt, I've been asked many times what I thought, and I don't know to this day the answer to that. Having met people who knew her, sometimes I thought she couldn't have ever been involved with a murder like that. And sometimes I've talked to people and thought, well, perhaps she was an unintentional accessory. The people she hung out with were real criminals.

H: In the 1970s you made two very big-budget films, *The Hindenburg* and *Star Trek*.

W: So, you know, I'm not the hottest old-time director around town now, in spite of what I've done. I'm not being besieged by offers from the majors. As a matter of fact, if I'm going to do another film, I'm going to have to develop it myself.

H: Richard Brooks was complaining about the same thing. Why don't the studios have respect for the older . . .

W: You know why, don't you? It's because so many of the younger guys who are making these things don't know our work. They don't know who we are.

H: Were executives different when you were younger?

W: I think so, yeah. I think there were more cognitive executives. There weren't as many studio musical chairs moving around. It's always been a business of raw evidence. Business has always been part of the blame. I don't think anybody agrees about this today, but I think the business end, the money-making end is just overpowering now. So it's really kind of heart-warming to us when occasionally a *Driving Miss Daisy,* a *Dead Poets Society* or a *Field of Dreams* will come along. And we say, well there is still a chance for a film of quality, a film about people to come out and do well. That gives you courage.

H: Your films often seem politically balanced toward the left, but somehow you've remained uncontroversial. How has that happened?

W: I don't know.

H: The modesty of your character?

W: I suppose so. I am a fairly modest guy, you know. I don't throw myself around a lot and try to find places or ways to get in the news. I've been asked about how I made out in the McCarthy period, and I was part of the left, I'd been a member of a number of organizations that HUAC [House Un-American Activities Committee] had deemed questionable, but I suppose I didn't belong to enough of them to really arouse suspicion. Unfortunately and sadly, I had to witness a lot of it. The paranoia often went beyond reason.

H: Very early on in your career you worked very closely with Orson Welles. You have been celebrated for your editing work on *Citizen Kane* and then criticized for being instrumental in RKO's infamous cutting of *The Magnificent Ambersons.* Would you tell me about working with Welles? When did you first meet him?

W: Well, I had been at RKO for a few years and had just finished editing a picture, so all of us who worked on it were out celebrating that weekend in late 1939. And the following Monday morning I get a call from my boss, Jimmy Wilkerson. He calls and says that Orson Welles has been making what he told the studio were tests for his new film. And after he had made about three tests the studio realized that he had actually begun shooting scenes for his picture. So once they found out he was doing that, they decided to give him the green light. And at the time he had an older editor, and I guess he felt he wanted someone younger on the picture, more his own age. So my boss tells me to go down and meet him where he's shooting in Culver City. So I went down there to what I think were the old Selznick Studios and he was in the midst of shooting the scene where he has the barbecue on the beach for Susan Alexander. And so the assistant went in and told him I was there, and he came out. And the first time I saw him he was dressed as the old Kane—he looked like an old man. So we chatted for a few minutes. Evidently he took to my looks and the fact I was about his age, and that was it.

H: What was it like cutting *Kane?*

W: Well, there was really nothing that extraordinary about it. It was like cutting any other film. I had to go down to the set a time or two to watch it all. And I sat with him while he looked at the rushes and made his selections at the end of the day. On the rushes, if he'd make two or three takes of something, he'd select his takes and make any other comments that he felt were needed: this or that changed, this shortened. And I'd go to my cutting room and when we had all the sequences finished, and put together, I'd show them to him at the end of the day, and the next day he'd have more comments to make. He never came to the editing room to tell me what cuts to make.

H: Did you know much about his collaboration with Herman J. Mankiewicz on the screenplay?

W: Not at all. I've been asked about that because of the whole controversy that came up.

H: Pauline Kael's "Raising Kane" essay?

W: Yes, and I have to say very honestly that I couldn't tell you anything about it, because when I came on the picture he was already shooting. There was the script with two names, and that was it. There was never any discussion about it. But I never saw Mankiewicz on the set once. He was not around to my knowledge any time during the shooting. I do know that at one point, one day—I can't remember the scene though I think it had something to do with the Thatcher character—Orson was not very happy with the dialogue. He didn't like the way it was worded. He shut down production and went home, and he came in the next day with a new scene. I have a feeling he went home and rewrote it. It's almost academic to me, because Orson's stamp is so strongly on every frame of that film. That's his film. There's no question.

H: Welles has been praised for his innovative use of sound, which apparently he brought with him from radio. Did he ever talk to you about overlapping the dialogue?

W: No, he didn't do that too much. I mean, he did in the staging of a scene of course. You know, it was an extremely well planned film, and I didn't have a lot of tricky, special stuff in the editing room. It was well planned, well staged, well covered. I suppose the two areas we worked the most over in the cutting room were the old "March of Time" sequence, because we had to find all that stock footage, and then we had to take the film that he had shot and degrade it and scratch it up and dupe it and all to make it match the real stock footage. The other scene was the breakfast table scene because the whole rhythm of that was double cutting. The concept was there when he shot it. It was a brilliant concept, I think. But the whole rhythm of it, the speed of the whip pan, where the dialogue comes in and out, and the quick scenes come in and out over a period of weeks, months. Well, it all had to be done by trial and error. We cut several different versions of that scene. It was a tough one.

H: Did creating the structure of the film seem very complex at the time because its chronology jumps back and forth?

W: No, not really. I just followed Orson's notes and made a few suggestions here and there. I'll tell you, those were marvelous dailies.

H: Were you aware of the pressure William Randolph Hearst was applying to RKO to stop the release of the movie? I know that Louis B. Mayer offered to buy the negative from George Schaeffer at RKO.

W: I heard that story. I knew there was some pressure and, you know, you heard all kinds of things. There was a controversy, but I was busy working on the film. The only real exposure I had to any of that involved my one experience bringing the print of the film to New York, the fine cut to the screening room at Radio City where a group of RKO executives and their attorneys were gathered to see it. It was very formal and Orson was there really putting on the charm. Before the screening he gave this breathtaking impromptu speech about how the citizens of the United States had the right to see the film. He said that banning *Kane* would be a violation of freedom of speech, and then he went on to remind everyone of the rise of fascism in Germany and how censorship was indicative of totalitarianism. It was like something Charlie Kane himself would have come up with. It truly was Orson's finest performance. We all applauded.

H: When you were cutting *Kane* did you have the feeling you were working on something special?

W: Well, yes. You knew it was something special. I've been asked did we know it was going to be considered down the line the greatest American film ever made. And of course, you know, that's ridiculous. But we did know we were working on something special. You couldn't see those dailies coming in every day and not know this was going to be a very, very good film, certainly above average.

H: Were you surprised when it didn't do well at the box office?

W: Yeah, I was surprised and disappointed that the public wouldn't be a little more interested in it at the time.

H: Why do you think the Academy overlooked *Kane* for Best Picture in 1941?

W: There was always a little resentment around town in those days about Orson. They thought there was this young whipper-snapper coming up and going to show them how to make films—the crown prince. He got this fabulous deal at RKO, and there was a lot of jealousy around. And I think that got through into the Academy. It was a very embarrassing night—the Academy Awards that year. This was before we had the shows, and I was there because I was nominated. And when the first couple of nominations were announced for *Kane*, there were boos in the audience. It took voices from the rest of the crowd to shut them up.

H: Why did Orson Welles lose final cut on *The Magnificent Ambersons?*

W: He was out of the country doing a film in South America [*It's All True*, 1941–1942]. He couldn't be around. Had he been around I believe he would have retained final cut.

H: Would you talk about editing *Ambersons?*

W: Well, we finished it up. Of course, you know he had gone to South America, so I had to finish up the editing with Jack Moss, his associate. And we got it all done but the score, and got a print of it which I was scheduled to take down to Orson in Rio. I was very excited about that, and I got my passport and everything was ready, and then about three or four days before I was scheduled to leave the government put an embargo on any civilians flying out of the country. I wasn't in the service, so I couldn't leave. So we were forced to ship the print down to him. So he looked at it and sent me back a thirty-seven-page cable saying what he liked, didn't like, do this, do that, you know. And then we had two or three long-distance phone calls where we relayed to him the progress of the picture. And Jack and I followed most of his suggestions, what we felt were reasonable, possible. And the studio was getting nervous, you know, because they had a lot of money in this film for those days, and they wanted previews. And those went terribly, just terribly, people laughed at it, they walked out in droves. So they wanted the end cut.

H: What was the original length?

W: I don't remember. Over two hours, I guess. I don't know. We had a problem. The studio wanted something they could release, understandably. Orson wasn't there, so it was up to us to do what we could, so Jack and I worked together, and cut the print, trimmed and cut, created a few bridge sequences and tried to make it work, put on a new ending. Now I didn't reshoot the ending. I did one scene with George and his mother. We tried to retain everything that we could that was Orson. And I think the fact that it's come down through the years as something of a classic in its own right means we didn't completely misuse Orson's work. It was a victim of its times. Well, you know, we were shooting in an automobile factory at the time war was declared, December 7. So by the time it went into previews and release, six months later, the country was all geared up for war. Guys were going off to war and training camps and building airplanes and Liberty Ships and women were working in the factories and were all keyed up. Audiences just weren't in the mood to sit and look at the trials and tribulations of the establishment's automobile family at the early part of the century. It just wasn't reality. I think if it had come out a year before, it might have been different.

H: Was Welles irate when he returned from Rio?

W: I suppose he was upset. But again, that criticism isn't fair. Orson was never there! He didn't make himself available at all. At one point I had to fly all the way to Miami to meet him coming in from Rio just to finish my editing work. I could never get him to come to Los Angeles to do his narration for the film, because he had to be in Washington on a certain date, like mid-March or something and report to the State Department. I still hadn't finished the work on *Ambersons*, so I just put the film in cans and flew down to Miami where there was a small animation studio that had a recording room, and I worked with Orson for three days and three nights almost straight around the clock to get his work done and his narration finished. The last time I saw him was down at the ocean and he took off in one of those old amphibian planes with an RKO executive.

H: Did you ever talk about *Ambersons?*

W: No, I didn't see Orson to any degree after that. I ran into him a couple of times throughout the years. He was always very warm and we got along well when we worked together, but I never saw him after he came back from Rio. I was busy with my own career. And our paths just didn't cross.

H: Some have criticized Orson, saying he was undisciplined, and some say that Hollywood was to blame for misunderstanding him.

W: Two things. Lack of self-discipline and self-indulgence. Guaranteed that the only film that he ever made in which he had his total concentration was *Kane.* At the time his whole life was making that film. But then he went on to *Ambersons* and while he was shooting that he was doing a radio show every week and on top of that he decided to play the Turkish General in *Journey Into Fear.* So he was shooting all night on *Journey Into Fear* and directing *Ambersons* all day. I say, come on! That was his fault. Too bad.

Filmography (as director)

1944	*The Curse of the Cat People*
1944	*Mademoiselle Fifi*
1945	*The Body Snatcher*
1946	*A Game of Death*
1946	*Criminal Court*
1947	*Born to Kill*
1947	*Mystery in Mexico*
1948	*Blood on the Moon*
1949	*The Set-Up*
1950	*Two Flags West*
1950	*Three Secrets*
1951	*The House on Telegraph Hill*
1951	*The Day the Earth Stood Still*
1952	*Captive City*
1952	*Something for the Birds*
1952	*Desert Rats*

1952   *Destination Gobi*
1953   *So Big*
1954   *Executive Suite*
1955   *Helen of Troy*
1956   *Tribute to a Bad Man*
1956   *Somebody up There Likes Me*
1957   *This Could Be the Night*
1957   *Until They Sail*
1958   *Run Silent, Run Deep*
1958   *I Want to Live*
1959   *Odds Against Tomorrow*
1961   *West Side Story*
1962   *Two for the Seesaw*
1963   *The Haunting*
1965   *The Sound of Music*
1966   *The Sand Pebbles*
1968   *Star!*
1970   *The Andromeda Strain*
1973   *Two People*
1975   *The Hindenburg*
1977   *Audrey Rose*
1979   *Star Trek*
1988   *Rooftops*

JOHN MILIUS
The Gifted Barbarian

If one didn't know that John Milius was once a celebrated member of the Hollywood Brat Pack (along with Steven Spielberg, George Lucas and Francis Coppola) who emerged from USC film school as the most sought after screenwriter in the business, one might think that he was the slotted replacement for Manuel Noriega. Milius fancies himself a kind of a revolutionary on holiday who at any given moment might wreak havoc wherever he is, which is currently on the Paramount lot finishing up his latest film, *Flight of the Intruder* (1990). "I don't think I'll cause any trouble. At least not until I get back from my vacation," says the director, pulling on a thick stogie.

"Where are you going?" I ask, thinking he might follow Lucas and Spielberg to their favorite vacationing spot in Hawaii.

"Argentina," he replies with a smile that inflates his round cheeks outlined by a well-trimmed beard. "I have many friends there."

Call him a sensationalist, call him a war-mongering patriot, call him a guerrilla leader, it's probably all true. Milius is more than happy to tell you that he would never quite make the cut of the politically correct set. "I'm a mean son of a bitch with the heart of a deer," he says, leaning his burly fame forward to offer me a twelve-inch Cuban cigar.

In Milius's Paramount office hang the memorabilia of his filmmaking adventures, marking a turbulent career: a poster from *The Wind and the Lion* (1975), a surfboard from *Big Wednesday* (1978), a Soviet belt from *Red Dawn* (1984). In fact, his office is cluttered with so many posters, models and war toys that one thinks that Milius let his toys grow up, get bigger and more real around him rather than outgrowing them. It's not surprising that this controversial director was only nineteen years old when he began writing *Apocalypse Now*, now hailed as one of the greatest war movies of all time.

Born in St. Louis, Missouri, Milius moved to Southern California with his family where, as an adolescent, he found a passion for surfing. "It was like a religion," says the director. "It had a certain Zen quality. We were all living at an intensity which couldn't be substituted by any drug, or job, or even woman," he continues, admitting that he entered film school never expecting to do anything with his life other than catch the big wave.

Catch the big wave Milius did. After film school he wrote a number of impressive screenplays that made him one of the most successful screenwriters of his generation: *Jeremiah Johnson* (1972), *Judge Roy Bean* (1973), *Magnum Force* (1973) and *Apocalypse Now* (1979). Those screenplays gave him enough credibility to direct his own work. *Dillinger* (1973), *The Wind and the Lion* (1975), *Big Wednesday* (1978), *Farewell to the King* (1988) and most recently, the Vietnam adventure, *Flight of the Intruder* (1990), are just some of the films that have gained him attention as a talented but controversial writer/director.

"There's something very normal about war," he says with a mischievous smile. "It's as natural as breathing and eating," he continues, reminiscing about an early childhood experience when his father took him down to San Diego to visit the U.S.S. *Enterprise*, one of the U.S. Navy's greatest aircraft carriers. "Walking inside that carrier was like stepping back into the womb. It was very comforting," he adds, admitting that the experience contributed to his fascination with war.

HICKENLOOPER: You once said that you thought revenge was the driving motivation behind most people's actions. Do you still believe that?

MILIUS: A lot of it, but you know there's a white-hot anger in everyone. It's hard to get rid of, you know. I must have developed a lot of white-hot anger.

H: Who would you direct your anger against?

M: I think that what really pisses me off is hypocrisy—the big lie. I don't mind a villain if he enjoys being a villain and doesn't pretend to be anything else. I mean, I have friends in Hawaii who are murderers—professionals. They're among the closest friends I have. They don't lie about who they are. I can respect that. They have strong codes they live by. Now I don't condone what they do, so it is not a moral judgment. It's just a fact of honesty.

H: Do you think most people live a lie?

M: Yes. I think they love living a lie. And it's not that they love it, they just don't even think about it. They just have no codes. They'll do anything. I think kids are raised that way.

H: What about this business?

M: This business is totally that way. Ben Hecht said that the people in show business are "moral cripples." He said that in the thirties. He also called screenwriters a bunch of moral cripples and weaklings. He said that when he was recommending that Dos Passos come out to Hollywood and write screenplays, he said, "Surely you could take the money, food, and women from these moral cripples and degenerate screenwriters." Because that's what they are, you know. They'll do anything. They'll stab their friends. They've got no code, no strength. And of course he was already sucked into it himself. I consider it a degrading occupation, because everybody's writing a personal screenplay. It's, "Wow, my sister's writing a screenplay," or "Oh, so-and-so's writing a screenplay." Every actor is writing a screenplay. Everybody nowadays gets so much for them, you know, you hear about these bidding wars and stuff. It's out of control. I was the hottest screenwriter in Hollywood when I was twenty-five years old. And I've been the hottest three or four times since. And every time in between there are always these years when "This guy is the hottest thing that's ever lived," and "He just sold a screenplay for five hundred thousand dollars," which is a pittance now. And of course the movie never gets made or it gets made into a piece of shit. The guy disappears into drug addiction. And every year there's one of these new wunderkinds. And I've watched so many of them come and go, but I'm still here. I'm still at large. I'm still a dangerous man.

H: Very early in your career you were part of a very exclusive club known as the Hollywood Brat Pack: you, Spielberg, Lucas, Coppola.

M: All schmucks. There were a lot more talented people emerging in the early seventies. Martin Scorsese, Bob Rafelson, all those guys led our generation in the right path, you know, which no one else took. Francis Coppola did to some degree, but even Francis got rich off of a very good movie. He didn't get rich off a piece of shit like *Star Wars* or something.

H: But you're buddies with George Lucas.

M: I don't even know George Lucas anymore.

H: How has he changed?

M: He insulates himself up there at that compound of his; isolates his people. I have nothing to do with most of those guys anymore. I lead my own life.

H: What happened?

M: Everybody started out very idealistic. Then it turned into a civil war. In the end, it came down to revenge, you know, who could kill the other guy the dirtiest way. I mean everybody started out with these very idealistic ideas, and didn't realize what they were playing with, you know, so that when things came in like fame and wealth on such a grand scale, it fucked up their values. They were not prepared in any way to accept success and were kind of really ruined, morally ruined. And now these new kids out of USC film school are turning into what the business has become: they don't want to be morally ruined, they want to start out from moral ruination.

H: What was going on right after you and Lucas got out of USC film school?

M: Nobody felt they had a chance. I mean the idea of going to USC was that it was a haven for most of the people from the war. And they were going to study film for a couple years, and I was going to go surfing and lifeguard for a few years while I was learn-ing. It seemed like a neat thing, cinema school; and then I was going to join the Marine Corps and fly an F-4, and probably never come back. I had reconciled myself to that, you know, to leaving my impression on the ground somewhere in Southeast Asia. And that's why this movie *Flight of the Intruder* is sort of a fantasy, be-cause this is really what I always thought I should be doing, so there was this whole thing that there was an impermanence. No-body took film school too seriously. So any attempt on Hollywood, any attempt on a career was sort of taken with a certain kamikaze attitude. We were going to make a grand gesture, an assault against the powers that be, which in those days were people like Frank Sinatra because we had to know somebody like Frank Sinatra to get a job. At the time, USC film school had no credibility. In a way it was a lot better, because the people, though it was very much of a closed club, did respect experience and seniority, and they weren't so crazed for making anything that's new. And the hot generation then were guys who were pretty talented—Sidney Pollack and Mark Rydell, people like that.

H: Well, was your generation rebelling against the previous generation?

M: We thought we had something to say. We thought we were the revolutionary generation, and our idols were Godard and Fellini and people like that. We were going to make "cinema verité." It was the idea of "cinema truth," you know. And that was wonderful, but in the final analysis, my generation has basically produced popcorn and amusement park rides.

H: What happened?

M: They wanted money, they wanted that house in Bel Air, then they wanted power. Really most of the people in my generation had nothing whatever to say in their lives. And looking back, they didn't have an awful lot to say then either. If you're ever going to have something to say, you're going to have to say it when you're about twenty years old.

H: And your work?

M: My stuff comes from the heart, man.

H: Andrew Sarris called you "the gifted barbarian."

M: Yeah, that was the best thing anyone ever called me. Those were the days when critics liked me.

H: But Pauline Kael never liked your work, and you were pretty outspoken about her as well. Didn't you two have a get-together not too long ago?

M: I saw her in New York a couple years back and took her out to have some coffee. She was really nervous.

H: Will you talk a little bit about your relationship with film critics and how it's changed?

M: Now that I think of it, most critics hated me at the very beginning, and I hated critics. And I'll tell you, they still hate me as much as ever. They'll blast me whatever I do. But I don't waste my time hating them anymore. It's pointless. I've outlived whole generations of critics. Stanley Kubrick said, "It's just a difference of opinion." Even though they're out to get you, out to ruin you, have you selling apples in the street or whatever, you have to look at it as their opinion. I tend to romanticize my life. Most of the time I feel like an outlaw and they're the good people of the town that would like the Pinkertons to catch me. I just want a few more trains to rob.

H: What kind of influence do you think that whole movie brat pack had on the industry?

M: Well, enormous. The ones who had the most influence were Steven and George. They showed how much money is out there to take. That affected these people more than anything. They showed that the market was much bigger, that rather than make *Gone With the Wind* or *Bridge On the River Kwai*, you could make *E.T.* and you could triple the market, and create all this mindless junk. So it's like these guys found a bigger vein of ore. When I grew up the idea was, you know, if you make something like *Raiders of the Lost Ark*, you wouldn't make *Indiana Jones and the Temple of Doom*, because you'd done that. It was a cute little experiment. But Steven said, "Well, it's like owning a mine with all the silver. You've gotta bring the ore in and sell it." Now, people's whole careers are based on making *Die Hard II* or something like that. These movies have also made the attention span of audiences very short. They make movies stink. We don't even have "B" movies anymore, because they're now what we call "A" movies. Whole genres have been swept aside because they're not potentially profitable in this hand-over-fist way that was started by the *Star Wars* and *E.T.* phenomenon. The bottom line is that it's greed. In the end, those guys are just smothering the talent they may have had a long time ago. I still believe *Duel* is the best film Steven ever made. That movie had guts.

H: When Steven Spielberg received the Irving Thalberg Award, he said movies had to go back to the written word, that films should aspire to be a little more sophisticated than they currently are. Do you believe that?

M: I always thought that in the first place. As you can see, Spielberg went back to the written word with *Indiana Jones and the Last Crusade*.

H: Could you talk a little bit about your youth, growing up in California, surfing?

M: Well, that was probably the roots of my anarchy. Surfers were a lot different then than they are now. It was a lifestyle—the beatniks. There's a wonderful book written by Greg Knowle who's one of the greatest big wave surfers that's ever lived. I advise you to read it. He was one of my heroes when I was growing up. And he describes the certain freedom of living on the beach, living under the pier. There was sort of an antimaterialism that went with surfing, a real heightened sense of rebellion. The thing about beatniks and the whole Beat Generation is that they were very serious

about what they did. They were scholars. They made definite com-
mitments to a certain way of life. They weren't parasitical in any
way, whereas the hippies were totally parasitical. It was a real deg-
radation of the original ethic. But when you became a good surfer,
which took years and years to do, you became part of the life.
There was the commitment that you would go to Hawaii, to the
north shore, and you would risk your life riding big waves, because
this was like going to Mecca, you know. You were not truly faithful
unless you had gone to Sunset Beach and stroked into a wave that
was big enough to kill you. And once you rode it you could leave
and never ride it again. It was implicit in every surfer's consciousness that this was required. All this was leading up to that day
when you would find "the truth."

H: Do you think that directors have a responsiblity to uphold
some kind of social mores?

M: I think that directors should be people that have something
to say. Directors used to have a lot to say. John Ford was not afraid
of public opinion. He did what he liked. He put the life that he
found interesting and exciting on the screen. I think people today
are doing it for a secondary effect. They're sitting there putting on
the screen what they think is going to appeal to somebody.

H: To make money?

M: Make money. Get good reviews. They think first of what is
going to appeal. And we get this from the executives. They go over
the scripts and they say, "Now, don't get too right-wing, John!
Don't get too crazy here, you know. You can't have them say he
enjoys dropping bombs, because you know, there might be a cra-
zie like that." They're always sitting there saying, "What's gonna
happen? We don't want to get these guys to like the Navy too
much, 'cause this is the 1990s, and people aren't loyal to institutions anymore." I got a memo that actually said that.

H: Regarding *Flight of the Intruder*?

M: Yes, it said, "This is the 1990s. We don't want people to be too
loyal to institutions. Kids don't feel that's exciting."

H: Was there a fight to get *Flight of the Intruder* made?

M: There's always a fight. It's always a bitter struggle.

H: One time you said *Big Wednesday* was your most personal film. Is it still?

M: Yeah. Absolutely. How could it be more personal than that?

H: Will you talk about your writing process—what you physically do when you write, how many hours a day—what is your routine like?

M: Well, traditionally, I used to have it down that I would write six pages a day. And that takes about an hour. And I'd bullshit all day until I couldn't get away from it anymore, and then I'd sit down between five and six o'clock. I'd have to get to work so that when I went home I knew that I'd done something. Now it gets even more disciplined. Sometimes I come in and work for a little while, and then I go home. Now I tend to write more than six pages a day. I have some days I don't write anything, and then I'll write twenty pages. I'm not necessarily writing the same way now because I've been adapting this book. I have to adapt another book and then I'm gonna do an original. So, we probably won't be back to my old style until I go back to write another original again.

H: Before you started directing, were there any scripts that you got more pleasure from writing than others?

M: *Jeremiah Johnson* I enjoyed a good deal, and *Judge Roy Bean*. I felt that that was probably my best script of all of them, but the movie wasn't very good. It just didn't turn out. It was one of those Hollywood movies that happen to writers. The scripts get mixed up and changed. I mean, I like [John] Huston a great deal, but I think that I should have directed *Judge Roy Bean*. I don't think Huston's heart was in it. If your heart's in it, then you can do a good movie. If your heart isn't—who knows. Then you'd better have a good script and a good cast.

H: How would you have done it differently?

M: Oh, I would have done it much, much more raw, you know. My vision of it was a lot different than his. I don't even know whether it was more like a Ford movie or even a Sam Peckinpah–type movie.

H: How was it making the transition from writer to director?

M: It was really easy to direct. As a matter of fact, it was scandalously easy. I've been told that all of a sudden you can get yourself into a corner and shoot in such a way that you won't know how to get out of it. None of that happened to me. It was all real common sense. Even dealing with actors is real common-sense stuff. And I don't do fancy things with actors or anything. I've gotten good performances in my movies from just being straightforward with actors. Tell them what you want. Deal with what they're doing. It's just a matter of using common sense.

H: At what point did you decide that you wanted to direct?

M: After *Judge Roy Bean* I got the urge to do it. I found somebody who would take a chance. It was a big, big, big chance. And the odds are still the same. If you look at first-time directors' movies that are made today, most of them stink and just go right to cable. There are not too many auspicious directorial debuts. Most of them are just disastrously pedestrian, and it makes sense. It's a pretty big risk. You know, you hear these executives saying, "We want to get new vision, new stuff, the hot new thing." That's why they have so many lousy movies.

H: Do you consider directing other people's scripts?

M: Yeah, but I always end up rewriting them. I mean, *Red Dawn* was originally somebody else's script, and I rewrote it. And *Flight of the Intruder* is really somebody else's book that I rewrote.

H: Now with the spirit of *glasnost* prevailing in Europe and the fact that the Berlin Wall has come down, what are your thoughts about *Red Dawn*, which at its release in 1984 was considered a paranoid view of the Soviet menace.

M: Well, I thought it was a great adventure, great fantasy. I didn't mean for it to be political. It was a comic-book adventure.

H: But you took a lot of flack for it?

M: They really got angry about that one, didn't they? I thought it was pretty innocuous.

H: Some critics think that your greatest·film is *The Wind and the Lion*.

M: People love that film.

H: Did you have David Lean in mind when you were shooting it?

M: Absolutely. It's amazing that the knack of doing these things is not too hard if you have somebody to steal from, somebody to copy. That movie really looks good. I mean, they show it all the time with *Lawrence of Arabia*, and it looks like that film because I had Lean's film to look at. It's not so much that you steal shots, but you get the feeling, the mood.

H: The characters in your films are all sort of misfits. What kind of characters really appeal to you the most?

M: I like misfits. I like people who don't fit in, who are not too cool.

H: Would you talk a little bit about the Nick Nolte character in *Farewell to the King*?

M: Yeah, he's definitely one of those guys. He doesn't fit in any-where. I sort of like him because he's interesting in a world where every day you read how people go bad with power and wealth. But he's a guy who gets advantage and uses it for good effect. He's sort of a Lord Jim type.

H: Were you happy with the film?

M: Yes and no, it was bowdlerized. It's not my cut. The producers mutilated it. So that's been a real bitter wound. I've never made peace with that film.

H: What exactly was changed.

M: How he becomes king and a lot of the motivations at the end. The producers and Orion took a very simplistic view of it. It was very, very much more of a complex story, and it didn't necessarily take much more time. But they felt that they were great filmmakers.

H: Have you ever thought about working outside the studio parameter?

M: That one was sort of outside the studio parameter. You're either working for a machine or you're working for a couple of egotistical idiots. Actually, one of the worst battles I ever had, but in a way it worked very well, was with Dino De Laurentiis on *Conan the Barbarian*, and I think that's a very, very fully realized film. That's a good film. That's exactly pretty much what I wanted it to be.

H: How do you feel about writing scripts now for other directors?

M: I don't feel that bad about it. I just sort of come through. You know, I've been a director, so I know the process. When I was young and hadn't directed anything, I felt that a script was my vision—this pure thing that I felt I couldn't let anyone else touch—so I had to become a director to do it. And now I see that maybe my vision got done best by another director, for example, *Apocalypse Now*. So, maybe I was wrong. Now I'm happy to write for other directors, and if it comes out good, it comes out good. If it comes out bad, them's the breaks.

H: I wanted to talk about *Apocalypse Now* because it's been hailed as one of the few great American films of the last decade or so. Would you talk about the evolution of the script and what was going on in your own life at the time?

M: That really started back at USC when we were all planning on either avoiding or going to war. It really started in my writing class where the teacher, Irwin Blacker, said that *Heart of Darkness* had never been made into a film, that Orson Welles tried it and couldn't lick it, that someone else tried it and couldn't lick it. And, of course, that's when he said it couldn't be done. So naturally, as a nineteen-year-old, it was absolutely the first thing that I attempted to do. And I liked Conrad. I like Conrad for what he says, but I didn't like his style at all, so I sort of waded through his book. But I always liked the stories. I was really more of a Jack Kerouac man.

H: So, what happened?

M: Well, after I started *Apocalypse*, I wrote some other stuff for a while. I wrote *Jeremiah Johnson* and a few other things like that. Not much though, but I was making a living. I made fifteen, twenty thousand dollars a year, and that was a lot of money for a surfer, you know. I lived like a rajah. I was married, young, and had a kid. My wife worked and we had a little apartment, no responsibilities. It was a good life. So Francis said he always wanted to do this Vietnam thing. He said, "I've got this deal at Warner Bros. George Lucas is going to do a movie, a cheap movie. Why don't you guys do your Vietnam movie? The one that you've been writing, and George will direct it." So then I finished it. We got me a deal there: fifteen thousand dollars to write it, which was enough money then to live on a whole year. It was an incredible deal. It gave me an incredible amount of freedom. And it really changed the whole way that my career went, because I'd been offered another job rewriting a script that also was made called *Skin Game*. It was a little western about the slave trade or something, but it was a rewrite job. And so I got to do this instead. I got to do what I wanted to do. And that sort of steered me into the path of doing my own work and being a little more like a novelist. So that was an enormous break. So I wrote *Apocalypse Now*, and they read it, and they loved it, and they said, "On the basis of this, have you got anything else?" And I had *Jeremiah Johnson*, so they bought and made that, but then *Apocalypse* never got made, because people were really afraid of us actually making it. George and I came fairly close to making it then. We were gonna go to Vietnam and make it.

H: In Vietnam?

M: Yeah. We were gonna do it. Remember that at the time they were making movies like *Medium Cool*, and the whole idea was to make a movie in the verité style where you actually were there and shooting the movie among, you know, people doing the real events.

H: Not unlike Dziga Vertov.

M: Yes, and so we really wanted to go do it. We were going to make *Apocalypse Now* for a million and a half dollars in Vietnam. And we got all these connections. We got people who were generals in the Air Force, and people who were going to help us get around. And I remember, it was wonderful that all of these guys who were around Francis at the time who were hippies and extreme political radicals, who burned their draft cards because the idea of being killed was horrifying, they all wanted to go make this movie. They wanted to go to Vietnam without any protection whatsoever and hop around through the minefields, and every one of them wanted to go.

H: How close did it really come to getting made over there?

M: It came pretty close, but then the studio started saying, "Why are we sending these hippies over there? They're a bunch of nuts. Some of them will be killed. There's a real war over there. Those guys are really nuts." So they stopped us.
  The subject of the war also was an unpopular topic for Hollywood. I mean, this was a time when there were riots in the streets about the war, and a studio executive is the last person who's going to want to get involved in the middle of that. Hollywood isn't exactly known for its social courage.

H: When you wrote the screenplay did you have Conrad on your left side and the script on your right?

M: As a matter of fact, I never even reread *Heart of Darkness*. I read it when I was sixteen or seventeen years old, but then never read it again, just remembered it. But of course, that was just the beginning, because I worked on it for ten years. There was always some time during the year that I was rewriting *Apocalypse Now*. It was rewritten so many times, so many drafts, until finally when the movie was released I went into the theater and realized that a huge part of my life was gone. The script was written ten years before the film was ever released. That's a lot of time. I remember when Francis's daughter was seven years old and they asked her at school, "What does you father do?" she replied, "He makes *Apocalypse Now*." The script was older than she was.

H: Was the Lance Johnson surfer character autobiographical?

M: No, I just liked the idea of a surfer being there, you know. But I always thought that I would be Kurtz, man. I would be the guy who went up the river who sends the letter back home and says, "Sell the car. Sell the kids. I'm never coming home. Fuck you all."

H: Did you go to the Philippines for the shooting?

M: No, no. They never allowed me to go. Francis didn't want me to go. He was afraid of a coup. And there's really some seriousness in that, because there was a real plan by the United Artists executives to dump Francis. They really felt he was never going to finish the film, and so they said, "Well, we'll get Milius and throw a net on him. Get him in a straitjacket for Francis. Get Milius to take over and finish the film, get it done."

H: Did they actually approach you?

M: No, they wouldn't do that. They never approach the guy in the middle of a coup. He's always drafted after the Air Force has taken over the radio station.

H: Did you want to direct it?

M: Originally I wanted to direct it. I almost directed it several times right after *The Wind and the Lion*, but then Francis decided he wanted to direct it. And once he started on it, I saw that there was something going on that was better than any way I could have ever done it. And looking at the movie, he did a bigger and more visionary work than I would have ever done.

H: Some critics have called *Apocalypse Now* an antiwar film.

M: That's so silly! Making an antiwar film's like making an anti-rain film. The whole idea of antiwar is just ludicrous. Anyone who makes an antiwar film is not human, or doesn't understand human nature and is lying to himself. I mean, war is horrible. Robert E. Lee said it best at Fredericksburg, watching rank upon rank of Union troops being mowed down, "It's lucky that war is so horrible as it is, lest we love it so."

H: Some people believe we lost Vietnam because the White House didn't want a full commitment to the war. The Kurtz character says it succinctly when he talks about the political double standard of the war, how commanders don't want the soldiers to write "fuck" on their airplanes.

M: Yes, I think that *Apocalypse Now* still has certain truths in it that are probably the most vivid of any of the Vietnam films. It's got some real strong stuff. It's kind of a young man's film. I don't know if I could have written it today. If I was going to write a war film now, I'd go to war and I'd hope to write *War and Peace*. You've got to write something like *Apocalypse Now* when you're young.

H: Is that because you're more idealistic?

M: And you're full of white-hot anger and full of daring, and you go way out on a limb. You think you have answers when you're young. When you're older you begin to know you have no answers. Then you try and make some sense out of it all.

H: A hundred years from now how do you think historians will look upon the Vietnam War?

M: They'll look at it as a great big stupid folly, a mistake. But there's always great valor in a lost cause.

Filmography (as director)

1973   *Dillinger*
1975   *The Wind and the Lion*
1978   *Big Wednesday*

1982   *Conan the Barbarian*
1984   *Red Dawn*
1988   *Farewell to the King*
1991   *Flight of the Intruder*

RICHARD SCHICKEL

A Life Goes to the Movies

I was recently walking in Greenwich Village when I passed a side-walk bazaar of old books and magazines being peddled by a man in a knit cap. There by his feet lay an aging stack of *Life* magazines. I dusted off the covers and flipped through the brittle, yellowing pages looking for film reviews by Richard Schickel, one of American cinema's most insightful and revered critics who, for the past twenty-seven years, has been a writer for *Life* and then *Time* magazine.

I came across an issue of *Life* from the third week in August 1967. There in the front of the magazine on the editorial page, *Life's* managing editor George P. Hunt wrote about Schickel: "In the last two years, [he] has seen 300-odd movies and written 83 reviews for *Life*. Some of our readers will be in agreement; some will say 'Well, you blew it again, you idiot'; some will excoriate Schickel for being an old fogey ('You must be about 65, with white hair,' a teen-ager wrote last week); they will vilify him for his child-ish naïveté (one reader asked, 'Are you out of high school yet?'). We don't always agree with Dick either, but we respect his views."

I pick up another issue from that same year and come upon Schickel's review of *Bonnie and Clyde* (1967). "What?" I exclaim over the din of sidewalk congestion. "Is there a problem?" asks the man in the knit cap. "He didn't like *Bonnie and Clyde* . . . He hated it," I say perplexed by Schickel's disdain over what is generally consid-

198

ered to be director Arthur Penn's masterpiece. The man in the knit cap shrugs as I pay him two bits for both issues.

Twenty-three years after Hunt defended his colleague on the editorial page of *Life*, Schickel sits in his Los Angeles office, still a critic whose writing often goes against popular opinion. In 1989 he published a book of essays titled *Schickel on Film*, in which he questions public sympathy for the Hollywood Ten and attacks the sanctity of Charlie Chaplin's and John Ford's rank as the cinema's greatest artistic legends. Schickel is a little vexed that the book didn't create more of a stir.

"If a literary figure of my stature wrote such a book denigrating Hemingway or Faulkner, you can bet it would have been widely reviewed," comments the author who has also written compelling biographies of Walt Disney and D.W. Griffith. Schickel is a little disillusioned by the New York literati's apparent apathy toward serious film scholarship. "Perhaps it's that there's such a glut of silly film books, picture books and fan biographies that it's too much trouble to sort out the interesting from the mundane," he continues. He is now focusing his time on directing biographical documentaries on important figures in the American cinema, projects he shares with his wife and associate producer Carol Rubinstein.

In 1989 they produced "Gary Cooper: American Life, American Legend" and they are now working on a project that explores the career of Elia Kazan. "Writing, especially film reviewing, is something I'm becoming less and less interested in," says Schickel, making the distinction between the film reviewer and film critic. "If people will read my books, I'd like to continue writing about older films that meant something to me. That's the real challenge of the film critic." Schickel believes that marketing motion pictures has become so sophisticated that the value of reviewing new films has become moot. "There was a time when film reviewing was very exciting," he says, almost with a sigh of nostalgia.

HICKENLOOPER: What was your experience like working at *Life* magazine?

SCHICKEL: Oh, *Life* was great to work for.

H: Didn't the magazine have a special relationship with the studios?

S: Well, no, I think not as pertained to me. I think earlier they had had. In the sense that they had that kind of regular feature, "Life Goes to the Movies." They had an obvious mutual need to publicize movies and stars. One wanted to sell magazines, the other films, so I think there was a lot of trading. I wouldn't say that *Life* did any kind of heavy-duty reporting on the stars that they put on the covers. They were rather agreeable profiles, which wasn't any different than it is now at most magazines. I mean, there are very few articles or profiles of stars that are hard-hitting, investigative journalism. You know, I think there's a relationship between all magazines working in that area. In my time I've written cover stories for *Time*, interviews with stars, the whole thing, and I just don't care for it very much. The whole question of access to a star is a vexing one. It's vexing now. It was vexing then. But I'd say it's quite a bit more vexing now than it was in the heyday of *Life* in the sense that now the stars' publicists want guarantees before access is given if it's a major star like Tom Cruise or Jack Nicholson.

H: Cover guarantees?

S: Yes, and though most magazines will never engrave it in stone, if the celebrity is big enough and wants the cover, they'll probably give it to him or her. In the old days of the studio, the stars had to go wherever the studio heads kicked them. Nowadays, the stars are independent. They employ independent publicists who will negotiate very hard on behalf of their clients. So, I would say that, probably, a question of arranging a major story at any magazine, *Time*, *Vanity Fair* or whatever, gets down to some very hard bargaining.

H: In your book *Intimate Strangers* you talk about the "cult of personality" and the phenomenon of celebrity. Would you talk a little bit about the book?

S: Well, stars have always been pedestaled as mythological figures. In other words, they've become what the gods were to the Greeks. They've become a kind of twentieth-century mythology. The great stars have a capacity to represent a distillation of certain ideals that people aspire to at different times in history. In other words, it's possible Clark Gable would not be a great star today, but in his particular era, notably the 1930s, he was a great star because he ideally represented in his person both male and female yearnings about masculinity. I think John Wayne and Clint Eastwood represented it at some point in our history. Certainly Mary Pickford represented femininity in her time and Marilyn Monroe in hers. There's a whole group of female stars in the 1930s—Claudette Colbert, Myrna Loy, Irene Dunne and Jean Arthur—which, taken as a group, represented a significant change in the definition of female ideals in our society. It's certainly different from the stars of previous eras, theatrical stars of the nineteenth century. There's not the same intimacy with them, as though you feel you know these people—a phenomenon which is simply created by the magnification of their image. Uniquely, movies have both intimacy and scale. The trouble with television stars and why TV doesn't have the same impact is that it's all intimacy. There's no scale to it. It's interesting how important television is; however, it's still the movie star who fulfills this socio-psychological need to aspire to certain ideals.

H: Do you think this "mythology" was responsible for the election of Ronald Reagan, or at least contributed to his success?

S: No, Reagan was certainly not a great movie star. He was a stayer. We have a need for a man of mutable talent. It was that he was an agreeable man. Week in and week out he did not offend you. Week in and week out he did not offend most people. That's all there is to it.

H: In your book *Schickel on Film*, you wrote that there is a distinction between film reviewer and film critic.

S: Yes, it's very primitive. A critic's a person who sits down and thoughtfully contemplates a movie that's maybe ten or twenty or fifty years old. He has the reasonable supposition that his readers will have seen the movie. The reviewer is writing immediately. Chances are most people will not have seen the movie he's discussing. It's that simple. You know, reviewing is just the first word on a movie. It's not the last word. From my point of view, I'd rather write criticism than reviews. I find it more agreeable. I like to take a little more space, a little more time to contemplate the pictures, go into more detail on maybe eighty or ninety lines in the magazine. When you're young, the thought of being part of a dialogue about a brand-new movie is kind of exciting. And you want to strut your stuff and show off a little bit. But now that I'm older, I'd rather think about older movies with some kind of historical perspective.

H: Do you ever change your opinions about a film over a period of time?

S: Yes. Certainly my estimation of *Bonnie and Clyde* has risen over the years compared to my initial notice. I think that would also be true of *Chinatown*. I also think there are movies that I liked at one time and have encountered since then and said, "Why did I like that?" So, you know, that kind of thing happens a lot.

H: Do you think one's appreciation of older movies is relative to the kind of films that are released later?

S: Well, you know, there's a nostalgic factor that you have to be wary of. You don't want to be in this sort of weird position of imagination where there's this great Golden Age of movies. It's like last year, there was all this hoopla over Hollywood's fiftieth anniversary celebrating the movies of 1939. "It was the greatest year for movies." Well, it was a pretty good year, certainly for American movies. But take a look at the entire list of releases of 1939, and it might not look like such a golden year. It's sort of silly. And I don't want to ever get trapped in the notion that the first fifteen years of the sound era were the great years that can never be duplicated again. I think the new technology of that period, certainly the thirties, was very stimulating. It brought a whole new group of people into the movie business. And it had a great devotion to some kind of literary values by which I don't mean adapting best sellers. Writers like Preston Sturges, Noam Johnson and Ben Hecht—those were intelligent men with a good ear for witty dialogue, and Sturges was, I think, something of a genius. I think they were all stirred by the possibilities of sound pictures, because it played into their values and they were newspaper men who tried their hands at novels and playwriting.

I've just been reading a collection of Johnson's letters and they're very illuminating. This was an intelligent newspaper man who'd done some short fiction for popular magazines, got into screenwriting and found himself very happy. He was intrigued by the craft of it. He worked very hard and devotedly for what he was doing, and I think that spirit animated Hollywood in that period. There were perhaps very few people who said, "Oh, this is going to be the Elizabethan age of movies, and I want to be a part of it." But then again, I think there was an almost semiconscious awareness of the possibilities of movies and movie making. And I think they responded to it. There was stir and bustle and mutual stimulation happening. And to that degree I think it was a better age than this current age of movie making.

H: In what direction do you think the cinema would have gone if sound had never come along?

S: Well, as you know, the late twenties became very visually so-phisticated. They were mastering a way of telling quite complex stories in truly visual terms. There are people who regret that that was cut off for five or six years during the transition movies— which I find unbearable to watch. The studios were so worried about recording the sound properly that dialogue was read slowly, making performances wooden. Consequently, the films were very very slow. I don't share the nostalgia for silent movies that some people have. Most of the people who are fanatical about silent films are cultists now. I mean, I wrote an extensive biography of D.W. Griffith, watched his entire body of work several times, and I wouldn't care if I saw another one of his films ever again. Granted, he orchestrated a certain set of technologies that created a new cinematic vocabulary, but his films are basically painful to look at. My own preference for movies lies in the dialogue comedies of the thirties and forties culminating in Sturges, as opposed to the silent comedians, though I do have a very high regard for Buster Keaton. I don't have much regard for Chaplin. Harold Lloyd is okay—but I certainly don't think that that was the Golden Age of the movies, if that's the word.

H: Your dislike of Chaplin certainly places you in a minority.

S: Chaplin is bullshit. You know, there are wonderful moments in Chaplin, but the wonderful moments tend to be in his earliest films—with a few exceptions.

H: In your book *Schickel on Film*, you give him credit as a performer, but not much as a director.

S: As a director he was a hopeless jerk. The worst. He had no sense of screen technique. His films are lessons in how to photograph himself, and that's the entire battle.

H: Yes, but wasn't he able to evoke a sense of pathos that no other filmmaker had done up to that point?

S: I don't think so. Griffith had plenty of pathos. There was plenty of pathos in silent movies. It was developed in the easy way. There was more of a kind of tragic, poetic sense in the movies in those days than there subsequently has ever been. But also, you have to remember that they were working off that vision of theatrical melodrama which had contained a great deal of sentiment, pathos. And Chaplin was no less different because he embodies the values of a little child. He was the cult of the child. The cult of innocence and all that crap.

H: Why has it been only recently that critics are paying attention to Keaton?

S: Well, I have a feeling that there are certain figures in movie history that the literati got behind; popular figures who were wonderful to write essays about. My sense of the early history of movies was that there were a large number of people waiting for a Chaplin. He was someone who was easy to write about. Of course, well into his career, they became disappointed with several of his features. In fact, he just went on and did what he'd always done. He hadn't declined that much. He was easy to write about. Garbo is another figure like that. She was somebody you could speculate on, write about, so she, like Chaplin, became a far greater figure than she deserved to be. I mean, Jesus, they were insufferable! Keaton, who really was a wonderful director, and really had a sense of the possibilities inherent in movies for comedy, as opposed to mere self-preservation, was an unpretentious man. He did not court these people. And Chaplin did—he very clearly courted the good opinion of the world's elite, by which I mean not just literary figures, but political figures.

H: Do you think the sound picture set back the developing visual aesthetic of the motion picture?

S: I think you could go through all the movies of the early sound era and keep finding felicities, visual felicities. King Vidor, who was probably the biggest victim of the silent-to-sound transition, who had all kinds of trouble with dialogue, but who in my opinion was also the great American silent picture maker, had these smashing visual sequences in his early sound films. And even in *Duel in the Sun*, especially that scene which includes the great gathering of the clan at the railhead, there are several stunningly orchestrated visual sequences. But overall, yes, I think there was a bit of a setback strictly in visual terms. Many of the comedies and dramas of the early thirties are visually uninteresting. And in the early sound days, the camera was limited in what it could do in consideration of the microphones picking up dialogue. However, I don't think it was a fatal setback because it wasn't very long before John Ford, Howard Hawks, Fritz Lang and Orson Welles started giving us wonderful-looking films in the late thirties and early forties.

H: It's interesting to observe the evolution of cinematic vocabulary from, let's say, the Lumière Brothers through someone like Tony Scott. It would be interesting to take an audience out of a theater in 1915 and put them into a movie like *Days of Thunder*. I wonder how they would respond visually to what they were seeing.

S: Well, *Days of Thunder* is not unattractive, visually speaking. It understands that you don't have to have lingering shots of mechanics working on cars. It used very rapid montage—quick cuts of guys very rapidly changing tires. We understand it very quickly. I would say that the biggest thing that's happened since the forties is the rapidity with which information, visual information, can be pushed out in a movie and the audience will understand it. I always think of that typical forties sequence with the hero—let's imagine he's a detective—who has to go interview the suspect, and there are shots of him getting into the car, driving the car, getting out of the car, he goes up to the door where somebody opens it. We no longer really have to do that. Now you can say I'll go interview Jane Doe, and the next thing you're in the house and he's interviewing Jane Doe. All those other shots that people thought had to be there so the audience could absorb what was happening are no longer necessary. We now read it very quickly and that's a function of television. We don't need all that boring stuff anymore. So, to that degree even the uneducated eye is more sophisticated visually. And you know, I don't think it's MTV. It's everything. Movies have been around for a hundred years now. We have absorbed that and we can now skip a lot of the stuff that in the twenties, thirties and forties were standard.

H: Has the accelerated rate of storytelling had an effect on the literary content of films?

S: Well, I suppose so. To a degree that if you're moving very rapidly, imparting a lot of visual information very quickly, there are very few dialogue scenes anymore in any movies. I'll tell you what it does prevent: the kind of pleasures of Sturgesian dialogue where the weird little guy in the corner of the frame who usually has a wonderful line will now find himself on the cutting room floor. You lose many of the funny little moments and subtleties which the old movies had. If Sturges were alive I'm not sure he would be happy working today. Especially if he couldn't get in all those funny little moments. What we've lost today are people with a real ear for that kind of writing, if you will, which is based on observation. The big thing about Sturges is that he'd had all those years away from America, so when he came back it was like coming to a foreign country. He heard the humor in our banalities in a way that a person who hadn't had so much experience away didn't hear. I should compare him to Vladimir Nabokov who had that too. He was a Russian emigré who had a gift for language, and he came here and heard the way we talked freshly. He saw our landscape freshly. And I think Sturges had that quality that I think very few people do. They had a much larger range of reference and so did their work. I think the range of reference in movies has dropped considerably. For example, there was a Cagney, boy-meets-girl movie about two screenwriters. There were Proust jokes in it. Now, I mean, I don't know if anybody would do a Proust joke in a modern movie. Somebody would say, "Aw, nobody will get it." But somehow in 1937 or '38, whenever the picture was made, it was "Sure, that's funny." Now I don't know whether all of America heard that joke or not, but they said "Oh, that's fine. Somebody's going to get it." And it was part of the texture of the movie.

H: What are your thoughts on the American cinema of the late sixties and early seventies, which I've been touting as Hollywood's last Golden Age?

S: Hmmm . . . well, that's interesting. I was talking to Arthur Penn about a month or so ago and he said he had a distinct sense at that point that during that period, truly the last vestiges of the old style of doing movies had disappeared. The last contract player, the last contract director and writer had disappeared. But they had not yet locked themselves into this present kind of block-buster syndrome.

There seems to have been a lot of openness then. The point that Arthur was making was that at the time he was shooting *Bonnie and Clyde* the other picture that was being shot on the same lot at Warner Brothers was *Camelot*. He said, "You know, it's interesting. The same management had taken these two risks. They could not have been more opposed." And yet that might be a good example of the spirit of the moment—that you could go with *Camelot* or you could go with *Bonnie and Clyde* and have a shot. There was an openness. The studios weren't quite locked into the notion of the commercial formula being the road to success as they seem to be today. And after all, *Bonnie and Clyde* was a substantial commercial success. That's another interesting thing about that movie. It opened very well despite some studio hesitation over it. All I would say is that I think there was a sense of discovery in the late sixties and early seventies of the movies as an art form. And that's stupid, because most people should have known that as far back as the twenties. But there was suddenly this "Ah, movies are important. Movie critics are important. Movie chat is important. Directors are important." There was a rise in the number of star directors. There had been a number of star directors before that, but suddenly we were interested in a lot of people who became known to the public as directors.

H: Were Andrew Sarris and the fellows at *Cahiers du Cinéma* a major force behind this?

S: Partially, and I think there was even a sense of this on the part of the directors themselves, that they wanted to be like Howard Hawks or whoever. They wanted to be auteurs. There was this whole redefinition of what director was. But more than that, this sense that movies are important, that movies are an art form, that movies are something that serious people can get serious about, in many ways animated Hollywood. There was a freeing up there. Again, I don't want to get into calling it a "Golden Age," because I'm not sure it was all that golden an age, but being a critic then, there was a very strong sense of the possibility of surprise at all times. Sometimes the surprise worked out, like *Easy Rider*, and sometimes it didn't, like *The Last Movie*. But there was a liveliness to it. The last time I saw Pauline Kael we both agreed that it was a lot more fun back then than it is now, because things were in general less formulaic, or there was greater hope—maybe this is a better way to put it. There was greater hope that you wouldn't see something formulaic. There were going to be formulaic movies of course, but there was a sense that at any given moment something would be different. Something would be odd. Something would be not quite like anything you'd seen before. And I think that was an important thing. It was sure important in my life. It made it more fun.

H: Would you take four directors who started very promisingly during the seventies and talk about the progression of their careers: Francis Ford Coppola, Peter Bogdanovich, Woody Allen and Martin Scorsese?

S: Well, Scorsese and Allen are the only ones who have consistently behaved as film artists. Both of them continue reaching out beyond their previous successes. They climb, with greater or lesser degree of success, for something that's new to them or interesting to them without abandoning their roots. Marty will always be a guy interested in urban life, and that's true of him. There's an intensity about his work and a constant ambitious reaching out which is also true of Woody. He's really trying very hard to go beyond simply being funny. He's criticized for it, but I praise him for taking the risk. I like his ambition. And I think some of his films which have been chastised will look rather good in a decade or so.

Bogdanovich is hard to talk about. His career and personal life have become this weird combination of disaster and success. I'm not sure where Peter got lost or what happened to him. I've often suspected that some people who worshipped Welles, like Peter did, courted disaster so they could be more like him. But Peter's talented. There are just so many ways to go wrong in this business. And with Francis Coppola, he got himself into some kind of ego trip in terms of his own studio, restaurants, magazines, wineries and these new technologies that he wanted to experiment with— all this stuff forced him to overextend himself and I think distracted him and I think continues to distract him from the content of his work. Both Coppola and Bogdanovich have fallen victim to all the things that we mean by that tired cliché of "going Hollywood." There are so many ways that this business can do you in without your quite knowing it while it's happening. When you're hot, everyone will indulge you, and sometimes maybe that's the thing you mustn't let them do.

What I think saved Scorsese and Woody Allen is that they stayed in New York. They kept their feet on the earth. It's as simple as that. You know, they're still in the rub and mix of a difficult place—difficult in the sense of everyday survival. They both live in Manhattan and hear something other than last week's grosses. They're confronting people from all walks of life and not from the inside of an air-conditioned BMW, but from the subways, buses and taxis. They don't isolate themselves in a Bel Air mansion. In New York there's always visual and intellectual stimulation. California's beautiful, but it doesn't offer you the same kind of contact with human life that exists on the streets of Manhattan. I was talking to Elia Kazan and he said he felt insulated in Los Angeles. It's easy for people to lose sense of themselves there. He said that in New York "if I get depressed I go out and walk around the streets and I always see something that gets me going." It sounds simple but it's true. If you walk around the streets in L.A. you're not going to see anything but the sidewalk because there's nobody

walking on it. Being in constant contact with people is very important. And I think the temptation toward isolation is disastrous for
anybody who has ambitions toward artistic statement. I think that
it's a disaster that the movie business left New York.

H: I wanted to go back to your book *Schickel on Film*, which I
found very provocative, particularly your denigration of Chaplin
and Ford. Why didn't your book raise a few eyebrows?

S: Oh, I don't know. I'm so sick of book publishing and the
whole scene—don't even get me started. I'll tell you that I do believe that there is a substantial literary prejudice against serious
writing about movies. If the literary establishment comes to it at
all, it's to try to patronize it or pat in on the head. As far as I'm
concerned, that book is as substantial as anything Irving Howe has
ever written. His collection of essays would be seriously reviewed
all over the goddamned place. But my book wasn't. It is a bitter-
ness to me and disappointment to me. I despise the literary community. I despise their attitude toward film. I don't really intend to
write any more books because it's labor intensive and unprofit-
able, both of which are acceptable to me if at least what you write
is taken seriously and debated, is discussed, gets into the stir of
culture. But this kind of thing is reprehensible to me.

H: I found what you wrote about the Hollywood Ten intriguing.
You seem to take an unpopular, if not revisionist, look at the
House Un-American Activities Committee during the late forties
and early fifties.

S: Nothing that HUAC did was despicable! It's actually not that
revisionist in the sense that I was born and raised in it, in the anti-
Stalinist left tradition. There's a naïveté about American communism as if they were just a little bit more liberal than some of us
were, which is just not true. And I guess I just got a little bit concerned in the sense that it seemed to me that young people were
missing the point. I mean these were real issues and I had certain
beliefs that the Stalinist left was courting martyrdom, and once
they achieved martyrdom, they would do so at the expense of their
former enemies. Elia Kazan, perhaps the major American director
of that era, is not taken seriously as a director in the film commu-

nity because he's tainted by this stuff. I mean, I bet there's more cinéaste writing about Bud Veticher than there is about Elia Kazan, and we're talking about the implementor of major new schools of acting in both theater and film. And the thought that nobody writes books about him is ridiculous.

H: What do you think about someone like Dalton Trumbo, who was one of those martyred?

S: Dalton never courted that martyrdom. I knew Trumbo and I liked him enormously, and it's clear to me that he was long done with the Stalinist left probably by the time that happened. But, you know, his sense of honor demanded that he stay with the Ten. But I mean, he was constantly lecturing at them, saying "Leave it alone. It's over now. We all made mistakes." All I was trying to do in that piece was say "Hey guys, you know what? There's another way to look at the Hollywood Ten. The reverence for this particular group of injustice collectors is probably somewhat misplaced." This does not make me say that I think HUAC is anything but gross nonsense of a particular kind just as much as Jesse Helms is more or less the same thing in this campaign against the NEA. To me it's the same trip, except that now it's an allegedly aesthetic position instead of an allegedly political one. But it's all know-nothingism on a huge scale, and I've always been opposed to any kind of government subvention of the arts. Because it's inevitable that this will happen. It happened in the WPA when Orson Welles tried to perform *The Cradle Will Rock* on Broadway. Artists should just want to stay away from those people. Their money is tainted and it will eventually lead you to what we're seeing at this particular moment in history. You're better off without it.

H: But I'm still not sure if I understand your defense of HUAC. Weren't they just creating another witch hunt like Jesse Helms?

S: Yes, but when those of the Hollywood Ten began propounding a revolutionary point of view, they should have been prepared for the consequences, which is that the nonrevolutionary whole will pick on you. You're no longer a liberal. You're a revolutionist. What happens to revolutionists in most countries is unspeakable. They go to Siberia or they get tortured. I think once you embrace a revolutionary ideology, you had better be prepared for the consequences of that, which in the United States are rather mild. If you ask me do I think Congress has the right to silence these people, there's an ambiguous right there of which I disapprove as a liberal. I mean, I don't think the propagation of revolutionary views in the United States is a very dangerous activity. But I don't think you dare claim martyrdom if you're ever hounded, because in point of fact, it was an antidemocratic point of view. It was pro-Stalinist, which borderlines fascism. Just witness the history of Russia. So, the Hollywood Ten lost ten years of work. That's the price you pay for having that point of view. I don't know why it comes as a surprise to anybody. Do you really think you can go around propagating a Stalinist point of view and have no consequences to pay for that? And the consequences strike me as rather mild. In point of fact, since none of them were particularly good screenwriters, they all got posthumous fame, more so than writers who were much more apt at their trade than these guys were.

H: In your essay on Chaplin you talked about the decline of film criticism over the past ten years. Would you talk about that?

S: Is it a decline or were we all deluded back then? I don't know. Sure, there's a decline in the sense that film criticism has basically just become a branch of marketing. That's a function of this alleged criticism on television which is some kind of performance— they are performers no less than the performers they are reviewing. Does that, to some degree, lessen the quality of the dialogue about movies? Sure, I think it does, but there are still those of us who are writing in print, seriously attempting to come to grips with movies—both present and past.

H: Were shows like "Sneak Previews" and "Entertainment Tonight" the forces that contributed to the decline of film criticism?

S: Probably. But Roger Ebert is very sophisticated observer of movies. Though I don't read any of the Chicago papers, from what I've read of his in magazines and so forth, I find that he's a very intelligent man with quite a good sense about the movies. That kind of banter that he does on television doesn't strike me as his best mode. On the other hand, it's a mark of his intelligence that he's probably the first millionaire movie critic in the history of mankind. And I suppose that in all our remarks about him there's envy. I mean, you know, why didn't I think of that or why don't I have the personality that's adaptable for that kind of work? It would be agreeable to be that well paid for venting your feelings, however hastily, however simply.

H: How was film criticism changed since you began?

S: Well, I think to begin with the media in general were just naive about it. They said, "Let's have a voice sounding out about movies. That's something we haven't done much of in the past." So you started to have guys do sound bite reviewing for local television. I mean some of us became sort of little stars of that kind of writing. I think the tendency now is for a much more feature approach to it, much more personality oriented. I don't detect that any magazines now are real long on criticism. The pressure is more toward a shorter, quicker, bitier kind of reviewing, or toward a softer kind of reviewing where they wrap a trend or a personality into the story. In other words, it was possible to practice, not pure criticism, but a truer kind of reviewing in the sixties and seventies. It was very acceptable to the readers, and it was acceptable to the editors. I think the trend is away from that now.

H: Has the film critic fallen victim to the phenomenon of the "cult of personality." In other words, have their personas become larger than their opinions?

S: I suppose Siskel and Ebert are probably the best example of that. I suppose what people resent is that they've become the standard bearers of the profession. And maybe that's not so bad because certainly Ebert is as good as they can get in that particular incarnation.

H: In 1979 there was an interesting article in *New West* magazine about film critics' incestuous relationships with the film industry.

S: Oh, *that*! I was interviewed for it. People are always trying to find the critic writing the screenplay for the guy he's just given a good review to. It's bullshit. I think at the time the piece came out, Jay Cocks, who had gone to NYU with Marty Scorsese, was working on a project but was quite open and public about it. There was also a guy at *Newsweek,* Paul Zimmerman, who just wanted to write screenplays, but I don't think he was in the tank then. I mean, it's not as if you're in the old studio system and they've got you under a seven-year contract and you've sold movies on the side. All you can say is "I guess Jay shouldn't review any more movies of Marty's for his readers."

I don't see anything wrong with the critic trying to get into movies. François Truffaut did it, Bogdanovich did it. In fact, I see everything right with it, if you want to know the truth. If you're very interested in the medium, it would be very hard not to involve yourself with the medium. I know something about the process of putting films together. And I like the knowledge. I never fancied myself a screenwriter, but you know, if somebody asked me to do one and it was something that interested me, I'd probably do it. I don't see anything wrong with it, because I don't see where the corruption comes in. I can't stand the kind of journalism where people incessantly just dig for the dirt, especially where there is no dirt to begin with. The more I've worked with the television and film industry, the more sympathetic I've become to the problems that come with it. It really is very difficult. And if that makes me a slightly softer critic, then so be it. Certainly I have sympathy for creative people struggling through the minefields of moviemaking. For on top of all the aesthetic issues, there are the economic issues which are constantly fighting against a director's individual choice of expression. You know, it's a miracle that anybody gets anything done that's halfway decent.

Books by Richard Schickel

1960   *The World of Carnegie Hall*
1984   *D. W. Griffith: An American Life*
1985   *The Disney Version*
1986   *Intimate Strangers: The Culture of Celebrity*
1986   *Lena* (with Lena Horne)
1987   *Carnegie Hall: The First Hundred Years* (with Michael Walsh)
1987   *Striking Poses: Photographs from the Kobal Collection* (text only)
1989   *Schickel on Film*
1990   *Hollywood at Home: A Family Album 1950–1965* (text only)

III

The New Transatlantic Cinema

STEPHEN FREARS
Bloody Mindedness

"Southern California is so deliciously decadent," Stephen Frears says, commenting on his sumptuous three-room suite at the Bel Air Hotel. "There are so many bloody rooms in here, I don't know which one we should go into," he continues, walking through the living room in his pajamas, his hair slightly disheveled. We finally choose the terrace where he brings out some peanuts and Coca-Cola. "There's just so much of everything in L.A. And you Americans do so well enjoying it. Back in London, if you have money, you live with your head in a hole," he adds, half attracted and half repelled by the city's opulence.

Though Frears continues to live in a modest neighborhood in the north end of London, within the last five years he has achieved a great deal of success in the United States, first with his British-financed independent film, *My Beautiful Laundrette* (1986), and most recently with the Academy Award–nominated *Dangerous Liaisons* (1988). As we speak he is excited about the good advance word on his newest endeavor, *The Grifters* (1990), his first film to be shot on location in the United States. "I like Americans. I enjoy looking at a particular piece of American life," Frears says of this film about a group of con artists. "Americans are very straightforward. They'll tell you exactly what they feel. The Englishman . . . well, it's tough being an Englishman," adds the director.

Born in 1941 into a middle-class family, Frears grew up in

Leicester, England, a town he found "dull and oppressive, but mostly dull." At the age of eighteen he was sent to a state-run school where he met the headmaster who instilled in Frears a desire for knowledge about literature, politics and the world. From there he went on to Cambridge to study law in the early 1960s, a time in which the school was filled with such undiscovered talents as John Cleese, Eric Idle, David Frost and Dudley Moore. "So much was going on in the world around us that at the time the pursuit of law seemed tedious and unimportant. My generation became a generation of dilettantes. We not only turned our back on public life, we made fun of it." From law school Frears drifted from working at the Royal Court Theater with Albert Finney, to assisting film directors such as Karel Reisz and Lindsay Anderson, and eventually to directing his own films for the BBC.

Frears's first feature work became known in America in 1971 when his film *Gumshoe* was hailed by critics as a hilarious parody of the American gangster genre. However, it wasn't until fourteen years later, when *My Beautiful Laundrette* (1986) became a hit in the United States, that Frears was discovered as a viable new director with a very different point of view. "People talk about this black hole in my career during the 1970s," says Frears. "Well, I was working steadily for British television, learning my craft." His fourteen years there allowed him to work with some of the best writers in England—David Hare, Tom Stoppard, Neville Smith, Adrian Mitchell—with all of whom he created a number of impressive films, including *Bloody Kids* (1979), *Saigon: Year of the Cat* (1983) and *The Hit* (1984).

In 1985 Frears embarked on a more ambitious project. Financed by Channel 4 in London, *My Beautiful Laundrette* told the story of two homosexual entrepreneurs who run a laundromat in a run-down section of London. The film was a great success in the United States, and Frears immediately followed it up with *Prick Up Your Ears*, a biographical account of playwright Joe Orton's life and murder, and *Sammy and Rosie Get Laid*, the story of a Pakistani man and an English woman living in an interracial London slum. Based on the success of those three films Frears was courted by Warner Bros. to direct *Dangerous Liaisons*, his biggest budgeted film to date. "It was appealing because it was elegant sleaze. It was the film to turn me into a popular entertainment director."

After a few minutes chatting with Frears, I realize that he is not going to be an easy interview. I find that his often laconic answers to my questions are indicative of his English reserve. His gentle manners will only occasionally give me a little insight. I decided to start from the beginning.

HICKENLOOPER: I know you went to Cambridge where you received a law degree . . .

FREARS: A very good one.

H: You were there at the same time as Dudley Moore and John Cleese?

F: Dudley was ahead of me. I was there with David Frost and for three years I sat in the same room as John Cleese. And then one day I walked into a theater and there was this man performing with whom I had sat in a classroom for three years. Cleese was simply brilliant on stage.

H: Were you attracted to the theater at that time?

F: I wasn't very happy at that time in my life. I didn't really seriously think about the theater then. I knew that I didn't want to practice law. In fact, I don't know why I ever studied law. I suppose I did because I was the child of professional parents.

H: At the time, were your parents aware of your interest in theater?

F: Oh yes.

H: Did they discourage it?

F: Not in an unpleasant way. There was full employment in those days. I don't really remember having conversations about what I was going to do. I mean, if my mother were alive, I would still be having conversations about what I was going to do [laughs]. She would now be worried that I didn't have a proper job. When I was at Cambridge the atmosphere was very dilettante. People talked about how this was going to be the last bit of education you're ever going to have so you shouldn't be really training for a career. It was really the end of the gentlemen's era. Now, of course, there's massive unemployment.

H: In 1967 you directed your first short, *The Burning*. How did that all come about?

F: Well, it really all started at the Royal Court, which is really what I wanted to do. So I started working there where I was really out of my depth. There I met Karel Reisz and I went to work with him. And he introduced me to Albert Finney, so I began to work with him, and I just wanted to make a short film. So I found some interesting material and discovered that there was a fund at the British Film Institute which was administered by Bruce Beresford [laughs]. I don't think he much approved of me but I got some money out of that. And then after I made *The Burning*, I started to get jobs, one of which was assisting Lindsay Anderson. He's a re-markable man. I was very fortunate.

H: Your first feature film, *Gumshoe*, came to the United States in 1971. I read that that was the film which was supposed to launch your career abroad.

F: Well, I don't know if I ever thought like that. I mean, it did get shown over here but it was very limited. I was incredibly inexperi-enced. I had no master plan. I still don't have. I was just going about my wits. I was very unformed, almost amoebic. *Gumshoe* was a stroke of luck. I just happened to walk in off the streets with a wonderful script. And after that I was out of a job until the BBC hired me to direct again.

H: Were you given free rein in British television?

F: Not at all. The drama department at the BBC was a very well run place. They commissioned stuff from the best writers in En-gland and I would be one of the directors they would send it to. I did it job by job.

H: I once read that you said if you wanted to make a theatrical film in England, you would have to make it for an American audi-ence. What did you mean by that?

F: Well, the problem with Britain is that it has such a small population. You can't finance films in Britain from home-video sales. You have to make them for export. I know this now that I'm a little more lucid about the business. If you want to make a film about Britain for British audiences, my advice would be to make it for television. I'm just describing the reality of the situation. You'll get money if people feel they can sell it abroad, but there are only a few films that do well in Britain and get their money back. Overall, right now the situation in Britain is quite hard.

H: Alan Parker, Ridley Scott and Tony Scott are English directors who came from commercials, an entirely different background than yours. Do you think it may have been easier for them to adapt to American filmmaking than it was for you?

F: Well, I came from the background where films and plays were concerned with society. Since British society was the only thing we knew about, clearly that was one of our preoccupations. I guess advertising films are different. Also I came from a very political background at Cambridge. I was part of that large movement that concerned the whole world, namely protesting the Vietnam War, whereas advertising celebrates American virtues, so I guess it was easier for them. In that sense, I would say that I changed more than they have.

H: *The Hit* is one of your most interesting English films. Would you tell me about the origin of that project?

F: *The Hit* began because I was working with Ian McKellen, and I kept saying why don't we make a popular film. It was about that time in the early eighties that I started to want to make more popular films. I got fed up with I was doing.

H: Because it wasn't lucrative?

F: Maybe that was part of it. I also just got fed up with the size of the television screen. I just wanted to expand a bit, not just to make more money, but to have more fun, more opportunities.

H: Was that a film you thought might appeal to American audiences?

F: No, but it was a film that I thought would be popular because it was in a popular genre. So I rather foolishly pursued that, but it really didn't mean anything.

H: *Saigon: The Year of the Cat* is also quite a good film. What was it about David Hare's script that appealed to you?

F: I became friends with David, and again, it was more ambitious, bigger material to get your hands on. I began to get fed up with this tunnel vision on England.

H: Was there something unique about the English experience in Saigon at the time of the Vietnam War?

F: Well, David went to Saigon during the war. What was appealing to me was the love story in the foreground, and critics kept saying, "How can you make a film about these people when there's this huge war going on?"—which seemed to be a rather peculiar thing to say. But of course, it was attractive, an English woman in that situation. It seemed to me to be a kind of *Casablanca*-like story in its romantic way.

H: What is your working relationship usually like with the writer while you're shooting a film?

F: Well, I like to have the writer on the set, you know, in case we need to adjust a scene or something. But usually it's very clear; he writes it, I shoot it. I never threaten the authorship. I would never presume to do so.

H: You never do script work?

F: No. The writing is their bit.

H: That's very curious because I find you such a distinctive filmmaker.

F: I wouldn't know where to begin to explain that. I mean, I'm flattered that you think so. What I can say is that I'm good at choosing scripts. I work with good writers.

H: What's so uncanny is that your style comes through so clearly even when you're dealing with writers of such high caliber.

F: Well, I think that if you don't have a good writer, you're in trouble. I come from the writer's theater. Writers, in England, are the ones who are thought to have ideas.

H: *My Beautiful Laundrette* was financed by Channel 4 in England. Was the creation of Channel 4 in 1981 a very hopeful thing for British filmmakers?

F: Channel 4 perpetuated the values of the BBC at a time when they were rather slipping away. It took life in Britain seriously and they were my friends. At first, I was rather foolishly skeptical about it, but then I thought, no, this is a really good place.

H: You made *My Beautiful Laundrette* for British television. Was there anything in the back of your mind saying that this film might work for American audiences?

F: There was nothing in the back of my mind, quite the opposite. At the time I made the film the ambition among directors at Channel 4 was so strong for making films and wanting to put them in the cinema that a lot of my friends got into trouble, and it was slightly embarrassing. So when the script to *My Beautiful Laundrette* came along, I said, well, let's not do that because I could see the pain they were all in, so I knew that was what you had to avoid. Even after it was finished, I was always skeptical.

H: Both the protagonists in the film are homosexuals. Did you feel that you had to deal with this sensitively?

F: Quite the opposite. Not at all. It was a radical film. You had to have radical relationships. And people thought it was rather wonderful. It helped make homosexuality more acceptable. It showed homosexuality as not being so tormented, so painful, not leading to madness or death. It made it rather charming like *Butch Cassidy and the Sundance Kid*. It's rather naughty, isn't it?

H: One of the wonderful things about the film is that these two men are entrepreneurs who rather seem to enjoy their corruption. The character of the Pakistani boy is shown in an unflattering light throughout most of the film, but nevertheless one gets the feeling that you're sympathetic to him.

F: Yes, in a very perverse way, I suppose you're right. I loved the suits he was wearing as though he was waiting to be a mobster his entire lifetime. The trouble is that the corruption in the film is quite enjoyable.

H: Was that your indictment of the Thatcher era in Britain?

F: I thought the film was rather good on economics, a good comment on entrepreneurial society. That is what really interested me about it. It was written by a naughty boy. Alan is rather a naughty boy. There's really nothing more than that.

H: Would you talk about your interest in Joe Orton? How faithful did you want to be about the facts of his life in *Prick Up Your Ears*?

F: As faithful as necessary. It's very, very confusing making a film about real people. You know most of the time the actors don't look like the people they're portraying. Gary [Oldman] in some uncanny way looked like Joe. Also, I came from the same town as Joe so I was always intrigued by his work.

H: The Alan Bennett script for *Prick Up Your Ears* was criticized for having been a little too conventional.

F: What do you mean?

H: Well, the use of narration was criticized for being too conventional a device in telling the story about someone as unconventional as Joe Orton.

F: Well, we had to tell a story and the audience had to understand the chronology of events.

H: Were you ever tempted to tell his story in more of an Ortonesque tradition?

F: Well, I think we did some of that. I think some of the sequences were very Orton-like. I mean, we worked straight from his diaries and plays.

H: There's a certain similarity of tone in your body of work, in that you push the drama very far, so that it almost becomes absurdist. You create an interesting dichotomy between the real and the surreal.

F: Well, I suppose that just comes from my background, perhaps at Cambridge, perhaps in life. It could come from being partway between Europe and America. One cinema is analytic and the other is action-dominated.

H: Among actors you have a reputation of being fairly democratic. You solicit suggestions from your actors regularly.

F: The actors know more about the characters than I do.

H: What is your rehearsal process like?

F: Well, I'm not very good rehearsing with marks on floors. I like the actors to break the ice really, familiarize themselves with each other. I like it when they relax and joke with one another. Anything they want to do I'll do, because it seems to me to only make sense when I see the people in the right place.

H: Why did you choose to shoot *Dangerous Liaisons* with an American instead of a British cast?

F: Leaving aside the actors who originally created the parts on stage in London, I thought if you did it with English actors it would end up as sort of a comedy of manners. And I thought it should be about passion and feelings. First of all, it has nothing to do with the English, it has everything to do with the French. So if you had been able to do it with French actors that would have been one thing, but I thought it was an absolutely wonderful story that people would love if you made it accessible. And the way I wanted to go was making it about feelings and making it accessible. What I wasn't interested in was sort of a correct, English la-dee-da type film. I wasn't interested in making a costume type film.

What I liked about this was that underneath it all it was about feelings that everyone could understand.

H: Are American actors more equipped to make those kinds of films?

F: Well, I suppose that I felt English actors would be more walled up in the manners and procedures of society and American actors would be more concerned with feelings.

H: Does that have something to do with the fact that British actors are generally more classically trained?

F: Yes, it's all part of my rebellion against Britishness, Englishness, which seems to dictate a lot of my actions. I felt that I was violating the mold. You have to smash something. You have to break a leg. You have to violate everything and start with a clean slate in a way. So whatever is existing, we'll smash that and we'll get going.

H: I understand that you clashed with John Malkovich on the set?

F: No, well, John is a highly intelligent man. It's quite complicated. I had to learn that John wasn't like an English actor. Clash is the wrong word. I had to learn what American actors offered, which isn't the same as English actors, and I had to think on my feet. And there was no point in expecting that John would be able to work as an English actor.

H: His character comes across as a kind of antihero, a sympathetic antagonist. Were you ever afraid of the character going to far, being pushed beyond the realm of sympathy for the audience?

F: Well, you see, the play had been running for a long time. And Christopher Hampton, who wrote the play and the screenplay, knew what had worked with audiences when it was on the stage, so we had a tremendous amount of information as to how audiences responded. Anyway, as soon as I read it, it became apparent that the worse people behaved, the more fun it was, I'm ashamed to say. So we were always rather confident.

H: I was intrigued by the shooting style you chose for that film.

F: Well, there's an old American myth: "Nail them to the floor and light them." Originally, I thought I was going to shoot it in a more distant style. But it just wasn't working and I kept hearing the camera operator saying, "Well, can we go in closer?" And gradually we went in closer and then, of course, you see that in rushes, and you see which shots come to life and where the vitality is. Well, of course every time John spoke, he told a lie. The lines always had more complex meanings. And you saw that complexity in the close-ups, so that's when we realized that's how we should continue shooting it. It was just the opposite of shooting Anjelica [Huston] on *The Grifters*. Anjelica has these incredible legs. And I thought why just shoot her face, when it's the whole thing that's extraordinary. So I'll adapt to include other bits of her body instead of doing just a mid-shot.

H: So on some of your films you shoot in the style of mise-en-scène as André Bazin defined it and sometimes you shoot using close-ups and montage?

F: Well, I'd actually love to do it all in that sort of depth of field, but films aren't made like that anymore.

H: Why can't they be made that way?

F: Because the world is moving too quickly. I don't know, people won't sit still for it. You just don't do it. You cover. You keep the camera close to the actors. It may well be the influence of television. They aren't made that way now.

H: The dueling sequence in *Dangerous Liaisons* was wonderfully shot.

F: It was a bit of Michael Curtiz's *Robin Hood*, wasn't it? A very, very good stunt man arranged it and John and Keanu worked on it and I sort of subverted it for the camera [laughs]. I remember that there was an arch, and I remember being taken down there and thinking, this is just like a fight between two gangs in New York, people fighting in arches and things like that, so I made it very rough, sloppy. The feelings of the film made it impossible to be courtly, because the movie is all about feelings. It wasn't buried beneath a mask of manners.

H: That's very interesting because it's one of the few costume dramas that I can think of that resists that highly stylized look. It's a nice contrast.

F: Well, that's because I think people find those kinds of films quite dull. They're art rather than drama. You see those films and it brings out the Philistine in you [laughs]. You want to go home and cut two fingers off.

H: Milos Forman also shot a version of *Les Liaisons Dangereuses* which came out as *Valmont*. Were you shooting simultaneously?

F: He started shooting the day after I saw the first rough cut of my film.

H: Was there pressure for you to get your film out before he got his out?

F: Yes, early on. I said, "Look, I may not have made as many films as Milos, but I'm faster than him." I knew that because of my experience in television. They said, "But what if they hire five editors?" I said, "I'll still be faster." The main thing, of course, is that if the film turned out well, they didn't want it competing with *Valmont* for the same awards. Warner Brothers wanted to release it in a separate year from *Valmont*.

H: Is there anything in your work that you think is distinctly English?

F: You mean in the last American ones? Well, perhaps my rebelliousness or bloody mindedness, but I really don't know how to talk about it. My films seem to be about repressed feelings, or the frustration that your feelings are repressed, coming out in a sort of mischievousness. I'm reluctant to really say more than that. It's very difficult being an Englishman, as John Cleese said.

H: Would you talk about your most recent project, *The Grifters*, your first shot on location in the United States? I understand that Martin Scorsese produced it.

F: I was sent the book by Martin and I liked it very much. It's a hard-boiled melodrama about an outrageous lot of juvenile offenders. I thought it would make a wonderful film. I once read an interview with Fred Zinnemann and he talked about directing B-movies and then graduating to A-movies. And I think that I thought, well, I'm in a new school, I better direct a B-movie. I'll start at the bottom [laughs], so I'll make a B-movie. People always ask me what kind of film do I want to make, and I always tell them that I have nothing. There are no books on my shelf that I want to make. I really get involved in a project, the material, or that world when somebody sends me a project that I like. *The Grifters* came from a genre of cheap films and cheap paperbacks and I saw it as a way in, I suppose. It looked like fun so I did it.

H: Did you feel that you had to immerse yourself in American popular culture before making the film in order to get a handle on the genre?

F: Well, I feel that my life is already immersed enough in American popular culture. The world is saturated by it. What I had to do is try to understand a small bit of American life and who these people were. I had to ask myself, well, who are these people, where do they live and what kind of cars do they drive? It was the actual realization of these characters that was difficult.

H: Will you continue making films in the United States?

F: Well, the British film industry is virtually dead. And I'm having a good time working over here. It's very, very interesting. And I can't find anything in Britain right now. Now that may well be because I don't want to find anything in Britain right now [laughs].

Filmography (distributed in the United States)

1967   *The Burning*
1971   *Gumshoe*

1979   *Bloody Kids*
1983   *Saigon: Year of the Cat*
1984   *The Hit*
1986   *My Beautiful Laundrette*
1987   *Prick Up Your Ears*
1987   *Sammy and Rosie Get Laid*
1988   *Dangerous Liaisons*
1990   *The Grifters*

WIM WENDERS
Wings Over Berlin

The New German Cinema, a movement which produced a generation of radical filmmakers interested in exploring Germany's post-
war identity (Werner Herzog, Rainer Werner Fassbinder, Volker
Schlondorff, among others), has one member, Wim Wenders, who
also examines American sensibilities and culture which he believes began absorbing his own country after the Second World
War. Wenders, whose film *Paris, Texas* (1984) is perhaps his most
widely seen work in the United States, began his career in Germany with the idea that America was taking on a great role in
defining the political and cultural future, and not just of his own
nation, but in all of Europe.

"It's not something that we resisted," says Wenders, whose oeuvre reflects the ubiquity of American influence in his country,
whether it is evident in his use of Dennis Hopper in *The American
Friend* (1977), Allen Goorwitz in *The State of Things* (1983) or Peter
Falk in *Wings of Desire* (1988).

Wenders was born in Düsseldorf at the close of World War II.
Having grown up going to American movies, he says, "Nobody
cared about German films when I was a boy. They virtually didn't
exist. All we had were American movies and they were
wonderful."

Having spent much of his youth in Germany, the director says
that his generation grew up feeling alienated from the rest of the

world. "It seemed inappropriate that we shouldered the memory of Nazism and the Holocaust, that we were compelled to carry the brunt of the guilt." Consequently, many of Wenders's films deal with themes of alienation. His work is also frequently colored by indignation and melancholy, whether it's delicate as in *Alice in the Cities* (1974), freewheeling as in *Kings of the Road* (1976), out of balance as in *The State of Things* (1983), or whether the principal character in the film has just learned about his impending death, as Bruno Ganz's character does in *The American Friend* or as Nicholas Ray does in *Lightning Over Water* (1980).

Wanting to get a better perspective on himself and Germany, Wenders ventured to the United States in the early 1980s. In Hollywood he became acquainted with film maverick Francis Coppola and his American Zoetrope Studios where Wenders was introduced to a style of filmmaking to which he was completely unaccustomed. The result was the rather unsuccessful mystery-thriller-fantasy *Hammett* (1982), about film noir author Dashiell Hammett. Two years later he directed Sam Shepard's script of *Paris, Texas*, a highly stylized contemporary western about lost relationships among mother, father and son separated in the Southwest.

Wenders finally returned to Germany in 1988, where in Berlin he made perhaps his most critically successful film, *Wings of Desire*. For the first time it seemed that the German director was being praised for instilling in his audience life-affirming themes. One critic wrote, "Berlin, the most fated of locations, seems to infuse [Wenders] with a new vigor and suggests the possibility of a new beginning."

Preparing his newest film, *Until the End of Time* (1991), which will take him to seventeen different locations from America to Europe to Australia, Wenders found a few minutes to spare with me over the phone from Germany.

HICKENLOOPER: As a director your work is far from conventional. What do you like most about making films?

WENDERS: Well, my work is not that far from usual. I tell a story with images. In fact, the thing I enjoy most about directing is working in a language of images. I want to tell stories that can be told visually. I think that filmmaking invented its method of storytelling a long time ago and that there is probably very little to be improved upon there.

H: So is it impossible to be original?

W: Not impossible, but originality now is rare in the cinema, and it isn't worth striving for because most work that does this is egocentric and pretentious. What is most enjoyable about the cinema is simply working with a language that is classical in the sense that the image is understood by everyone. I'm not at all interested in innovating film language, making it more aesthetic. I love film history, and you're better off learning from those who preceded you.

H: You have a well-documented dislike for the methods of film distribution, particularly in the United States. Now with your success internationally, how do you get your films out?

W: I will always produce my own films and avoid finding myself at the distributor's mercy. You must become a producer if you want any control over the fate of your work. Otherwise, it becomes another man's film and he does with it what he pleases. I only had one experience like that and I will never repeat it.

H: That must have been when you directed *Hammett* for Francis Coppola back in '81. How did that experience change you as a director?

W: Well, that project took a large portion of my life—four years—but while I was doing it, fortunately, I was able to shoot two other films, *The State of Things* and Nick's film, *Lightning Over Water*. So I never really found myself overwhelmed by Hollywood. When *Hammett* finally ended, I wasn't as disoriented as I had been on a couple of my other films. Perhaps the experience of making *The State of Things*, which was sort of simultaneously coming to terms with what was happening to me while I made *Hammett*, gave me a clear head.

H: Was *The State of Things* autobiographical?

W: Yes, in the sense that it was my tenth film and I wanted it to be a comment on the state of the cinema in general and on my American experiences, particularly on *Hammett*. It is not autobiographical in the sense that the character of Friedrich is only half like me. Half of him is very different.

H: I understand that that film has a unique origin?

W: In the beginning of 1981, I was in Europe after having spent considerable time shooting *Hammett* for Zoetrope Studios. In Paris I was told that I would have three months off before I would be needed back in Hollywood. All of a sudden I found myself with a lot of free time. So before heading back to the U.S. I stopped off in Lisbon to visit friends who were working with Raul Ruiz on his film *The Territory*. I brought with me some spare film stock because I heard they were having some financial trouble. So I visited the set, met the French-Portuguese crew and the cinematographer, Henri Alekan. I was so impressed by the way he captured the Portuguese landscape, the city of Lisbon, all of it, that I immediately had a desire to make my own film there and nowhere else. So after being there a few days, I asked Alekan if he would be interested in making another film right after this one. He was game and so were the actors and producer. So I returned to New York, talked to my partner, Chris Sievernich, at Gray City, and told him he had to go back to Germany and raise money, for we would begin shooting in ten days. So I immediately started writing a film entitled *The State of Things*, and after a week I had the contours of the story, a crew and a cast and enough money to shoot for two weeks. In the end I shot in black and white for six weeks, four in Portugal and two in Hollywood, and all without a script. It became this kind of crazy adventure between two continents, sometimes a horror film, sometimes film noir, following no rules at all, which is also exactly how we made it too.

H: What was your experience like working on *The State of Things* versus working on *Hammett*?

W: Well, working on *Hammett* was a totally different approach to making films. It was shot in a studio with a producer [Francis Coppola] who considered himself the center of the film—very different from anything I was used to in Europe. Before *Hammett* I was my own producer on all my films. That film is kind of like what happened to a lot of the European directors who came to work in Hollywood in the thirties and forties. They lost control. However, I don't want to give the wrong impression. There wasn't a war between Francis and me. It was just a war between two different ideas of filmmaking—someone who had made eight films in Europe under totally different circumstances and a completely different tradition, and someone who wanted to re-establish the studio system. I think that he had too much desire for control, and in a way, that's what directing is all about. But I think he wants control in a way that exceeds what an ordinary director might want.

H: Did he interfere with your shooting?

W: No, I'm not saying that he didn't let me direct the film. He never interfered with anything during the physical production, but he was very much involved with the scriptwriting process and the casting.

H: What was his contribution to the screenplay like?

W: Well, working with Francis is always risky. With a story he never goes a safe way, which I think is wonderful. That's why I enjoyed making the film, because it wasn't a straight detective story. It was a comment on the genre—a biography of a man's fantasy. And I am very happy to have had the opportunity to try and do that. I knew that it would be a great challenge when Francis Coppola invited me to make the film for him.

H: Was it hard for you to go back to after shooting was suspended?

W: I had to be able to come back and finish *Hammett,* and I did it strictly according to the rules, abiding by both Francis and Zoetrope. I shot very fast—over ninety-five percent of the film in four weeks for under two million dollars. That averaged to about thirty-five setups per day. And as a director, I learned more from Francis in those four years than I had making any of my other films and acting as my own producer.

H: Would you ever go back to work for Coppola?

W: Well, Zoetrope doesn't exist anymore, at least the way it used to, so I don't know if Francis is hiring. And if he were, I don't think so, but that's not because of Francis. There are factors apart from him that would discourage me.

H: What do you see as the major difference between films made in America and films made in Europe?

W: Hollywood filmmaking has become more and more about power and control. It's really not about telling stories. That's just a pretense. But ironically the fundamental difference between making films in Europe versus America is in how the screenplay is dealt with. From my experiences in Germany and France, the script is something that is constantly scrutinized by the film made from it. Americans are far more practical. For them the screen play is a blueprint and it must be adhered to rigidly in fear of the whole house falling down. In a sense, all of the creative energy goes into the screenplay so one could say that the film already exists before the film even begins shooting. You lose spontaneity. But in Germany and France I think that filmmaking is regarded as an adventure in itself.

H: Like when Werner Herzog took his cast and crew on quite an adventure while shooting *Fitzcarraldo* in the middle of the Amazon jungle?

W: Yes, if that were an American picture it probably would have been shot on a soundstage. I, myself, decided to embark on an adventure while making *The State of Things, King of the Road* and *The American Friend,* in which there was very little screenplay to work from, just initial situations that we had to develop. The films had to discover their own story. It was like writing with the camera. American films are also much more expensive to make and they have to make three times as much money as they cost just to return the initial investment. In Hollywood films are heavily linked to the concept of money and business; in Germany they're still somewhat considered an art form. I hope.

H: Who are your major influences?

W: Ozu primarily. I am also attracted to [Anthony] Mann, Robert Bresson and Jean Renoir. Their stories work best for my own particular taste, style and imagination. And then of course there are the American directors without a doubt: Sam Fuller, Nicholas Ray, Howard Hawks, Alfred Hitchcock and especially John Ford. Perhaps I am closer to the American cinema than the European cinema. For example, I admire many films that came out of the French New Wave, but I admire them with reservations because they were films reflecting or reacting to what was going on in the American cinema. Perhaps it was not so much reservation, but envy. I also wanted to be doing what they were doing. I was particularly struck by Jean-Luc Godard's *Made in the U.S.A.*

H: What do you think about the generation of German filmmakers just preceding Hitler: Fritz Lang, F.W. Murnau, Ernst Lubitsch, Josef von Sternberg? Can you relate to them?

W: Lang is the best, but they were all brilliant. They lived in a German world that has long since vanished. My generation of filmmakers didn't have that tradition, so we had to be courageous, perhaps even naive. We had to acknowledge that an audience for our films did not exist. At the time very few people had faith in our filmmaking or any other German tradition, whether it be literature or painting.

H: Many of your films seem intrigued by American culture? Why is this?

W: Well, after the war, American culture colonized our subconscious. American influence permeated every square inch of western Europe, which is very unusual because I believe Europe and America at their essence are truly different in their view of things. If you look at *The State of Things* you will see my disposition. It's all about the conflict between European and American sensibilities, and I think I would like to see the two remain separate. I'd like to maintain a perspective on both the United States and Germany. I don't believe both should become the same thing, and I see that happening as borders break down and as American influence becomes more prominent. Perhaps with the reunification of Germany my country will have better control over its own identity.

H: *Paris, Texas* was filmed in the United States. How do you relate that film to your other work?

W: First, I think *Paris, Texas* deals with American culture more than my other films. It's really about American dreams and myths, and for me the core of America is located in this mythical landscape which is the American West. In terms of story content, I think the main character of Travis [Harry Dean Stanton] went further than any of my other characters had gone up until that point. I wanted to find some new territory and try a story I had never done before, a love story which is something my other characters had never achieved, with the exception of the angel in *Wings of Desire*. I felt good about *Paris, Texas* and in a way felt that it was a culmination of my earlier work.

H: I was curious about the male characters and their relationship to the female characters in *Paris, Texas*. There almost always seems to be a real lack of communication.

W: The men are not able to see the Nastassia Kinski character the way she really is. In the film Travis frequently refers to a "sickness" that his father has, but what I am suggesting here is a real male sickness in that men can't really understand women for who they are. They prefer to go by images of women on billboards, or on television ads or in movies, all male-dominated mediums. And you'll see that Kinski is dressed in the kind of clothes that portray a male-projected image. Men love women on the screen, not in the flesh. This is how my idea came for the scene between Travis and his wife in the peep house—the whole concept of the two-way mirror shows Travis looking at his wife the way most people watch a movie. The mirror is like a screen. The first time he really knows her is when he looks away and closes his eyes.

H: Why did you cast Nastassia Kinski?

W: She was perfect casting because her image as a sensual, erotic symbol preceded who she really was as a person. And I knew at the time that that was troubling her. I knew when I cast her that she was very eager to show a human side. She wanted to prove to audiences that she was an actress with three dimensions.

H: Is *Paris, Texas* a tragedy?

W: It's interesting that you should ask that, because to be honest, for a while I didn't really know if it was a tragedy. At one point I thought it might be, but now my attitude has changed. Now I don't think the end is tragic. Though a family is never reconciled, you have a mother and son who are together again—which is life-affirming. And you have Travis, who isn't as lost as he was at the beginning.

H: But wouldn't an American audience see the breaking up of a family unit as inherently tragic?

W: I don't think so.

H: But in order for it to be comic, wouldn't an audience want a typical happy ending where everyone is reunited?

W: If you always give people what they want in movies, if you give them what they are taught to long for, in a sense you destroy their longing, which is not always good. You see, if I'd gone with an ending that shows the family together, people would have this illusion affirmed, and they would come out of the theater hating their own families. They would make no connection between their own personal lives and the film. The audience must be allowed to come to terms with their own notions of family—their ideals about family in relation to reality, not Hollywood cinema. If you look at television in America, you will see the family ideally romanticized. And audiences wanting to sustain illusions don't have to think, which is exactly what television does. My intention was to make a film that asked questions: Is it better for some families to split apart? I think in some cases, yes. So *Paris, Texas* is not a tragedy, because I think it is real. You see, I'm not interested in tragedy—things that are sad. I'm interested in real.

H: Is *Wings of Desire* real?

W: If you believe in angels. And I must admit, it was an ambitious venture once I started taking angels seriously. I soon found it very challenging once I realized how endless the possibilities became in the language of film. In terms of its reality, *Wings of Desire* is as life-affirming, but in a different way, as *Paris, Texas.*

H: What inspired you to make *Wings of Desire?*

W: Well, on the very last day of shooting *Paris, Texas* I took Nastassia, Harry Dean and Dean [Stockwell] and Aurore Clement and the little boy to a beach in Galveston. It was only the five of them, myself and a Super 8 camera, and we shot the home-movie sequence that you see in the middle of the film. And that's the only real happy moment together when the Nastassia character and the Stanton character are a family. Otherwise the film is really about a relationship that has already come to an end. And it was on this day of shooting that I realized my next film had begun. I realized that *Wings of Desire* would be a kind of preamble to romance. It would be full of life.

H: So *Wings of Desire* is a lot more optimistic than your earlier work?

W: Well, I intentionally tried to be optimistic before making that film. I almost adopted it like a method, and very strangely, I found that I enjoyed it. I didn't find it naive or suspect. I felt it real and honest, so by trying I became an optimist, which is why the Bruno Ganz character gets what he wants. He becomes human.

H: You made two films in Berlin: *Wings of Desire* and *Summer in the City.* In both films there seems to be a kind of obsession with the concept of city. For example, the old man taking the angel through a razed portion of Berlin showing him where he used to live.

W: In *Wings of Desire* the city becomes an important character. The city has a past, like the angel, and is viewed in relationship to history. This is something I had no concept of while making *Summer in the City.* There was only the city itself, its presence. Hans Zischler is released from prison and he has no past. He lives completely in the present so there is no depth of character or place. He has no use for the city. In *Wings of Desire* characters may go astray in the present day but they all have histories, memories, they are human beings. In *Wings of Desire* Berlin has a memory, a far reaching past. Berlin is really highly responsible for that film.

In a way Berlin is responsible for my being back in Germany. If it hadn't been for Berlin I wouldn't have gone back and there wouldn't be any *Wings of Desire*. It couldn't take place in any other city.

H: Did you get tired of America?

W: No, I love America. It is very much a home to me as well. I just felt that after *Paris, Texas* I would begin repeating myself as a filmmaker, working in America.

H: What did you learn during your seven years in the U.S.? Do you feel that you know America well?

W: Absolutely not. In fact it is more complex to me now than it was when I first arrived. The more I stayed in the U.S. the more my concept of America seemed to be a projection of other people's hopes and ideas. My own thoughts and ideas didn't seem like my own. It was very strange, so after making several films set in America, I thought it was time to move on to somewhere else. I felt that if I stayed in the U.S. my films would all start being like *Paris, Texas*. By being away from Germany for so long, I started to finally feel German in my heart. Perhaps my absence is what it took to find that.

H: Now that you're back in Germany what are your feelings about your own role in the "New German Cinema"?

W: Well, first of all, "The New German Cinema" is a label invented by the American press, not us. And I must admit that at one time I really didn't think that my films or Werner's [Herzog] or Rainer's [Fassbinder] could be put in a category that could relate to any kind of "Germanness." I thought our films were isolated. When I started making films in the early 1970s I felt I was working from nothing. It was like we had no history to work from. The generation before us was destroyed by Hitler. In some ways we thought there was no longer anything you could call "German." And as filmmakers we saw film simply as "cinema." But now that I'm back in Germany I realize that that is exactly what being German was in the 1970s, so in that sense, we were all part of something.

Filmography

1971   *The Goalie's Anxiety at the Penalty Kick*
1972   *The Scarlet Letter*
1974   *Alice in the Cities*
1975   *Wrong Movement*
1976   *Kings of the Road*
1977   *The American Friend*
1980   *Lightning Over Water* (documentary)
1982   *Hammett*
1983   *The State of Things*
1984   *Tokyo-Ga* (documentary)
1984   *Aus der Familie der Panzereschen* (documentary)
1984   *Paris, Texas*
1988   *Wings of Desire*
1991   *Until the End of Time*

KEN RUSSELL

The Victorian Dreamer

If Ken Russell weren't one of Britain's most respected and controversial filmmakers, one could easily envision him as a character in a Lewis Carroll novel. While I spoke to him by telephone, I couldn't help but picture myself as Alice lost in Wonderland, sitting under a giant mushroom, listening to the benevolent caterpillar laconically throwing out riddles and answers that jumped around my questions like fish swimming up the stream of consciousness. Russell is a tough director to interview, but in the end one can't help but get a sense of the passion he has for his work— an artist's passion that is difficult to articulate but easy to feel.

His films convey the same kind of ardor. Critics who scrutinize his movies, many of which are biographical accounts of other artists' lives, often find themselves outraged and condemn Russell for his sensationalistic portrayals and often fantastic historical inaccuracies. In Genoa, Italy, where he was directing opera for the first time, his interpretation of Mephistopheles infuriated the Italians so much that a riot broke out during the performance. But Russell dismisses this particular attack as being very Italian, choosing to see himself as a director led only by his love for the subject he renders, not by the politics it may breed.

Born July 3, 1927, in Southampton, England, Russell worked in the British merchant navy and served with the RAF before joining the Ny Norsk Ballet as a dancer in 1950. The following year he moved into acting and, after some training in photography, be-came a free-lance still photographer, contributing to *Picture Post* and other illustrated magazines. In the late fifties he directed a number of amateur short films, the quality of which opened doors for him at the BBC. There he embarked on a series of fictionalized biographies of such famous composers as Elgar, Prokofiev, De-bussy, Bartók, Delius and Richard Strauss and of the dancer Isa-dora Duncan. These TV films, which were praised for their imagi-nation, extravagance, mixture of fact and fantasy, and criticized for their self-indulgence and lack of traditional form, paved his way to feature filmmaking.

For the past twenty-five years Russell has dedicated most of his work to portraying other artists on film. With the exception of a brief but tumultuous working career in the United States, culmi-nating in the making of Paddy Chayefsky's science fiction script, *Altered States*, in addition to the less successful thriller, *Crimes of Passion*, Russell has lavished most of his genius on biographical films about the lives of composers. Whether it's Tchaikovsky in *The Music Lovers* (1970), Mahler in *Mahler* (1974) or the portrayal of such literary figures as Byron and Shelley in *Gothic* (1987), or films based on the work of great literary figures, like D.H. Lawrence's *Women in Love* (1969) and *The Rainbow* (1989), Aldous Huxley's *The Devils* [of Loudon] (1971) and Bram Stoker's *Lair of the White Worm* (1988), Russell continues to outrage and delight with his flamboy-ance and unpredictable excesses.

HICKENLOOPER: Back during your days with the BBC you de-lighted, stunned and upset television audiences with a number of documentaries about the lives of Strauss, Duncan, Prokofiev and Bartok.

RUSSELL: They were fictionalized.

H: Your work has been called sensationalistic. For you, what are the differences between documentary and feature filmmaking?

R: I don't like to categorize like that. Every film has its own unique approach. Each film has its own special requirements, so I never like to differentiate between documentary and fiction. To

me they are films, whether they're about Mahler or a D.H. Lawrence novel.

H: But you've been criticized for treating history cavalierly.

R: What is history but a group of assumptions? I work
intuitively.

H: So you don't believe that a filmmaker can be historically
accurate?

R: There is no such thing as historical accuracy. I'm currently
working on my next film which is more or less an autobiography,
and there's no way on earth it will be historically accurate. It's
impossible. It's all so subjective. If someone were going to make a
film about my life or write a biography of me and they referred to
information that had been printed in books, magazines and newspapers, the whole thing would be a tissue of lies. Nobody knows
the real me and I've never seen the real me written about. So there
is no such thing as historical accuracy. What is most important as a
filmmaker is to get to the spirit of what you're trying to put on the
screen. The spirit of music, the spirit of Mahler, the spirit of D.H.
Lawrence, that's what I'm into. That's the truth, the artistic truth,
not the mundane. Who cares about whether he got up at nine
o'clock in the morning and went to bed at eleven? That tells you
absolutely nothing about anyone. If you want to get the whole
truth you would have to know them every day of their lives, every
hour, second by second, every tenth of a second by tenth of a second. You see, people usually equate the truth with dullness. If it's
dull and boring, then it's likely to be true. Well, that's not the way I
think.

H: When critics berate a film like *The Music Lovers* for its sensationalistic portrayal of Tchaikovsky, while music professionals like
conductor André Previn praise it as being the greatest film ever
made about music, who do you listen to and how do you gauge
your own work?

R: Well, who needs it? I get accused all the time of distorting
history, that I'm untrue to these people, that I loathe all of them.
But then someone comes along, like Shostakovich, and says it was

the best film about a composer he'd ever seen. He thought it was a great tribute. I prefer to go with that rather than with the critics who hated me for showing the Gestapo throw Mahler into an incinerator. But then Klaus Tinstead, who I think is the greatest Mahler conductor alive today, thinks not only that *Mahler* is the best film about a composer he's ever seen, but that it's one of the best films he's ever seen period. He said I'd captured the essence of Mahler's prophecy in the march movement, the allegro of the Sixth Symphony. One is usually criticized by people who know little about the subject. I make these films because I love these people. Consequently, it's always the aficionados, the people who fully understand the subjects I am portraying, who praise my films. For instance, when *The Devils* was released, the only people who objected to it were the irreligious. The fact that it's on the curriculum of Loyola Marymount University as a good example of a truthful and imaginative representation of a real event says something, I'm sure. The Catholics know their own business.

H: Why do you like making films about artists?

R: I think they deal in mysteries just the way I think life is a mystery. Artists somehow make mysteries concrete, make them more tangible. They interpret the ineffable for the rest of us.

H: In *Gothic* you're once again courting the Romantics. Would you explain your attraction to Shelley and Byron and the other artists of that period?

R: Well, I suppose it's like getting together to have drinks with some old friends—Shelley, Tchaikovsky and Byron. I look at them all as my contemporaries. In my social life I've always mixed with artists and musicians and they're all sort of a crazy lot. So I'm sure there's nothing profound about Shelley or Byron just because they're "Romantics." An art movement is one entity despite what epoch it's from.

H: But you have faith in them and their work?

R: That entirely depends on whether we're talking about artists or *artists.* And just because I may believe in them doesn't mean I wear blinkers and think they're all wonderful. They're like anyone else, and their relation to their work fascinates me.

H: As a director, what do you think an artist's relationship to his work should be?

R: It should be pure dedication to the work. Filmmaking is a very difficult art form. You've got to convince sixty other people of your vision, your point of view, whereas if you're a painter you've just got a pot of paint and a canvas. It's up to you. Filmmaking is a difficult job. It's from morning to night. And you think about it maybe a year before you actually do the film. In the case of my latest project, *The Rainbow*, which is a prequel to *Women in Love*, it took eight years before I actually did it. A piece of art, whether it's a film, a painting or a story, is not something to be undertaken lightly, at least not by me anyway.

H: When you're directing a biographical film like *The Music Lovers*, *Mahler* or *Gothic*, who are you making the film for? Is it for a general audience or scholars?

R: First of all, I don't think there's any such thing as a general audience. I mean, I make it for myself and I hope that if it entertains me, it will entertain someone else.

H: You've been called a director who tries to bridge highbrow art with popular art. Do you agree with that?

R: I worked at the BBC for ten years and we were told we had to communicate. I was working on this arts program and we were dealing with esoteric subjects, but were also dealing with a mass audience who'd never heard of Debussy, Bartók or Strauss. And we weren't supposed to talk down to this television audience, instead we tried to fire them up with our own enthusiasm for these artists. And on this program there were half a dozen directors who all had backgrounds in music, painting or literature. It was like doing your own hobby. It was like making a film just for the sheer excitement, the exuberance, of seeing it on the screen. And the trick of it was to try and communicate that.

H: You think high art and popular culture can mix with success?

R: Yeah, I'm sure they can.

H: At one time you said you never made your films for commercial purposes. Do you ever feel pressure from the studio to make your films more mainstream, and, if you do, how do you continue to make films that are very original?

R: I don't know if I exactly said that, but you know, one hopes that people are going to see the film. I suppose by commercial I meant *Friday the 13th* type films which are totally cynical.

H: Do you ever feel pressure from the studio to control your work?

R: Well, they have an input on the casting so from that perspective there is a certain amount of studio influence.

H: Many of your films have English casts. Is this something that you prefer?

R: No, not really. Frequently it just turns out that way. *Lair of the White Worm* had an English cast because it was an English film with English people, except maybe [Catherine] Oxenberg. I still don't know what she is. But in general, I think that a good actor is a good actor. I suppose that some Americans take themselves a bit too seriously.

H: In England your success has been fabulous whereas in the U.S. it has not. What do you think the differences are between English audiences and American audiences?

R: Well, they speak different languages.

H: Could you be more specific?

R: Well, I think that is an English statement.

H: *Altered States* was a very American film, with an American cast and an American writer. How was the experience of making this film different from some of your others?

R: Well, it was the only film on which I ever had an unlimited budget. That was nice and it was American too.

H: You mentioned *Lair of the White Worm*. What attracted you to Bram Stoker's novel and why did you make that film?

R: Vestron, with whom I had a three-picture deal, were keen for me to make a film about Dracula. I had written a script on Dracula several years ago which they read and liked, but there were problems with the rights because they were held by another company that had become extinct. There was also the problem of there already being 338 films based on Dracula, so I thought it might be a better idea to make some changes, you know, retain the fangs but get rid of the bat. Coincidentally, at that time, someone asked me what I thought of *Lair of the White Worm* and I was ashamed to admit that I had never read it. I didn't know of its existence, so I immediately read it and found myself quite taken by it. I didn't think it was as good as *Dracula*, but I certainly felt that it had potential. At the same time I was getting a little tired of the Victorian Gothic period, so I updated the story and wrote it on spec for Vestron. They liked it, so they asked me to do it.

H: The film has a lot of humor in it. Were you parodying the novel?

R: No, no, it's not a parody of the novel, but it is a parody of horror films in general. You see, I couldn't be entirely faithful to the tone of the novel because it isn't very good, certainly not as well constructed as *Dracula*. I mean, Stoker must have been ill when he wrote it. I felt all I could take was the basic premise, and it had a good basic premise. It's nice to get out of Transylvania.

H: When you updated the novel, what kind of changes did you make?

R: Very little apart from the sports cars. The setting already worked because I put it in a kind of primitive society, a feudal society. I had a lord of the manor and not much had changed except the uniform in the five hundred years since the life of his ancestor, one of the knights who slew the dragon. I mean, the country girls were still country girls who were terribly simple. It was pretty primitive to begin with so there was really no need to update it that much.

H: *Women in Love* is still praised as one of your best films. Why do you think it stands above the others?

R: To me it doesn't, but we probably shouldn't say that. It may be okay in itself, but trying to get a six-hundred-page novel into two hours is a real problem. It has some very good performances in it and it was very outspoken about relationships. I hope that I went into them in depth much more than most other films had done by that time.

H: You once said, "All good entertainment shocks people." Someone like Bertolt Brecht may have done this for political reasons, to make an audience aware that they were watching theater, and Jean-Luc Godard might do this to break the illusion of reality that film creates. Why do you believe this? Why do you think films should shock people?

R: I think they should be shocked into an awareness, a kind of awareness of enjoyment, to liven them up and show that they can actually share in the excitement.

H: Do you think your films are manipulative, or are you working against that?

R: I don't know what they are. I just make them. I don't analyze my films. I've been making them for thirty years. That's just how I do them. They just present themselves in their own way. Of course, they have to communicate, they have to be cinematic, they have to flow, they have to do all sorts of things.

H: Over the past few years you've directed a number of operas. What was it like for you to come out of feature filmmaking and go into another form of drama that didn't require cameras.

R: Well, it's a totally different approach to film. There aren't many films where you can shoot in chronological order, scene by scene. But when you rehearse an opera, that's generally what you do. This enables the actors to watch their characters grow as they develop on stage. In film you've always got to make an inspired guess, because you often shoot the last scene first and the first scene last. Everything in between is like a jigsaw puzzle. So from that point of view, directing an opera is much more interesting. It's like having the soundtrack already finished. You just set the action to the soundtrack and watch it happen. It's totally different from film, but it's similar enough that when you do go back to directing movies, you can look at it with a fresh eye. I would imagine that each benefits from the other.

H: Specifically, what did you enjoy the most about directing opera?

R: The fact that it's out of your hands, it's live. On the first night of a film, you know exactly what you're going to see—though if you see it in a cinema theater, it most likely won't be in focus, so you probably won't see anything! You know you'll see the door open and in will come Glenda Jackson, and you'll know she'll close the door all on cue because it was filmed that way. But in opera you never know what's going to happen. You're a captive audience on the first night. You don't know if the orchestra will play badly or inspiringly. At the same time, when it works, there's a certain magic which you don't get in film. And that's due to the fact that film is obviously a mechanical process. It's done with electricity, with amps, watts and volts, whereas opera is done with just sheer vocal power.

H: You mentioned that you often don't know what's going to happen on stage. That seems to be true for the audience too. I understand one of your operas caused a riot in Genoa.

R: I don't know what's going to happen, but whatever it is I always hope that it will be exciting because the opera company has asked me there for that very reason.

H: In 1986 you started Sitting Duck Productions, which focused its energies on making music videos. How did that come about?

R: Dick Clark rang me up and asked me to make a music video for him.

H: Are you still making music videos?

R: No, I'm too busy now. I've sort of phased it out.

H: At the time you seemed rather excited about it.

R: Well, I was, but like everything else you always find that there are snags. I discovered that I was being a bit too literary with the lyrics. My approach only suited certain songs. It didn't suit them all and I began to feel that I didn't know what people wanted. I felt that we were talking different languages, so I stopped.

H: At the time you felt that the music video would have a great impact on narrative feature filmmaking.

R: I think that it has and it hasn't. It has, but at a cost. A lot of music video directors are brilliant on the two-minute or four-minute format, but you can't keep up that bombardment of images for over an hour and a half and not expect the audience to get punch drunk. So I think it has diminishing returns. Not many promo directors have bridged the gap to feature filmmaking.

H: I read that you constructed your films like symphonies.

R: If it suits the film, yes. Despite the fact that I can't read a note of music, I try to start with the soundtrack first—you see, that's the most difficult part. Because once you have the soundtrack, you have the movie. Music is architecture to me so I always try to get a musical or architectural sense for the film. In the opening scenes there's the development section: first, second subject, etc. I'm really conscious of it. For example, I did *Mahler* in rondo form. There was a statement, the sections in the railway train, then variations with episodes interlinking the journey. In *Lair of the White Worm*, and nobody's noticed it yet, I've done something that I don't think anyone else has ever done since Hitchcock—I never cut away from the actuality. You never cut away from somebody who's not immediately involved with what you're seeing on the screen, so time is continuous in the film. I don't think that's been done too much. Also nobody has seemed to figure out the dream sequence. In Freudian hindsight, if you understand the dream, you understand the mystery, which is why the hero of the film gets the solution. He doesn't consciously analyze his dream or even remember it actively, but he subconsciously remembers it and acts upon it. And the audience can do that. I certainly didn't mean for the dream sequence to be just a series of pretty pictures. It tells the whole of what happened. It tells who everyone is and what they're up to. It's a mystery, but it's solvable. I haven't read a review that says the dream is interesting because it meant this. Nobody said that. Now, whether the critics are too lazy to bother or just think it's an obsession doesn't matter. If you look, the whole mystery of the story is there.

H: Is the dream sequence in the novel?

R: No.

H: To me it was a collective flashback of what had happened in that exact place when the Romans were in Britain.

R: Yes, absolutely—memory, hallucinations, all that was part of it, but the dream was a dream as such. And the dream as a dream we are told has a meaning.

Filmography

1964	*French Dressing*
1967	*Billion Dollar Brain*
1969	*Women in Love*
1970	*The Music Lovers*
1971	*The Devils*
1971	*The Boy Friend*
1972	*Savage Messiah*
1974	*Mahler*
1975	*Tommy*
1975	*Lisztomania*
1977	*Valentino*
1978	*Clouds of Glory*
1980	*Altered States*
1984	*Crimes of Passion*

1987 *Gothic*
1988 *Salome's Last Dance*
1988 *Lair of the White Worm*
1989 *The Rainbow*

PAUL VERHOEVEN
The Vitality of Existence

After the phenomenal success of his two latest American films, *RoboCop* (1987) and *Total Recall* (1990), Paul Verhoeven sits comfortably in his modest West Hollywood office. The stillness in the room is suddenly broken by the exuberance that booms from the director's conversation. As he signals his assistant to "boot up" the office espresso machine, I notice that his commanding gestures and thick accent give him that touch of savoir-faire characteristic of many European filmmakers.

"See how far Tower Records is?" he says pointing to the building directly across Sunset Boulevard. "That's the distance my house was from where the Germans launched their V1 and V2 rockets," he continues, his eyes wide with anticipation as if it were still 1943.

Born in the Netherlands shortly before the outbreak of World War II, Verhoeven grew up during the German occupation in a part of Holland known as the Hague. After the war he came to love American movies, but by the time he entered the University of Leiden he had decided to study mathematics. After spending a short time in the military, where he worked in the film department making documentaries, he was offered a position directing for Dutch television.

In 1971 Verhoeven was given the opportunity to direct his first feature film, *Business Is Business*, a charming comedy about Amsterdam's red-light district; however, it wasn't until three years later that Verhoeven achieved international recognition with his second film, *Turkish Delight* (1974). An outrageous love story about an irascible young artist and a rebellious young lady, the film went on to be nominated for an Academy Award for Best Foreign Film of 1974. The picture was the second he made with producer Rob Houwer, and the first he made with screenwriter Gerard Soetemann, both of whom went on to work with Verhoeven on *Cathy Tippel* (1975) and then *Soldier of Orange* (1978), a profoundly disturbing war film based on Erik Hazelhoff's famous story, one which Verhoeven could relate to through his own childhood memories.

Before emigrating to the United States in 1984, Verhoeven made two of his most widely known Dutch films, *Spetters* (1981), about unbridled adolescents in Amsterdam, and *The Fourth Man* (1984), a provocative, surrealistic thriller that employs religious imagery to tell a story about a voluptuous young beautician who murders her lovers after marrying them. The following year Verhoeven made his American debut with *Flesh and Blood* (1985). Though the film proved to be a disaster at the box office, he went on to direct two of Hollywood's highest grossing films, *RoboCop* and *Total Recall*.

HICKENLOOPER: Your films are highly physical and emotional, often blatantly filled with symbolism. Are you conscious of this in your treatment of religion, war, whatever it may be in your work?

VERHOEVEN: As a director, my goal is to be completely open. Just look at how I portray sex in my films. They're considered shocking and obscene because I like to carefully examine human sexuality. It has to be realistic, otherwise it is bullshit. I really like documentaries; therefore, reality is important to me when I do fiction. It is often related to my own life, my Dutch background. The art scene in Holland has always attempted to be realistic. The Dutch painters of four hundred years ago were meticulously realistic. The example I always like to use is a marvelous painting by Hieronymus Bosch titled *The Prodigal Son*. It is a painting of a brothel, and in the corner is a man pissing against a wall. You would never, never find something like that in an Italian, French or English painting of that epoch. The Dutch have always been more scientific, interested in detail; certainly less idealistic and more realistic. The sex scenes in *The Fourth Man* and *Turkish Delight* were based on real experiences I had or a friend had. It's very personal. Of course, I must admit that I love to shock audiences.

H: Was that your intention in *The Fourth Man?*

V: No, that film had more to do with my vision of religion. In my opinion Christianity is nothing more than one of many interpretations of reality, neither more nor less. Ideally, it would be nice to believe that there is a God somewhere out there, but it looks to me as if the whole Christian religion is a major symptom of schizophrenia in half the world's population: civilizations scrambling to rationalize their chaotic existence. Subsequently, Christianity has a tendency to look like magic or the occult. And I liked that ambiguity, because I wanted my audience to take something home with them. I wanted them to wonder, "What is religion really?"

H: In *The Fourth Man*, as in many of your films, you often have a cavalier, if not black comic, approach to violence.

V: Well, with respect to *The Fourth Man* and its religious theme, you have to remember that Christianity is a religion grounded in one of the most violent acts of murder—the crucifixion. Otherwise, religion wouldn't have had any kind of impact. With regards to the irony of the violence, much of that probably comes from my childhood experiences during and immediately following the Second World War.

H: You lived through the German occupation?

V: Very much so. In fact, if it hadn't been for the German occupation and then the American occupation I would have never been a filmmaker.

H: How so?

V: Well, during the bombings, going to the movies was not all that convenient, so when you did go you really loved it, even if the film was German propagandistic shit. Then in 1945 we were liberated by the Americans, and in the years afterwards the only thing you could see were American movies—these action, horror and science fiction movies. And because there was no cinema industry in Holland, it seemed like another world. I wanted to do nothing but see movies. So by coincidence, when I was seventeen or eighteen, I was given a 16mm camera from an uncle. As a hobby I started experimenting, but then I became more interested in painting. However, here I was studying at a university for mathematics. It was a very confusing situation because I was doing mathematics, I wanted to be a painter and I started filmmaking as a hobby. But then I got involved with a film group at the university, so from a little hobby it became a real hobby where I was spending a lot of time doing it.

In 1964 I finished my studies as a mathematician, but then had to go into the military service for two years, and although they wanted to send me to study rocket science in Germany, I started to find out if there were other possibilities. I got myself moved into the film department in the Navy, then for two years I started becoming more professional as a film director. I did documentaries for both the Navy and the Marines, so when I came out of the service I decided to become a real film director. It took me a couple of years before a television producer, who was impressed with all the action in my films, gave me a children's television series in 1968 called "Floris"—something like Ivanhoe or Robin Hood in Holland. That was really the first time I became a film director, and that series was seen by a German/Dutch film producer in 1970, and he gave me my first picture in 1971.

H: As you first began to direct, did you ever find yourself applying your background in mathematics or painting?

V: Whatever you study in the university, whether it is psychology, sociology, philosophy, it really programs your brain for solving problems. And in film you can find that very useful. For me, because I'm such an organized guy, by concentrating on mathematics for six or seven years, I think that I improved my proficiency considerably. You know, Eisenstein also had a degree in mathematics, or chemistry, and Pudovkin even . . . all coming from the university. And I'm sure that my style and Eisenstein's have a lot in common. It's not really on the surface, but if you study it shot by shot, you'll see where I took my clues from Eisenstein really.

H: And like Eisenstein, you seem to have strong political views in your work, no matter how iconoclastic.

V: Politics are of no interest to me. I have no real political beliefs. I find everything fascinating. I do find the political beliefs of the United States interesting. I find the fact that media and government made such a big deal out of Jim and Tammy Bakker and the flag-burning issue interesting. But what I'm really fascinated by is the uncommon and common individual. What interests me in exploring religion and politics is how easily a person can fall or crack under tension. You get a very sharp focus on someone; it's like looking at someone under a microscope. They will react.

H: When did you first get recognized for your work?

V: In 1974 I made *Turkish Delight*, as I said, a very open, sexual, audacious film. It got an Oscar nomination for Best Foreign Film, and immediately afterwards I got phone calls from the American film industry. But I was afraid to go to the United States at that age.

H: How old were you then?

V: I was thirty-three or thirty-four, and I thought that I was doing pretty well in Holland. I had a lot of fun there, good people around me, nice crews and cast, and up to *Soldier of Orange*, I was pretty happy there. *Soldier of Orange* was the last film that was made without really big problems—that was 1978.

H: How did you get involved with that project?

V: I got a book, an autobiography by Erik Hazelhoff that appeared in 1972, and he had lived through that war period. It was his real account of what happened at that time. Immediately there were a lot of people interested . . . I was. So my scriptwriter found it for me. He said this is a great book, we should do it. At that point he wanted to do it as a television series, but we couldn't get the money together, so for three, four, five years we looked at it, worked on it, tried to get the money. My regular feature producer,

Rob Houwer, thought it was too big of a project to do as a feature, and thought it would be too expensive. So we postponed it and postponed it, until 1977. After having had three enormous successes in Holland, we made contact with the prince of the Netherlands—Prince Bernard—consort to Queen Juliana. He wanted to get the film . . . what do you call it in English? He became the honorary advisor to the film—honorary protector of the film.

H: A kind of honorary executive producer?

V: No, it's a very interesting thing. For example, the KLM is also under the royal protection of the Queen and the Prince—it doesn't mean anything really—it's just an honorary title. So when the Prince thought it was an interesting film, he gave it his honorary protection title. From that moment on, all the doors in Holland opened, more or less, to do this film; because at the same time, the Prince was the General, head of the Netherlands defense forces—the army. He could make a phone call to all the military, and say, help these people. So the producer had enough money, and the doors opened because the Prince was backing the picture. The film was made for two million dollars, but would have cost four or five if we had done it the regular way. But because we were under the protection of the Prince and the Queen, the project suddenly moved forward.

H: Obviously, the original material by Erik Hazelhoff interested you. But did your own experience, or your parents' experience with the German occupation have any influence on . . . ?

V: I experienced that when I was a kid, of course. And I was living in The Hague, which was bombed continuously. I was seven or eight when the war finished, so I have a very vivid memory of it—walking along the street, seeing the burning houses, sitting at the table, and the house opposite you is bombed, and the windows blast into your room, and being forced to walk on the bellies of dead people because there was tear gas in your eyes. I mean, The Hague was the center of the German occupation, and V1 and V2 rockets were fired from a distance very close to our house, so I have an extremely vivid memory of the war.

Then I went to Leiden as a university student where I lived on the same street that the author of *Soldier of Orange* lived on, but he had lived there twenty years earlier. And I went through the same initiation process that the main character goes through—the hair-cutting, the humiliation. Although he was twenty during the war, and I was six or seven, the war was still the same. The war always for me was, well, kind of like *Hope and Glory*. It was a big, fun war. I love war. I mean, not as an adult, or as a father of children, but as a kid. That's part of your attitude as a kid, of course. When the bombs hit, you'd say "Great! No school today." It was like that watching the V1 rocket. If you weren't aware of the death they caused, they were the most exciting things you'd ever seen. For me war was a wonderful presentation of seeing rockets fly up, and planes bombing, of people being killed. I mean, I was seven, yeah? It was like living in an amazing movie. I didn't know anything. You don't realize that. You see people thrown out in the street, into cars. You don't realize that they're taking away four or five million people, the children. If I'd been Jewish my experience would have been quite different.

So for me the feeling that is conveyed in *Soldier of Orange* is that war is an adventure. And there's this classic line in the picture when the main character, Rutger Hauer—before the war starts—and this guy, my main hero, says, "Well, what? There's a war? That's not bad . . . that's nice, that's funny." You see, the writer of the book is really an adventurer who likes these kinds of things. Of course, he thought that the Germans should be thrown out, but on the other hand, he also thinks it's fun. It's not a heavy film. I think it's even a kind of humanistic film, because it makes all these statements based on the fact that the main guy is somebody who is not antifascist in the first place. He hates the Germans, but he has no political statement to make. He just says, you shouldn't be here. A lot of the resistance people in Holland liked it. It was, okay, let's kill the Germans, let's throw them out. A lot of people were like that. When you were in the resistance, you had all these wonderful women couriers who brought letters around; so you fucked them, and next you went with the gun and killed Germans. And that normally isn't spoken out that much.

H: Rutger Hauer plays the protagonist in your film. He's also had significant parts in a number of your other films. When did you two start working together?

V: I met Rutger in 1968. He was the hero of my "Ivanhoe" series. I found him in a small theater group in northern Holland where somebody mentioned his name. We went to him, or he came to us, and he was this blond Nordic guy who was excellent for the part. We worked a year on this series, and then he did the male lead in *Turkish Delight*. On that project it became clear that he was our man for *Soldier of Orange*. By the time we began that project, I had known Rutger already for ten years, so we were very close, and I think he was the only guy in Holland who could have done this. Still, we did test him very profoundly because the character of the writer is much more of an aristocratic guy. The writer himself is an aristocratic man, and Rutger is much more of a . . . coming from the mud, you might say.

H: Rustic?

V: Rustic. That's the word. So it wasn't clear that he would be able to do it, but then we started testing, and he transformed so well that there was no doubt that he should do that part. We decided to take him.

H: Your last project together was your American debut film *Flesh and Blood*. Do you have plans to work together in the future?

V: Well, yes. But we had a terrible fight on *Flesh and Blood*. And our relationship and friendship was ruined during that picture. We hated each other so much at the end of the picture that it's going to take a couple of years to bring us together, but I would certainly like to work with him.

H: Critically, it would seem that his best work has been with you.

V: Right. And I think we can do great work together again, but in *Flesh and Blood* we couldn't work together. I think that making the transition to the American cinema put too much stress on both of us. Deep in my heart . . . I dream about Rutger once per month, I think. And it's not always a nice dream. Last I remember, a couple of weeks ago, I dreamt that I blasted his head off, so I'm sure there are some feelings of revenge or whatever you want to call it—friendship, deep involvement with somebody who you work with fifteen, seventeen years. It's really stupid, after all this time, to have all this animosity between us, and I really would like it to be resolved at a certain moment in our lives when we're both more adult, perhaps.

H: When you deal with actors on the set, do you ever want to evoke something specific from their performances?

V: No, because I'm not coming from the theater at all. I don't like the theater, I never go to the theater. I hate it. I think it's boring; so my direction of actors is really based on what I think it should look like. And I don't use any psychology, manipulation methods. I just say what I want, and although I am not an actor, I can certainly indicate by exaggerating what I want. It works pretty well.

H: Do you rehearse with your actors?

V: Sometimes, yes. For *The Fourth Man* I did a lot of rehearsing, but for *Soldier of Orange* we maybe rehearsed once, and nothing for *Turkish Delight*. In *The Fourth Man* we did a lot of rehearsing because it was such a difficult movie for the actors. I did some rehearsing on *RoboCop* because of Peter Weller's strange Robo-movements and stuff, but not dialogue rehearsal. I think that if a film goes really into depth with character, then it's okay. But if it's an adventure story with a lot of movement, then I think the actor and the director should go into physical training for a couple of months. That's a better preparation than looking through the dialogue. I'm not that kind of a director.

H: What kind of director are you? Who has most influenced your work?

V: I think the directors who influenced me the most were Eisenstein and Fellini. But perhaps even more, David Lean. I consider David Lean the most important director for me. *Dr. Zhivago, Bridge on the River Kwai*, these are movies that cannot even be made anymore, or perhaps it's just that no one wants to make them anymore. Of course, Kurosawa—I just bought *Rashomon* and *Seven Sa-*

murai again—is a very important director who still makes great films. And then, of course, I studied Hitchcock very profoundly, as you can see in *The Fourth Man*. *North by Northwest* and *Vertigo* are pictures I can watch forever, shot by shot, and there you have the major influences. I also studied Spielberg . . . I studied *Jaws* very well. But the strengths of the others were a major influence when I was younger, when I was much more interested in the work of others, because then you have not done so much yourself. So I was studying Fellini and Lean and Hitchcock and Eisenstein, and from Eisenstein mostly *Ivan the Terrible*.

H: When you're considering material for your next project, do you read a lot of novels or do you prefer original screenplays?

V: In Europe it was more reading novels. Here it is more screenplays, because you've got so many screenplays that you don't have time to look at books anymore. That's the problem, I suppose. I try to read books, but in fact, I'm not really a fan of novels anymore, because of all this fantasy stuff. I'd really prefer to read an autobiography of Patton or Hitler or the Buddha, or something like that, than read a straight novel. The reality of life is much more attractive to me at this moment than fiction. Although I do read fiction, and especially in the United States, the work I do here seems to be much more fiction than I ever did in Holland. *Soldier of Orange*, although taking freedom with reality, is not taking one hundred percent freedom. It's really seventy percent based on reality. Its characters are, the story line is—a lot of the incidents—are really true, based on reality.

H: Did you find the transition to American filmmaking difficult?

V: No. I am extremely lucky to have a great producer, Jon Davison. He protected me extremely well. We had big fights, but I think he's a wonderful producer. I would sign for every picture that he would offer me. He gave me the best people for *RoboCop*. He said, okay, this is a good guy, and this is a good guy. He made us team up, and he realized that I was making a transition. He coached me and gave me continuous feedback on every movie that I made—if it was European or American. And then after a couple of months, after a half year, you get more and more confident. I think the fact that *RoboCop* was a success and showed that I could make a certain American movie is credited to a large degree to Jon Davison and Ed Newmeier.

H: Did you have any reservations about doing an action movie like *RoboCop* or *Total Recall?*

V: When Orion offered me *RoboCop*, I was not interested. I only saw a very idiotic action movie, and I hate action and science fiction movies. But Orion asked me to take a second look at the script. They kept emphasizing that it was about the indestructibility of the human spirit, of the individual—a very American concept. So I became interested in that, and my wife also encouraged me to do it. She reminded me of how much I liked *Frankenstein:* the idea of a monster searching for himself. The same concept applied to *RoboCop*, so I did it. With *Total Recall,* I found that the script reminded be of my childhood dreams and pleasures. However, the physical making of the film had nothing to do with that. The task was so overwhelming that I felt trapped in a nightmare. I easily got frustrated and found myself yelling and screaming at people. Arnold [Schwarzenegger] was really good to me. He told me to laugh it off. So I learned to live with the fact that all movies will have their production problems. The script was wonderful. It took some work to convince Carolco to let me do it. I particularly liked the way that life on an isolated place like Mars would be more vital. There would be much more antagonism and excitement, so many possibilities. Imaging myself in that kind of setting would make me feel much more alive. Directing it certainly made me feel alive.

H: Do you find a significant difference between directing in the United States and directing in Holland?

V: There is no difference, really. The problems are always the same. You always lack ten percent of the budget. You always want a little bit more.

H: Do you have more creative freedom in Holland?

V: I didn't feel that. *RoboCop* was Orion, and Orion gave me a lot of freedom. The only difference I would say is that the work I'm doing now seems to be much more technical than the stuff I did in Holland. There really is much more diversity here. In casting, for example, there are more people to choose from. There are more ethnic qualities. I mean, the world seems to be larger here. The whole world is here. In Holland you have the feeling that it's just part of the world. You can find so many different characters, there is so much you can express here that you couldn't express in Holland. I don't want to say that the work would be any better or more profound, but it's more diverse I think. In Holland they quickly grew intolerant of my work. The critics started calling me a decadent pervert who misrepresented Dutch culture. *Spetters* had the worst response I ever got. I attempted to make a serious film about human behavior and I got crucified. An anti-*Spetters* committee was formed, which said the film was antifeminist, antigay and antiinvalid. It wasn't true. I was simply trying to be honest in portraying the way people act, and often it is antigay, antifeminist, antiinvalid. Of course, this is outrageous, unethical behavior, but it is behavior, so I portrayed it, and certainly at no one's expense. So, the answer to your question is no, I didn't feel that I had more creative freedom in Holland. Perhaps I was not politically correct enough.

H: Did you get the same kind of resistance after making your last Dutch film, *The Fourth Man*?

V: Well, the violence of course, nobody liked that. In the *The Fourth Man*, however, we did think it would be interesting to look at homosexuality again. This time, however, we used it only as a plot point, establishing that homosexuality shouldn't be seen anymore as something special. So no one objected. In fact, after that film, people thought I was a homosexual myself, as if because you are interested in something, it must be you—a "you are what you eat" kind of thing.

H: How closely do you work with your writer?

V: Very close.

H: Do you receive co-credit for any of the screenplays?

V: I don't like to take credit for everything. However, I did write a lot in Holland, co-wrote a lot, but in fact my name is only attached to *Soldier of Orange*. It was one of the only credits that I took, because I thought that I did a lot there. But it's easy to co-write, yeah? I think you have to give the credit to the guy who goes through this initial process of feeling completely lonely, and having his empty paper, and trying to fill it in. I think that's the real creativity. Now me, I have all these wonderful extra ideas, but I think it's still second. The credit should go to the writer.

H: I understand that the original novelist of *The Fourth Man* based the story on real incidents, and then romanticized some of them.

V: That is true. However, we significantly changed the book for the better. Most of it, though, does have something to do with the author, Gerard Reve, his attitudes, his character. He is an alcoholic, he is a homosexual. And we talked to him frequently about the details in his life. He really did meet a woman like the Christine character. In fact, when we were shooting in a local bar, she was there. She has a beauty salon. She was in her mid-forties when we were making the film, and looked very good.

H: Would you ever return to Holland to direct a picture?

V: I think there are one or two things I could do there, and which I can't do here because I could never get the money—either too personal or too specific. But, generally, I think I'm better off in the United States for the time being.

Filmography

1971 *Business Is Business*
1974 *Turkish Delight*
1975 *Cathy Tippel*
1978 *Soldier of Orange*
1981 *Spetters*

1984   *The Fourth Man*
1985   *Flesh and Blood*
1987   *RoboCop*
1990   *Total Recall*

LOUIS MALLE

Impression Filmmaker

Louis Malle strides down a Southern California sidewalk awash in hot sunlight. He squints as he self-consciously readjusts his sunglasses. The summer-bleached skies of Hollywood are a world away from the winter grays and Corot blues he is used to in his native France. M. Malle admits that in Los Angeles he has always felt like a fish out of water.

"I'm not very comfortable here, but I *am* really interested," he says as we step into some shade from the unrelenting heat. "I've been thinking about doing a documentary about Hollywood for years . . . I think people in this town are mutants. They're a different species. Sadly enough, this is a city of despair; not material or economic despair, but rather a spiritual and ethical despair which stems from lifestyles saturated by popular culture. Los Angeles has its own mini-culture that has grown to serve as the rhetoric for the rest of the industrial world."

Although Malle's comments might sound like those of a filmmaker embittered by an industry that has failed to appreciate his work, some of his most successful films have been made under the Hollywood umbrella. His provocative dramas, *Pretty Baby* (1978), *Atlantic City* (1980) and *Alamo Bay* (1985), were all produced in the United States and widely distributed by major studios. Malle has also been honored by the Academy of Motion Pictures Arts and Sciences: in 1988, his *Au Revoir Les Enfants* (1988), an autobiographical account of his childhood relationship with a mysterious Jewish boy who was being hidden from the German Gestapo, was nominated for Best Foreign Film.

Au Revoir Les Enfants, however, was not Malle's first project honored by the Academy. In 1981, *Atlantic City* was nominated for an Oscar, and in 1956, when he was twenty-three, his undersea film, *The Silent World*, received an Academy Award for Best Documentary, a distinction he shared with his co-director, oceanographer Jacques-Yves Cousteau, who discovered Malle right out of the French film school, I.D.H.E.C. There the young director had studied cinematography after majoring in political science at the Sorbonne, which was preceded by an austere Catholic education at the Jesuit college in Fontainebleau. He was born into one of France's wealthiest industrialist families, and Malle says, guffawing, "I knew that fate would somehow bring me into the cinema."

After *The Silent World*, Malle's later assignments introduced him to feature films. Following a brief apprenticeship with Robert Bresson, he directed a number of very successful dramas during a period which would come to be recognized as the height of the French New Wave. Though he didn't at that time achieve the same critical status as Truffaut, Godard or Resnais, Malle's films were praised for their poignant and often explicit look at human relationships. His highly acclaimed *The Lovers* (1958) drew controversy for its uninhibited exploration of human sexuality, while *The Fire Within* (1963) was praised for its sensitively told story about the life of a suicidal alcoholic. Both films firmly established Malle's reputation in France and abroad as a highly versatile director.

Malle returned to documentary filmmaking in 1969, directing two powerful portraits of poverty in India. Afterwards he set up shop in France for his most talked-about dramatic film, *Lacombe, Lucien* (1973), a provocative character study of a French collaborator and his relationship with the Gestapo, a film which is considered by many to be Malle's greatest work to date.

In 1977 the French auteur moved to the United States where he directed opera and theater in addition to film. He also delved back into documentary filmmaking with two insightful portraits of America's heartland, *God's Country* (1985) and *And the Pursuit of Happiness* (1986). When Malle's work fit no particular genre, he made one up. Perhaps his most fascinating English language film is *My Dinner with André* (1981), one of the only commercially successful films in the American cinema to completely ignore traditional narrative form. With the exception of the opening scene, the entire film takes place in continuous real time during a casual dinner conversation between two somewhat eccentric individuals. Malle engineered each camera move so as to create the illusion of a completely improvised dinner conversation.

Stepping out of the sun, Malle and I look for a place to sit down and begin the interview. Malle once again talks about how strange it is to be back in Los Angeles. This time, however, it is not business, but a personal visit to see his wife, actress Candice Bergen, who is starring in her own television show. "Paris, New York, Los Angeles," he says with a sad face, "long-distance marriages are very difficult."

Just then, Malle breaks into a smile as he reaches into his satchel and pulls out an aged black and white photograph of a younger version of himself (bearded) with Jean-Luc Godard and François Truffaut. "This was at Cannes in 1968, shortly after the Cinémathèque incident and the general strikes." I intently study the photograph of Malle and Truffaut sitting in folding chairs, nonchalantly looking up at the ceiling, while Godard shouts into their ears, gesticulating wildly. "It was a very crazy time," he adds, chuckling. It is then that I learn that Malle is rendering this turbulent period in French history in his most recent film *May Fools* (1990).

HICKENLOOPER: Would you tell me something about *May Fools?*

MALLE: Well, it's really about my life then. Shortly before the strikes I had been making a documentary in India [*Calcutta*]. I had been there for a long time and then coming back seemed very disorienting. I had to take five weeks, six weeks to get myself together because between India and May '68 I didn't know where I was. And then everything just exploded in Paris, at the university, at the Cinémathèque with the "Langlois Affair." Suddenly it seemed that the very utopian experience of May '68 was not so much about ideology or politics but rather about a different way of looking at things. Of course, it didn't go very far. It wasn't long before people took their holidays and everything was back to the way it was before. But there was sort of a dream that lasted for six weeks. I was very prepared for that after six months in India. But my project about May '68 is not about May '68 in Paris. It's taking place in a very remote part of France in a house in the country, and the family has gathered there for a funeral, and meanwhile all this unrest is happening in Paris, but it's like a distant echo for them.

H: Are you writing it yourself?

M: Yeah, I'm trying to because it's always easier for me to write alone.

H: I'm surprised. I always think of you working with someone else. You've collaborated with the same writer more than once.

M: Actually, I'm keeping in touch with Jean-Claude Carrière because we're old friends. I worked with him in the sixties and he helped me with *Au Revoir Les Enfants*. I sort of consulted him. And for this project, which I've tentatively titled *May Fools*, I think eventually I'm going to work more with him. You know, I spend an evening from time to time with him. But in a way, *May Fools* is also based on so many personal memories. It's certainly not as autobiographical as *Au Revoir Les Enfants*, but it's still inspired by family and memories of childhood. It's also about the end of an era. It's not that '68 was really by itself a turning point. I think in the sixties, in cities like Paris, they were already into a completely new approach, almost like a new culture; however, if you went into the outer provinces in France, you could find people still living the way their grandparents had lived in the nineteenth century. It was still a very traditional way of life and I think it's been all turned around in the seventies.

H: I'm sure the funeral becomes a kind of metaphor for the passing of that.

G: Yeah, I suppose. I'm not really trying to understand my metaphors. But one of the many points of the plot is whether this family is going to sell the house or not.

H: Do any of them aspire to go to the big city, Paris?

M: Well, a lot of these people come from the big city. They came back to this place where they don't come often anymore. One of them still lives there, and there are grandchildren and great grand-children. It's a mess.

H: Do you find it distracting to think about the metaphors you're working with as you use them and to think about the possible resonances of the story. Or do you prefer to leave that to the critics?

M: Oh, I definitely prefer to leave that to the critics, and sometimes they find them, but sometimes they find something else. You know, it comes to you because people who read your script might mention it. Usually it doesn't come to you up front, and I think it is dangerous if it does. Most of the time, the theme has always been more visual than anything else. And I've been dreaming for the last few months about this house which is a house that I know I'm not going to be able to use, but I'm referring precisely to a house that I've known many years back and the idea of these people stuck. It's a series of images more than anything else.

H: I understand that you do a lot of research for your films. Do you enjoy that process? Is it sometimes even difficult to stop with the research and begin the project?

M: To be honest with you my research on, for example, *Au Revoir Les Enfants* was minimal. For the simple reason that ten years before I had done enormous research for *Lacombe, Lucien*. The difference between *Lacombe* and *Au Revoir* was that *Lacombe* was about a character I was not familiar with, really very much a stranger to me, very much of a young man from a completely different world, different background. I did six months of research with a close friend of mine. It got so fascinating that at some point I had to stop. And I used that for *Au Revoir Les Enfants*. I had kept my files and I remember very well, and because *Au Revoir Les Enfants* was essentially based on my own memories, I just used the research to add another dimension to a scene, or to enrich a scene, for example, the scene in the restaurant which was originally a simple scene of my mother taking us out, taking us to this sort of very provincial restaurant in this little town. And then I remembered a story that came from the *Lacombe, Lucien* research of these drunk German Wehrmacht officers kicking out a French collaborator giving a hard time to everybody. So that helped me to come up with the scene of that very dignified, old man who happens to be Jewish. And also it helped me not only to refresh my own memory, but helped me try to be objective about what happened. I think it's a fairly accurate description of the way people lived and felt in 1944.

H: You said that you tried to create a stylistically objective approach in fear of the film becoming too sentimental.

M: I was terrified of becoming sentimental because the story was so easy to play sentimental. I had to almost fight myself. I don't think my films are sentimental, but in this case, and also because it was so close to me, I had to really hold back.

H: Is that why you waited thirty years to make the film?

M: That had to do with the choice of the voice. You know, I could have picked children with a lot more sweetness and charm, but I had to be careful during the shooting and in the editing room. You know, two more seconds on a close-up can sort of add a lot more. This is a very manipulative medium as we know well, especially in this town. It is so easy if you know a little bit about this medium to manipulate audiences with music, with a close-up, with editing. It's a Pavlovian medium in the sense that you can get almost any reaction mathematically. I think my only sort of rule of behavior has been to try to keep away from that cheap manipulation and try to impress the audience on a higher level and to trust them to make their own choices and not be forced. So I think eventually this was the strength of *Au Revoir Les Enfants* because it was so restrained. This is why everybody seems to find the ending devastating because it's been sort of building up but it's also very restrained. And it all comes out at the end as we reach this moment when Bonet is taken away and Julien knows he's never going to see him again. So there's a moment there which is pure, pure emotion and that's stayed with me for more than forty years. So I wanted things slowly mounting, going to the end and staying away from anything that would permit people to let go with their emotions. And I must say I've been amazed by the boy who plays Michel in *Au Revoir Les Enfants* because I ended up sort of giving him the part. What he did with it was great.

H: What was it like having him do things with it? I mean, were you tempted at times to say "Well, no it wasn't like that."

M: Well, I had to deal with that. It was a little difficult at the beginning. But very quickly I forgot that it was me, that it was my memory and I was just amazed that this boy, who was eleven years old in 1987, was so into it and so creative about it. And so I realized that it was completely uninteresting if he was close to the way I was or not. I was just watching something happening which was a perfect re-creation of the mood and the mentality and the emotions of the time, but at the same time, it was his own character that he had created for himself and from the screenplay. I never wanted to tell him, "Well, this is not the way I would have done it." Frankly, I don't even remember my childhood that well.

H: With respect to editing, traditionally there seem to be two schools of thought: Eisenstein's very popular theory of montage, in which a series of juxtaposed images creates a particular meaning, versus André Bazin's advocacy for mise-en-scène, in which all the action is contained within the framing of the shot. As a director, what are your approaches to editing?

M: I have always been tremendously interested in editing. It is a tool that gives you all the possibilities. Speaking as a documentary filmmaker, editing is always about "after." You don't write a screenplay. You just go out there and you shoot it. It's really from the hip sometimes. It's really improvised. That's the way I do it. And then the purgatory is the cutting room, because you spend months trying to put it together, and it's not so much trying to make sense of it, because there is no sense. The way you've shot it has a meaning. You just have to find it, order it, and clarify it, and it takes forever, because all the homework you've not done before, you have to do after. So I've been spending a lot of time in cutting rooms. When I did my India documentaries, I spent practically one year in a cutting room. That's all I was doing. We were under pressure because we had deadlines, so it was like still being in India. It was great. I really loved it. But now, for instance, with *Au Revoir Les Enfants*, I kept telling my editors, if you ever win an award for editing, I won't work with you anymore. That means your editing shows. Editing should not show. You spend a long time and you find out it's a question of two frames, more or less, or matching cuts, and that can take forever, but it's not meant to show. With *My Dinner With André* I had a terrible time editing, because André [Gregory] and Wally [Shawn], as good as they are, they're not really professional actors. André had, as you know, the longest speaking part in the history of filmmaking. André and Wally had written a marvelous script based on their own conversations, but I don't think they realized that nobody's ever had so many lines to say in a movie. There were ups and downs in there, and we had many takes, and I used a lot of reaction shots, especially in the first half hour. My big worry about the first half hour was people leaving the theater, because the beginning is this sort of endless monologue of André's, which was very important. And I wanted to take the distance with what André was saying and the perfect way to do it was to use Wally's reaction shots, and they were great. They would get a laugh, and we would get a distance from this very pompous approach to André's character before he mellows and becomes a little different. I think it works that way. I think we've succeeded in a way that would be almost unnoticed by the audience, and I think when people watch *My Dinner With André*, they think they see a continuum, but they don't really. You have no idea how many cuts there are. It's very cut, *My Dinner*. I knew it would be that way. It's basically two angles, except that sometimes it's here, sometimes it's there. It really varies minimally. I spent a lot of time rehearsing *My Dinner*, and it was not even rehearsal. I was actually shooting. We had two weeks of shooting. I reshot everything. The first week we worked six long days. The first three days were for the birds and I knew it.

H: Were you expecting that going in?

M: Yeah, but then we had an enormous amount of footage, and I remember, with the continuity girl, we spent a Sunday from seven in the morning until nine at night, with sandwiches, watching the stuff we'd shot. I knew that I would practically have to reshoot everything. The original footage gave me a sense of what was wrong. I realized if I wanted to get Wally funny, I would have to do it from that angle, slightly under him and from the left. If I wanted to have André sort of heroic I knew exactly how to do it, but it took me one week of shooting. It was not meant to show. It seems to be perfectly sloppy work, just putting a camera on one and a camera on the other, and they start discussing and you roll, when actually it was rehearsed, very studied. And, of course, the whole point was to give the sense that it was completely improvised, and that came a lot from the editing.

H: It was one of the first conventional, commercial films to take place in real time. I can only think of some others like Andy Warhol's *Empire* or Alfred Hitchcock's *Rope*. What kind of strategy did you have in mind for engaging the audience for such a long period of time in one location with only two characters?

M: We didn't really have a strategy. What took priority was locating the production money. It was very difficult, although we're talking about very little money. People would be interested. They'd say, "Ah yes, it sounds exciting," and they would read André's and Wally's script, and then say, "But this is not a movie!" and my only reaction was to say, "Well, you know, if I shoot it, it is a movie. [laughs] What can I tell you? I mean, it'll be a movie. What is a movie? A car chase? Okay, it's not a car chase." Everybody was very pessimistic about the commercial future of *My Dinner With André*. I thought it was a very interesting experience. I thought a few people would be interested, but I never figured that it would become such a cult film.

We discussed vaguely at the beginning, when I started working with André and Wally, about flashbacks, but we all agreed very quickly that it would be absurd. It was nice to have this opening before Wally gets to the restaurant, with Wally sort of fading out in the city of New York, and sort of remembering his youth, and so that was nice. But the moment he enters the restaurant and meets André at the bar, it's practically an hour and a half. It's practically the running time of the dinner. One of the first things we did once I rehearsed with them in my apartment in New York every afternoon for six weeks was to show them with a video camera what they were doing wrong. They had so little experience with films, so I thought a video camera would give them the best feedback.

André was spending three hours every morning learning his lines, although they were supposed to be his own lines, but still he had to learn them because actually they'd been completely transformed and rewritten. It's very interesting because it's a process of something that seems to be like cinema verité and becomes a very elaborate work of art to eventually appear improvised. So it was this slow process. I remember at some point I told them, "Well, we're going to go to a restaurant, The Ginger Man, where it more or less is supposed to happen, and we're going to sit, the three of us, and you're going to tell me your lines and we're going to run the screenplay." So we went to The Ginger Man and stopped after twenty minutes, because it didn't work. It was too noisy, the waiter came at the wrong time and they absolutely didn't have the concentration. We realized that the timing was completely wrong in real real time, so we had to sort of re-create a real time.

H: You've had a lot of success directing documentary films. Have you been criticized by other documentary filmmakers for your endeavors in fiction?

M: I don't think so. I know I'm not considered a pure documentary filmmaker. People like Jean Rouche or Chris Marker in France are real communicators as documentary filmmakers. And of course, you have to understand that most documentary filmmakers are at some point really tempted by fiction. Many of them try. In my case, I don't know what I am first, because I actually started in documentaries. I started with Jacques Cousteau, and I was his underwater cameraman. But my approach to documentaries is very different from Cousteau's and it's probably the reason why I've always been very uncomfortable with large crews. I like to work with the minimum possible number of people. I feel always more comfortable. Of course, *My Dinner With André*, that was a crew of fifteen. You need the people you need. I'm not saying that you can cut out certain key jobs on the set, but there's nothing more pleasurable for me than to go with my documentary crew, which is actually two plus me or me plus two. It's actually three people.

H: Was it difficult making the transition from documentaries to features?

M: My problem with filmmaking at the very beginning was with handling actors. When I came back from Cousteau after four years, I directed my first feature. Technically I could deal with any problem. I knew enough to discuss it with the soundman, the editor. I'd been doing all that because when I was working for Cousteau, it was practically a one-man crew. At the age of twenty-three or twenty-four, I had a real technical knowledge of my craft, but I knew very little about actors, and I remember my terror, during the first two or three features I did, was dealing with actors, because at that point I knew I was really only experienced in directing fishes [laughs]. It's very different, and how to handle actors is something you have to learn. The great advantage to working onstage is that you have much more time to spend with actors than you do in films. I directed a play of John Guare's six years ago and I asked for six weeks of rehearsal. I spent six really interesting weeks working with actors very closely and saw their work evolve. You never have that kind of luxury in films, although I always try to rehearse.

H: Do you think it's a necessity?

M: I don't believe in over-rehearsing on film. It's a different kind of work for the actor. A lot of stage directors want to direct films. It's often happened that they're not very successful, and vice versa. It's a different rhythm. It's a different experience altogether. It's a very different medium for me, the same way I'm really happy to take a 16mm camera and go back to the real world and shoot a documentary. I don't think it's very different, finally. It's always good for me, for my mental sanity, but on the other extreme, it's not always good work with actors, their egomania, their insecurity. But it's fascinating and very useful too. In film you don't have that much time. You end up in situations where you have to direct three actors in a scene and the three actors have to be directed differently, because they're different, their personalities are sometimes almost opposite. Some actors, you have to make them nervous because they're too confident. Other actors, you have to terrorize them, because that's what they want most. I would say they need to be fathered and sort of patted on the back and helped, and you have to hold them to the camera.

H: Does casting have a lot to do with the success of your films?

M: Yes, often. In the case of *My Dinner with André* it was very funny because I was constantly having to loop-the-loop because the film was more or less about André and Wally themselves. It started from this series of encounters after not seeing each other for several years. Being very close, they separated, then they split, then they came back together. They had done theater together and then they went their own ways. André started traveling and Wally started having his plays produced and staying in New York, you know, as they say in the film. And they decided to do something. Originally they wanted to do something on stage from their conversations so they taped those conversations. I think they had twenty-five hours of tape. And then Wally took it for two years and came up with a screenplay which is about these two characters who were André and Wally, but not quite André and Wally, but rather transposed. Eventually, they, André and Wally, would play those characters but not quite as André and Wally. And I read the script and I said, "Yes, I'll do it." I thought it was interesting and really challenging and I knew both of them quite well at the time. Wally even had a small part in *Atlantic City*. So we had our first meeting and I said, "You know, it doesn't have to be you playing those parts." I said we could conceive of Robert Redford and Dustin Hoffman.

H: What did they say to that?

M: They were shocked, but from the beginning I wanted to make it clear to them that they would have to approach acting the parts not as "It's me, I'm just playing my character, and I'm to be just honest to myself." I wanted them to become professional actors being asked to play a part. It became very confusing and it took a long time to get the necessary distance, but if not, it would have been a mess, because they would have been confused. And it was helped by the fact that thanks to Wally's writing there was a distance. It was very close to the way André speaks, but not quite. And I kept saying, I don't give a shit about what happened to you, André, in the Polish forest, I want you, André, the actor, to come and tell me how you feel about it. I kept sort of breaking this confusion between the character and the actor. I needed to. I realized very quickly, if not, I was not going to make any progress. I would be stuck in this messy confusion about who they are, and I really needed for them to be able to keep a distance so they could clearly look at their characters and their weaknesses. And I wanted André to be, not completely, but, almost completely ridiculous in the first twenty minutes. I think that was my input into the screenplay. If this film is going to work, we must get laughs. If we don't get laughs, it will be buried. The first time I read it, I laughed a number of times, but of course, they took it very seriously, especially André. Wally was much more into the humor of André's sometimes being so solemn. I said I injected those reaction shots to get laughs, but that would have been cheap if I had only done that. But I got André to understand that his character had to be pompous and then open up, so I needed the distance. If not, it would have been not a documentary and not fiction, but a mess.

H: *Au Revoir* comes at an interesting time in your career because usually one identifies films about childhood with a filmmaker just starting out or one who is at the end of his career. Coming square in the middle of your career, does it ever feel like you made *Au Revoir* too soon or too late in your life?

M: You know, it's funny because of course a lot of filmmakers, and the best known example is Truffaut, have started with their childhood or adolescent memories, but in recent years we've had a number of major filmmakers like Bergman, even Woody Allen, who have made films about their childhoods rather late in their careers. You know it's never mentioned but you have Bergman's *Fanny and Alexander*, Woody Allen's *Radio Days*, then Boorman's *Hope and Glory* and a couple of others. I was discussing it with Boorman and he said he'd been thinking about doing that film for years but it was only recently that he remembered exactly the way he felt as a child. I've always wanted to deal with the story behind *Au Revoir*. In my case it's a story that's particularly traumatic and I really wanted at some point to pass it on. For a strange reason, I don't know, I almost felt like I should buy time. I should really wait and save it. Then at some point my memory came back with vengeance. It became so obsessive. And the last couple of years when I was in the United States, when I was shooting *Alamo Bay* in those little towns on the Texas coast where you're really far away in a different world, my memories just came pouring back. So that's when I really started trying to think of a structure for *Au Revoir Les Enfants* in my spare time, which was very little—Sundays. I would try to put together an idea of a screenplay because I carried this memory for many years without being sure I could get a screenplay out of it. I didn't know how to approach it. I think at some point it seems natural, it's almost a Proustian way of dealing with memory and allowing things to open up. Things open up, meaning that suddenly little instances float to the surface from the deep. They sort of appear on the surface of your consciousness and you start saying, "Well, it becomes material you can use," when before you felt uncomfortable dealing with it. I remember I repressed a lot of things of my childhood, including this story of Bonet and 1944, for years until I was past thirty. I didn't even want to deal with it. I was not even talking about it to anybody. I don't know why but it felt like I didn't want to deal with it.

H: Was making the film cathartic? Do you feel less inhibited talking about it now?

M: It does come back more and more. As you get older, memory becomes almost omnipresent. It's bizarre. And that's why I'm sort of happy living in Paris these days because that's where all my memories are, and I walk and turn a corner and something comes back which took place in 1964. And I remember this corner and that there was somebody living in an apartment and then something else comes back. And then I'll walk some more and on the next block I'll see a café where I remember something from my past. So for me it's sort of the geography of my memory. Because I spent most of my adolescent and adult life in Paris, it's like walking into my past. So that's what I've been doing lately. That's why I'm working on *May Fools* [laughs], which of course is not taking place in Paris but is certainly loaded with personal memories. That's why lately I've enjoyed making films that deal with my memories. When I did *Au Revoir Les Enfants* I felt immense relief because suddenly I was working in my own past, on my own ground and in my own language. I felt it was a lot easier. I felt like I was a hundred percent in control, whereas in Hollywood I was at best eighty percent in control.

H: Do you see yourself ever coming back to Hollywood?

M: Only to do the documentary if I ever get around to it. You know, it's funny because I made a film about a city, which is a city of despair, of physical, economic despair, called *Calcutta*. And in those years I was thinking of doing a film about Los Angeles, another city of despair, obviously not economic or material despair, but of a mental or moral despair. I've always been struck by something very unique to this place which you sort of define as a kind of slow-motion paranoia. It's not the New York paranoia where everybody wants to kill, but there is a real paranoia here.

H: Insecurity?

M: Yeah, it's a new environment. I think Los Angeles is the city of the future. It think it is and has been defining the future and spreading it for the past twenty or thirty years. American popular culture comes from here, it doesn't come from New York, it comes a little bit from New York, but more on a subtler, sophisticated level. But the real popular culture comes from Los Angeles: movies, television, commercials, music, and not only that, but the way of life. You know, this obsession with health, all that stuff comes from here. You're really talking about a mini-culture that's the paradigm for the rest of the world. As I said before, I'm not really comfortable working or living here, but I'm really interested. Understand me. And working in fiction here is absolutely uninteresting because then you fall into all the traps. I did it once on *Crackers* and I'll never go that route again. I made all the mistakes, one-by-one, just like in a catalogue; number one, number two, number three, all the mistakes. But you know, I suppose everybody has to do it once. Eventually, they were very nice people, a nice writer, a nice producer, a nice studio, Universal, wonderful actors—that's what saved me from quitting actually. I had a great group of actors, Donald Sutherland, Sean Penn. They were a nice cast. What I'm saying is that it doesn't make very much sense for me to become another Hollywood director.

H: Creatively are you more restricted working in the United States than in France?

M: I think it has nothing to do with the system or the economy. I think it has to do with the fact that I'm more comfortable working in my own language.

H: Do the studios ever prevail on you to make changes?

M: No, well, some for *Crackers*. But really I have made all of my American films in complete freedom. I don't blame the system for being oppressive or destructive; I just blame myself for not being comfortable with the system and not being able to adjust. And when I was shooting *Crackers* there were 110 people on the crew and I didn't know what to do with them. They were always in the way [laughs]. I just don't understand Hollywood stages. You walk on people, there are so many of them. And they were changing almost every day because they were moving to another set. I mean, not the principals, not the camera crew. There were just so many people. I don't like to work that way. It's because I've learned to work a different way. If I were a young British director coming from commercials, I could easily adjust to the Hollywood way. But that's not my background and I don't regret it.

Filmography

1956   *The Silent World* (documentary)
1958   *Frantic*
1958   *The Lovers*
1960   *Zazie dans le Métro*
1962   *A Very Private Affair*
1963   *The Fire Within*
1965   *Viva Maria*
1967   *The Thief of Paris*
1968   *Spirits of The Dead*
1969   *Calcutta* (documentary)
1969   *Phantom India*
1971   *Murmur of the Heart*
1972   *Humain Trop Humain* (documentary)
1973   *Lacombe, Lucien*
1975   *Black Moon*
1978   *Pretty Baby*
1980   *Atlantic City*

1981 *My Dinner With André*
1984 *Crackers*
1985 *Alamo Bay*
1985 *God's Country* (documentary)
1986 *And the Pursuit of Happiness* (documentary)
1988 *Au Revoir Les Enfants*
1990 *May Fools*

ANNETTE INSDORF
A Sophist for the Screen

Annette Insdorf glides into a lecture hall at Columbia University with the magnetism of a screen actress. In the wake of her entry three hundred undergraduates fall silent. Though her image never appears on the silver screen, Insdorf frequently stands in front of one, for she is the highly celebrated film scholar whose frequent appearances and contributions to *The New York Times* and several major film publications have made her known to filmmakers, scholars and critics around the world.

Her students break open their notebooks as they await a screening of Howard Hawks's *Scarface* and Insdorf's animated lecture that will follow in her always overflowing course, Masterpieces in American Film History—better known to less serious film students as "Tuesday Afternoon at the Movies."

Insdorf is the new star professor and co-chair of Columbia University's Film Division, a title she shares with Academy Award-winning director Milos Forman. In addition to her accolades in New York, she also has the honor of having won a long battle to get film studies taken seriously in the Ivy League's most academically stubborn university, Yale. Cofounder of the Yale Film Studies Center, Insdorf served as an adjunct professor in American Studies at the college through the 1980s. A staunch believer in intelligent film scholarship, Insdorf drew hundreds of undergraduates into the new Film Studies major. At the same time she authored a compelling biography of François Truffaut (who praised it as "the most sensitive and intelligent book in the English language about my work"), in addition to *Indelible Shadows: Film and the Holocaust*, an examination of Nazi genocide through the eyes of world cinema.

Insdorf and I met just as she was finishing some work at Columbia before flying out for her annual visit to the Telluride Film Festival.

HICKENLOOPER: Well, my first question, appropriately enough, is about film school. There's somewhat of a controversy as to whether undergraduates should pursue film production as a core curriculum. I understand that UCLA has just dropped their undergraduate film department because they believe that a solid liberal arts program is much more important. Do you have any thoughts regarding film school for undergraduates?

INSDORF: My experiences teaching during the seventies and eighties lead me to believe that the best model existed at Yale University, namely to have at least one course open to undergraduates in which they could learn "the language of film." That was the title of the course as taught by Michael Roemer. In other words, to teach film production within the context of film analysis and history. It's true that there is a danger of undergraduates' studies becoming overly vocational if a student is allowed to major in film production. My sense is that the best films are made not by very young people, but by those who have lived and/or learned enough to have something to say. I firmly believe that there is a place for film studies on the undergraduate level, but I believe that the focus or the context should be a solid liberal arts curriculum with an emphasis on film history. I think that before a student holds a camera or splices celluloid he or she should have seen everything from *Citizen Kane* to *2001*.

H: What do you think are the major films or filmmakers that a student should study?

I: The danger in answering this kind of question is that one necessarily omits dozens of major names. But in terms of American film history, maybe I should answer purely personally. My Masterpieces in American Film History course covers the following: the original *Scarface*, Howard Hawks; the original *Stagecoach*, John Ford; *Citizen Kane*; Fritz Lang's *Fury*; Ernst Lubitsch's *To Be or Not to Be*; Preston Sturges's *Sullivan's Travels*; Howard Hawks's *The Big Sleep*; William Wyler's *The Best Years of Our Lives*; Elia Kazan's *On the Waterfront*; Alfred Hitchcock's *Psycho*; Gene Kelly's *Singin' in the Rain*; Billy Wilder's *Some Like It Hot*; Stanley Kubrick's *Paths of Glory*. Obviously the individual titles can change. Even some of the directors can be changed, but I believe that the major genres and the major periods of soundfilm in American film history should be explored in a classroom. Obviously I stopped around 1960, and I could give you a whole different slew of names for the sixties, seventies and eighties, but I believe that if you're teaching Masterpieces, the films should have stood the test of time, and maybe thirty years is about where we should start. Has it lasted through one whole generation? Here it gets very difficult because I love and appreciate the movies of so many countries, but if I had to say who I thought was the greatest director of all times it would be Jean Renoir, and the greatest film, *The Rules of the Game*.

H: Richard Schickel told me that he felt film scholarship, particularly in the literary world, was met with a certain condescending attitude. And he felt disillusioned to the point where he's thinking about giving up publishing critical work because he doesn't feel his work or anybody else's work is taken seriously.

I: I disagree. But I do think there is a horrifying gap between filmmaking and film scholarship as taught in universities, and then, in addition to that, there's a gap between film criticism and the more popular form of writing about film in both magazines and books. So there are at least three levels of film activity that one could delineate in the United States: people who write and make or direct films, who have very little in common usually with people who write about film in journals or books, and even less in common with thematicians and deconstructionists who often use film in their attempts to develop an often obfuscating language.

H: Why do you think that gap exists? If it exists less in the literary world, is it because film is much more of a business, and therefore attracts the more commercialized elements?

I: I think part of the reason for the gap is that you use the same basic language whether you are writing a novel or writing about a novel. It's a totally different language if you are using a camera, actors, celluloid and set design, than writing about the combination of those elements. There's a lot in film that resists the critical mind and pen. Film is not only technical and commercial, it is visceral. It evokes emotion from the spectator like no other creative medium. I also think the gap exists because filmmakers don't trust critics, and critics not only don't trust filmmakers but are sometimes condescending to them. And then you have the film scholars who occasionally don't understand or don't accept the popular nature of the medium and use films toward an end that filmmakers then revise with new kinds of work.

H: Why do you think filmmakers don't trust their critics? It seems like film criticism has much less power in terms of audience appeal than theater criticism.

I: Well, I think that one should never completely trust any critic or reviewer, including myself. Because ultimately the response to any given film is subjective, and the person who gets common space in a newspaper or magazine is not necessarily the one who can best evaluate the power or importance of a given motion picture. At best they can be guides for those who, on a busy evening, have to choose among a variety of films playing in their neighborhood. And my feeling is that the best critics are not reviewers. They're not the people who tell you, "Yes, go see this film" or "No, ignore this film because it's bad." It's the person who takes it for granted that the reader has seen a given film and is able to engage in some kind of, well, discourse with the reader. For example, I've never wanted to be a reviewer, despite offers, because I think it's a waste of time to write about what should best be forgotten.

H: I want to ask you about your experience at Yale. I know you were there for fifteen years. You were a graduate student there, and I was wondering how did a very serious academic institution like Yale, in the last fifteen years, change its perception of film as a serious course of study?

I: I think it evolved from a basic condescension and indifference to an increasing tolerance, if not respect. Initially some senior faculty and administrators assumed that film was too much fun to be taken seriously, and that there wasn't a sufficient body of work to warrant intensive analysis. However, some of the people who expressed such views were, frankly, defensive or insecure. They thought their own classes might be drained of students who would flock to the study of a more popular field. I think that what happened at Yale was that student demands combined with the quality of a faculty—I think we had very, very good teachers—resulted in the beginning of a serious program in film study.

H: Why did you leave?

I: The only reason I left was that by that point I was an adjunct professor teaching half-time at Yale and half-time at Columbia. And Columbia simply made me an offer I couldn't refuse—by giving me a full-time, full professorship, and a title of Director of Undergraduate Film Studies as well as Chairman of the Ph.D. Program in Film and Theater, with a mandate to create a solid program in film for undergraduates, not unlike the work I was part of at Yale.

H: It's ironic that an institution like Yale wouldn't at first take film seriously. Couldn't the university recognize the impact of someone like Chaplin, Ford or Welles, or that the medium is perhaps the most influential of all the arts?

I: Maybe it's too obvious. I'm not sure how to answer that question, because it's hard to generalize. Certainly many faculty members at Yale recognize not only the power of film, but the need to study it seriously. At the same time there must have been those who felt threatened by serious study of film, because it wouldn't be as much fun to go watch movies. I'm obviously being a bit facetious here, but I think they were so leery of anything that could be so popular. And don't forget that Yale, like Columbia, is an Ivy League institution, and it prides itself on a certain rigor and quality of education into which film didn't seem to fit for a long time. I mean, the respectability of film is a relatively recent phenomenon. But my contention is that its moment has come.

H: How do you think it will grow in the future?

I: I'm almost scared of how it's already growing, because since the time I left Yale, film studies have been proliferating in universities around the country. What frightens me is that it's often taught in departments of semiotics. And my feeling is that film is not an appendage of art history or English or mass communications or semiotics. It has its own terms, its own properties and limitations, its own ways of being experienced, and it deserves its own department. And . . . I worry when film students are well versed in Jacques Derrida but haven't seen a film by John Cassavetes.

H: Is Derrida still a strong influence in film criticism?

I: Let's just say that the French still exert something of a stronghold on film theory, and that much of film theory in the United States uses the French for a point of departure.

H: Does that force still come from *Cahiers du Cinéma?*

I: Less now than before. I think much less than before.

H: Speaking of which, I wanted to ask you about François Truffaut. You did write the most significant book on his work. He even said so himself. And you had a pretty well-known, well-documented relationship with him, several of his letters to you have been published in a book of his correspondences. Would you first tell me how you met and how you became interested in his work?

I: Well, it's the typical New York, late sixties story, namely a high school or college student in Manhattan has the joy of choosing among ten rival movie houses plus the Museum of Modern Art. And so one night she sees *Shoot the Piano Player*, can't stop laughing during certain scenes, and then finds herself crying during others; and upon leaving the theater realizes that she has had a very unusual and invigorating movie experience. Then she sees *The 400 Blows* and realizes that it is possible to make a film about a child that is unsentimental. And then she sees *Jules and Jim* and the treatment of romance blows her away, because it's tender and lyrical and poignant at the same time. And then she's lucky enough to go

THE NEW TRANSATLANTIC CINEMA

see *Stolen Kisses* and *The Wild Child*. Well, to make a long story short, such a person—namely me—realizes that Truffaut's films have a particular tone, a particular treatment of characters that is totally endearing and stimulating.

What happened, quite simply, is that when I was at Yale doing my Ph.D. in English, I realized not only that film was the area I felt most passionate about, but that I had a particular proclivity toward the French New Wave. This may, of course, be influenced by the fact that I was born in Paris and speak French. And of all the New Wave filmmakers, Truffaut was the one whose world I felt closest to. And I was at some conference where I was giving a paper, around 1975. I was asked about what I teach, and I was teaching the French New Wave at the time. And I told these people about why I loved Truffaut's work, and after ten minutes they stopped me and said, "Okay, okay, okay! How would you like to write a book about Truffaut for our new series?" And that's how it happened.

At that point I wrote to Truffaut to inform him that I was writing a book about his work and to ask him if we could meet. He wrote back a very polite but firm letter that suggested it was too early, that since he had not yet reached the age of Hitchcock at the time that Truffaut interviewed him for the famous interview book, *Hitchcock/Truffaut*, he would prefer that I write most of the book and then meet him. I agreed, but we began a correspondence, and he quite generously sent me articles and books that could be of help in my work. And we finally met during the New York Film Festival the year that he came to present *Story of Adele H.* And I went to meet him in the lobby of his hotel. I think he was even more scared than I was. We both laughed a lot in order to break the ice, so that was the beginning of our friendship. Eventually, I began translating for him during his visits to the United States. For example, when he came to speak at the American Film Institute's Life Achievement tribute to Alfred Hitchcock, I helped him translate his speech into English. Truffaut knew very little English to begin with, so when we translated his speech, we wanted it to sound a little broken, like a Frenchman trying to speak English, so that it wouldn't sound too translated. Then I translated a piece that he wrote in French for *The New York Times* because they had no one there to do it, and I essentially had to rewrite it in the offices of the

Times the day that it was submitted. And Truffaut was quite pleased with the results. When the *Times* wrote to him asking how to send payments—in other words, where to send him his checks—his answer was that I should receive the entire fee, not just the translator's fee, because he claimed that I had essentially written the piece. It was a very generous thing to do, and it began my career at the *Times*.

H: Could you talk a little bit about his special relationship with André Bazin, and how it developed into the auteur theory?

I: André Bazin was Truffaut's spiritual father, as well as one of the most incisive and sympathetic film critics of our time. I still consider him "of our time" because, after all, he died in 1959. He channeled a great deal of Truffaut's anarchic energies into film. He enabled Truffaut to write for various journals. And I think Truffaut, as well as many others of the French New Wave filmmakers, was deeply inspired by Bazin's humanistic appreciation of the film medium.

H: The auteur theory was introduced by Bazin, Truffaut and the fellows at *Cahiers du Cinéma*, then brought to the U.S. by Andrew Sarris. How do you think the theory holds up today? Are there still auteurs making films? Are there still recognizable styles among filmmakers?

I: Yes. Although many in Hollywood will tell you that the real auteur these days is the agent, or the person who creates the package, whether that's a producer or an executive producer. My own feeling is that a relatively new talent like Alan Rudolph, for example, is very much an auteur—someone whose films have an idiosyncratic personal style, recognizable from film to film. And actually, when you look at his work, the whole is greater than the sum of its parts. I'm a big fan of movies like *Choose Me, The Moderns, Trouble in Mind, Return Engagement, Welcome to L.A., Remember My Name.* Jonathan Demme is another one. Yes, he's an auteur. Whether it's the urban locale thing like *Married to the Mob* or *Something Wild.* On the other hand, if you think of some of the most respected directors working today, they are craftsmen more than auteurs. And here I would include Alan Pakula, Sidney Pollack,

Arthur Penn, Milos Forman, Steven Spielberg. They make very well-crafted films, good stories that are well told. But I'm not sure about their "personal vision," or consistent personal vision.

H: Of the directors that are working today, whose work do you think will endure the longest?

I: That's a horrible question to have to try and answer. So let's just say I'll talk about those whose work I'm already teaching in my classes. I have a course on film narrative, and I do include many films by contemporary directors. I know that Peter Weir is in there and Volker Schlondorff. I showed Bernardo Bertolucci's *The Conformist*, Philip Kaufman's *Unbearable Lightness of Being*. I showed Francis Coppola's *The Conversation*, Alain Resnais's *Hiroshima Mon Amour*, Wim Wenders's *The American Friend*, Richard Rush's *The Stunt Man*, Schlondorff's *Tin Drum*, Terrence Malick's *Badlands*, Robert Altman's *McCabe and Mrs. Miller*, and finally Krushtov Kistlovski's *Camera Buff*. He's the Polish director getting a lot of acclaim in Europe these days.

H: Martin Scorsese seems conspicuously absent.

I: I didn't teach him this term, but I did show *Taxi Driver* last term. I mean, I can extend the list slightly by using the cream of films from last year: so *Taxi Driver*, Resnais's *Providence*, Rudolph's *Choose Me*. In that class I also showed Istvan Szabo's *Mephisto*.

H: So is the auteur theory as alive and well, as it was twenty years ago?

I: Well, it depends as practiced by whom. It is no longer nearly as alive in the classrooms. The auteur theory is not used as much in show analysis; however, it is more alive than ever among audiences who flock, for example, to the name Spielberg—whether it's as director or producer. I mean, I think the name of a director is more recognizable today by the mass audience. Scorsese, Woody Allen, I mean those are names that people contend with.

H: Do you think television has desensitized audiences to the power of film?

I: It has limited attention spans. People who watch a lot of television become habituated to a commercial every ten or fifteen minutes, and that is not the proper attention span for a hundred-minute film.

H: Has film criticism begun to lower its standards?

I: Well, yeah. I mean, I don't think it's so much popular film criticism as television film criticism. Don't forget that TV critics have to be able to describe, analyze and recommend, or not recommend, a film all in approximately ninety seconds. And that simply does not allow for anything beyond a superficial gloss on a movie. And that has become the current main format for evaluating film.

H: It seems like film critics have reached a celebrity status almost equal to auteurs.

I: I think the recognizability of someone like Roger Ebert is greater than most directors. I was walking with him one day at the Telluride Film Festival a few years ago, and on the same street there were many well-known directors and actors. It was to Roger that everyone ran up to speak and to get an opinion.

H: Do you think that kind of visibility undermines serious film scholarship?

I: Well, again, I think there is a sizable gap between what Roger Ebert does and film scholarship as practiced by scholars and professors. I don't think Roger Ebert would even pretend to be a serious scholar.

H: But he's written some serious pieces.

I: Absolutely, but they are what I would call film criticism as opposed to film scholarship. I'm making a slight and perhaps false distinction here, but I think Roger knows that he's writing for the masses. And many film scholars assume that they're writing only for a small coterie of their peers.

H: In the introduction of your book, *Indelible Shadows*, you quoted Elie Wiesel—there really can't be a Holocaust literature. Would you explain his statement?

I: The idea is that there is profound incompatibility between something as overwhelming and terrifying as the Holocaust and the aesthetics of a written language. If it's literature, it can't be about Auschwitz. And if it's about Auschwitz it can't be literature. His own work gives the lie to the fact. But he's trying to say the Holocaust is too incomprehensible and overwhelming to be the raw material of art. I'm not sure that I agree with him, but I respect the reasons for his statement. But I do think that it is possible for images to suggest what words are too limited to convey.

H: But you do suggest that there are problems with the use of archival footage of the Nazis and the Holocaust.

I: Sure, because archival footage depends upon who had the cameras, who was in control, what kinds of images did they want their viewers to see. So they captured on camera only what fulfilled their purposes. One can hardly accept those images as the total reality of the situation. I mean, the victims could not visually or photographically document the situation.

H: Do you think that Hollywood has been able to make any kind of acceptable film about the Holocaust?

I: I think it is possible in Hollywood to make a very respectable film. I mean, even last year we saw the *Music Box* and *Triumph of the Spirit*, which is not, strictly speaking, Hollywood. It was made independently. But I think they're extremely well-intentioned and dramatically effective depictions of aspects of the Holocaust experience.

H: You had talked about the problems of commercial interruptions with television mini-series like "Holocaust."

I: Well, I mean, it's pretty obvious that if you are watching horrifying scenes of Jews being herded into a gas chamber, and you suddenly break for a commercial and dilute the tension as you go off to get a beer while the commercial for Lysol comes on, there's something wrong.

H: How do films like "Holocaust" educate people?

I: Basically, film as a medium can prepare us for horrors that we could never face directly. If we see the reflection on screen of things that we need to overcome, then perhaps these motion pictures will enable us, almost as if it were a rehearsal, to deal with the darker aspects of existence once they are upon us.

H: How do you look at films like Leni Riefenstahl's *Triumph of the Will* and *Olympiad*, which are praised for their aesthetic accomplishments but which were major contributors to the Nazi propaganda machine?

I: One can appreciate certain artistry but never forget the ideology behind and within the frame. I think it's quite important to be aware of how film can manipulate. And *Triumph of the Will* is an all-too-good example of how a so-called documentary is, in fact, filled with staged footage. And that should be pointed out to people in the classroom.

H: How has the New German Cinema dealt with the Holocaust?

I: It has been indirect rather than direct. It has to do with characters struggling with their legacy. I suggest in my books that the Holocaust hovers in the background of films like *Aguirre, the Wrath of God*. But very few German filmmakers have dealt head-on with the Holocaust in terms of the relationship between Nazis and Jews. But an increasing number of filmmakers have manifested what I would call "the new German guilt." I think they're all grappling with the image of a father and the image of the fatherland. And many of the films deal with rootlessness and power balances. And I think much of this can be traced to an awareness of manipulation, of how manipulation manifested itself throughout World War II. You know, the way that the media controlled citizens.

H: How do the German filmmaker immigrants—particularly Wim Wenders and Werner Herzog, who have made films in the United States—differ from the German immigrants of the thirties like Fritz Lang, Ernst Lubitsch and Joseph von Sternberg?

I: The German directors of the thirties were more easily absorbed into the Hollywood machinery. I think they had less of a
choice, you see. They were fleeing an oppressive regime, and they
couldn't go off and make personal auteur statements and raise the
money to do so. I think in the case of Wenders, Schlondorff and
Herzog, they've made some English-language films but hardly Hollywood. They've managed to retain their idiosyncratic individual-
ity. Schlondorff, of course, is an exception in that he is a crafts-
man. I think that he is closer to the model of the professional
director who interprets other people's screenplays with visual bril-
liance. But . . . I guess I'm being too abstract. Let me think of a title.
Wenders's *Hammett* was clearly a compromise, but the *State of
Things*—that was not Hollywood. It was just English language. And
Paris, Texas—I don't know quite what to say. It clearly was not a
Hollywood film. And that's one of the reasons it did so badly at the
box office in the U.S.

H: As a writer and teacher about film, do you have any aspirations to get involved in production yourself?

I: Yes, I'm now screenwriting with a friend of mine. And I just
executive-produced a short film which won the Palme d'Or at
Cannes.

H: Congratulations. Any desire to direct?

I: It might be the next natural step. But one thing at a time, yes?

Books by Annette Insdorf

1978   *François Truffaut*
1983   *Indelible Shadows: Film and the Holocaust*

IV

The Rising Respectability of the B-Movie

JOHN SAYLES
Declaration of Independence

John Sayles, the man who has led the vanguard of American independent filmmaking for the past decade, is about to catch a plane
to Milan, where he'll spend the next few weeks working as an actor,
a role he's now playing often. Having performed in his own films
(*Return of the Secaucus Seven* [1980], *Lianna* [1982], *Brother From Another Planet* [1984], *Eight Men Out* [1988], and *Matewan* [1987]), Sayles
is also making cameo appearances in his friends' work. In 1987 he
played the somewhat restrained New Jersey motorcycle cop who
confronts Melanie Griffith and Jeff Daniels in Jonathan Demme's
Something Wild.

But fans of John Sayles recognize him primarily as America's
prolific, New Jersey-based writer/director. Born in Schenectady,
New York, in 1950, he had an appetite for storytelling even as a
schoolboy. "It was like getting high grades for lying," he says, admitting that he never thought about being a writer while growing
up. His passions were with sports. "I wanted to be an outfielder. A
writer was somebody who sat behind the backstop with a score-
card." An avid baseball aficionado, Sayles admits that "Most of
what I learned about style, I learned from Roberto Clemente."

Exempt from the draft during the Vietnam War because of a
spinal injury, he enrolled at Williams College. "I majored in everything outside of the classroom—intramural sports, movies and
summer stock theater." On the side he continued to write and soon

301

realized that it might be a way to earn a living. At age 25, three years after graduating, his notion was realized when his short story "I-80 Nebraska" was published in the *Atlantic Monthly* and shortly thereafter won an O. Henry Award. Then, in 1977, his second published novel, *Union Dues*, was nominated for a National Book Award. After supporting himself as a writer, in addition to a variety of odd jobs that included meat-packing and laboring, Sayles thought he'd try his luck in the movies. Transplanting himself to Los Angeles, he shacked up in a motel and began writing low-budget exploitation scripts for Roger Corman, the king of the B-movie and mentor, early in their careers, to such successful filmmakers as Martin Scorsese, Francis Coppola and Peter Bogdanovich. In 1979 Sayles took his "bread money" earned from writing scripts, moved back to New Jersey and invested it in his first directing endeavor. The following year he burst onto the filmmaking scene with a modest $60,000 feature called *Return of the Secaucus Seven*, a 16mm sleeper which ended up on most of the year's Ten Best lists in addition to winning the Best Screenplay award from the Los Angeles Film Critics.

For the past eight years, Sayles has forged ahead directing inexpensive, independent films that often attract more positive critical attention than many of Hollywood's multimillion-dollar extravaganzas. In 1987 he was awarded the prestigious MacArthur Award, known as the "Genius Award," which guarantees him a tax-free $30,000 per year for five years to pursue any creative endeavor he chooses. *Los Gusanos*, his first novel since *Union Dues*, is among his numerous projects, which include two of his biggest film productions to date. Applying his low-budget philosophy of independent filmmaking, Sayles stretched two eight-million-dollar budgets (his largest ever) to look like twenty-million-dollar movies. The results were *Eight Men Out*, an elegantly crafted period film that recounts baseball's notorious Chicago Black Sox scandal, and *Matewan*, a frightening, realistic look at a bloody coal miners' strike—two moments in history set one year apart that Sayles believes helped change the face of America.

HICKENLOOPER: What initially interested you in the 1919 Black Sox scandal?

SAYLES: I had heard about it growing up. Every once in a while

I'd hear a snatch about that major-league baseball team, way back when, that threw the Series for gambler's money. When you're a little kid, you're not really sure whether there was a team called the Black Sox or if it was really the White Sox and then they got named the Black Sox or what. That was always kind of intriguing to me. Then twelve or thirteen years ago, I read Eliot Asinof's book *Eight Men Out*, and really felt like, wow, this makes a lot of things come clear. As complicated as that conspiracy and scandal was, he did legwork and tracked down the players who were still living and would talk to him. He got some who initially wouldn't talk to him. They wouldn't come forth and probably in the end revealed stuff to the parties involved that they didn't know themselves, because so many people were holding out on each other. It was a terrible conspiracy. Once they agreed to do it, everybody kind of stopped talking to each other. They certainly didn't get together years later to have a reunion and say, "Yeah, well, who did get the money? We were trying in the seventh game, weren't we?" So it always just seemed like a very interesting story that had a lot to do with not only baseball and its evolution, but also America and that period around 1919 to 1920. That time was a major turning point in America.

H: How do you think America changed in 1919?

S: Well, I'd say that the combination of World War I, the Black Sox scandal, the Fatty Arbuckle case and maybe a half dozen other sobering incidents of the time really helped bring America out from its childhood into what I like to think of as a disturbed adolescence. You know, there's that period in adolescence when kids think everything is stupid and everything that they were told was the truth before is a lie. There's a real cynicism that sets in during that period. And I think the Black Sox scandal was one of the things that really helped lead America into the Roaring Twenties, into the cynicism of the Capone era, which the country really didn't come out of until the end of the Depression, the beginning of World War II. Roosevelt helped and some other things helped, but certainly the kind of public attitude that could allow for gangsters to take over in Chicago and New York, despite desperate measures like Prohibition, was the result of public cynicism run amok. And I really think the Black Sox scandal was one of the straws that broke the camel's back.

H: What kind of research did the film require?

S: I did quite a bit of research. I read about the Boston police strike. I had already been doing labor history which eventually turned into *Matewan*. I read a lot of the Chicago writers who grew up in that period. In order to get a better feeling for the dialogue of the time, I read a lot of Ring Lardner, James T. Farrell and Nelson Algren—people who were writing fiction in the thirties based on the characters they grew up with in the twenties. I read Dos Passos's *1919*. I read anything that had to do with baseball and gangsters in that era, from Elliot Ness books to *The Rise and Fall of the Jewish Gangster in America*. I learned that sociology was born in the Chicago of the twenties. It's probably the best documented city in the country, even better than New York City. Carl Sandburg, for instance, covered the big race riot that happened in 1920. Those documents are still around. *Eight Men Out* wasn't the first screenplay I ever wrote, but it did take twelve years to get to the screen. So I had plenty of time to do extra research while I'd have a little bread between my other movies.

H: Both *Matewan* and *Eight Men Out* deal with this great disillusionment of the late teens and early twenties. Were there any parallels you were trying to draw between both films?

S: Not so much. In its own strange way, *Matewan* is almost a post–Civil War movie because West Virginia was so isolated compared to Chicago. At the time, it was so isolated that the relationship between workers and owners was much more of a nineteenth-century class difference than a twentieth-century one. Even though the two films happened only one year apart, they're very different just because the conditions were so much more primitive in a town like Matewan. So that film is a little closer to a western, whereas *Eight Men Out* is set in Chicago, one of the most progressive cities of that time. That's one reason why the players realized early on that they were being treated unfairly. Even though they had a reasonably good deal compared to a coal miner of the period, they could still look around and see that Comiskey wasn't paying them what they were worth, even on the baseball market.

H: And in *Matewan?*

S: Well, in *Matewan* it's more of a life-and-death scenario. Who's gonna get killed and who's not? Like in the westerns, Joe Kenehan would say, "I used to be in the Army," and he would pick up his gun and take care of the guy—the classic Gary Cooper, John Wayne, a man's got to do what a man's got to do. I use that genre, but Joe is a pacifist, and consequently Joe loses, so that causes people to wonder if pacifism is the right answer. Maybe psychologically it was more important for the miners to strike back. I don't know, I just want to raise questions.

H: *Eight Men Out* has an ensemble cast. As the writer and director, were there any particular characters whom you wanted to highlight?

S: Well, when we were trying to raise the production money, what we held out for was the fact that the story is called *Eight Men Out* for a reason. It's not called *One Man Out* or *Two Men Out*. But in later drafts of the screenplay I tried to draw out the three characters I thought would be the most sympathetic to an audience: Eddie Cicotte, who was the older pitcher; Joe Jackson, who was pretty much the greatest player of his time and who didn't do anything to throw the game, but who took the money and didn't feel too good about it; and Buck Weaver, who was the guy who didn't tell on his friends and didn't do anything to throw the games but got kicked out anyway. In the writing, and quite a bit in the editing, I used those three guys as the emotional base that I wanted to keep touching. So if there were reaction shots, they very often went to those guys. Those are the three guys whose wives we meet, so we get a little more personal with them, a small glimpse into their home life. Those are the three guys about whom we thought the audience might say, "Well, those guys got screwed for sure. That might happen to me in that situation."

H: What kind of demands did you make on your actors while rehearsing *Eight Men Out?* Obviously there was a need to be historically accurate. Did you make them research their parts thoroughly?

S: I sent everybody a one-page outline of who I thought their character was and then left it up to them. Actors, if they want to be good, will do the extra work before rehearsals begin. Almost everybody went and looked up their character's background and stats. I know John Cusack, living in Chicago, tracked down a bunch of people who knew Buck Weaver, and I got these stories about everybody going out to the park and working on the particular skills they knew they would physically need. A bunch of them read other books or novels to get a better feeling for the period. Then we had Ken Barry come in. He was a major league outfielder with the White Sox and the Angels and a couple of other clubs and he had been coaching and managing in the minor leagues. We got him to lead a two-week training camp for the guys where he helped them work out some fundamentals. For instance, if there was a play that was going to go to right field, Ken would tell us who should be the cutoff man and what base this guy covers—all those things. He was our expert at throwing the ball or hitting it exactly where we wanted it on screen. So the guys not only had to go through mental preparation for who their characters were, but also a physical preparation for things they had to do at least once in front of the camera. And I told all of them to start practicing without a glove, or just with a winter glove because those tiny little mitts the major league used back in the twenties are much smaller than the gloves of today. You couldn't really do the one-handed kind of things with the older gloves.

H: Do you have any other films planned about the Black Sox and Matewan era?

S: Not in the near future. I think that the writing on the wall for me is to go back to making movies that are really, really cheap, what they're calling "no budget" features right now. And to do that you have to stay either awfully small or not do period movies.

H: Do you feel more comfortable with smaller budgets?

S: Not necessarily more comfortable. There's less economic weight on my back. I have to justify things a lot less with less money, but the thing is, with all my movies I've always had a little less than would have been nice. *Matewan* and *Eight Men Out*, which had the biggest budgets, were also my most ambitious movies. We were still shooting with the pace and the kind of labor intensity that we used with *Lianna* and *Brother From Another Planet*. We were just honking out millions to set up the day. It had to be really well planned in order to pull it off at all, but we had more people, and we spent a lot more money because there was a big art department budget and more characters and we were shooting on location. So I think I've been able to maintain a certain amount of independence, partly because I have a sense of how to make films in a cost-effective way and how to write the screenplay for the budget that I'm likely to be able to raise. You can tell your story in a lot of different ways. Very often when I'm writing a script, I'll change scenes or cancel scenes because I realize that I can't afford to shoot them.

H: You've financed your films both independently and with the major studios. What are the differences between working alone and working within the studio system?

S: Well, it varies really. Within a studio context, you are or you aren't independent. In the case of Orion, I think both sides—because *Eight Men Out* was something they had passed on a couple of times earlier—felt somewhat nervous about making their money back. I think eventually, just having seen some of the other movies I had made and what they cost, they realized that, yes, they can make a very good-looking picture for six or seven million dollars, and that it's not going to run over and end up costing twenty million. The casting that was possible at the time made it very attractive for them, so I think we both stated our positions clearly enough before we even went into it. It ended up being a very positive experience, an independent experience in a way, just with more money. They were very supportive and I never felt them breathing down my neck. It really depends on what the individual situation is. But under a studio you always have more money.

H: So, professionally you seem to lead two lives: One within the studio walls and one outside.

S: I've always felt like I've had one foot in Hollywood and one foot in New Jersey. Even now, I'm in the Writers' Guild, but I had to quit the Directors' Guild of America. So I can write for the studios, but I'm not allowed to direct for them. I think a lot of writers feel like an insider/outsider, even regional writers like William Faulkner—he felt like an outsider in his own community. Despite their understanding of their environment, they always remain estranged from it. That's a lot of what writers do: they try to let people see things that they've always taken for granted. Often, that's why you get interesting work when a foreign filmmaker comes to Hollywood to make a movie—the audience sees what strikes his eye first about their culture, and we might not ever see it because we see it every day.

H: All of your films seem so vastly different. *Baby, It's You* is a commercial Hollywood high-school love story while *Lianna* is a study of a middle-class lesbian relationship. Would you comment on your versatility?

S: Hmmm, well, I guess I just do what interests me at the time. I'm interested in a lot of stuff. I write like that too. In my novels, each chapter always captures a completely different point of view. I'm interested not so much in what I think about something, but in seeing things through someone else's perspective. For instance, I think that my work as an actor helped my writing. An actor has to explore a character through his own eyes. How does that character look at the world? If you go to a movie as a spectator, then you see certain things. If you go as a critic, then perhaps you look for certain things. And if you directed the film, then there would be a whole set of things that you'd see—going to the same theater, through the same door at the same time. Your eyes immediately would alight on different things. So it's always interesting to me to try and put myself inside people's heads—that's part of why my stories are so different.

H: Has your acting had an influence on your directing? For example, does your own status as an actor affecting your working relationship with other actors while you direct them?

S: The one thing I think both acting and writing have helped me with as a director is that they've given me a better idea of what an actor might need, whether it's just to provide a mood on the set or talking to the actor take by take, where you must steer them through a scene that they're having a hard time with. I've not only been in my own movies, but I've been in movies that other people have directed. I've been in a bunch of plays, and I have an idea, when I get lost, of what's helpful. When I'm uncomfortable, what is it that makes me uncomfortable? What is it that a director can do to help me out of a particular corner? What will make me feel like a complete character? Do I want to know more about myself, would I want to know more of who I was and what I was doing in the script? If that's the case, then as the writer, I'll change the script to bring that character out or I'll make sure that when I deal with that actor, I'll give him some background material that may not appear on the screen, and now and then we'll rehearse it. You know, we'll do those lines or improvise scenes even though they will never be seen by an audience.

H: How does it feel to have the reputation as the champion of independent filmmaking?

S: I hope it means that my independence from the studio struc-ture is not just physical, but aesthetic. I hope that with my work I can encourage other people to make films on their own without the pressure of the studio telling them to change the story or cast somebody who's an untalented schmuck. Twenty-five percent of the people out there must feel that there are stories they want to tell and will hold out, more or less, to make that story. And then there're twenty-five percent who are fooled by the studio into thinking that that's what they're doing. They're the kind of people you meet at a cocktail party and they're always apologizing for their movie because the studio pressured them or lied to them — it's all bullshit. I always say, "Fuck the studio, don't let them make your movie. Do something else. Make a cheaper movie." And then there are those who'd sell their mothers to make a nice living.

H: Your films don't have the same kind of slickness that is expected of much larger-budgeted studio pictures.

S: I want to put people up on the screen, and my style needs to serve that. When I have more money, like I did with *Eight Men Out* and *Matewan*, I don't try to make things slicker, but, sure, I can do more with the camera. For instance, with *Matewan* I got Haskell Wexler to shoot it, so I could get a hell of lot more done with him in seven weeks than I could with a less experienced director of photography who might be very good, but just doesn't have the experience to move more efficiently. More than slickness, I have trouble seeing that studio pictures tend not to have any kind of recognizable human behavior. You can refer to the world, but it can never be too upsetting. When I write a script for other people, I tend to think ahead about the kind of things that will come up with the executives. They don't like complex characters. For instance, in *Baby, It's You* one problem I had was making the woman smarter than the guy. You know that's one reason they're not going to stay together is that she's smarter than he is, and that's taboo in Hollywood movies.

H: When that film was released everyone was speculating that you had finally become a "Hollywood" director. What happened?

S: *Brother From Another Planet.* Look, there are two dozen movies I want to make and some of them are never going to be commercial enough for Hollywood because the story may be too controversial or just too small of a project for the studio to take on. I'd like to quote Robert Altman. He has a wonderful saying: "There's no such thing as a low-budget movie—there's only an appropriately budgeted movie." He's absolutely right and I'm sorry that *Baby, It's You* ended up like it did. I had a huge custody battle over the final cut of the film. The bottom line was that Paramount owned the rights and I got stuck with that in my contract. And it didn't help that we entirely disagreed over the direction of the film. For a while, I left the project and they did their own cut which they test-marketed, and, fortunately for me, it demographically didn't do any better than mine. By threatening that I wanted my name taken off as writer/director, they finally let me go with my version of the film. They probably thought they weren't going to make any money on it anyhow. They certainly didn't want the negative publicity in the trades, and it certainly wasn't going to put me on any studio "A" list for directors. It was just a bad experience. At that point I decided that I didn't want to direct anything unless I had complete casting control and control over final cut—which I got for my next studio picture, *Eight Men Out.*

H: It's amazing how you're able to maintain your individualistic, noncommercial style and at the same time reckon with the overwhelming furies of the motion picture business and its notion of film as a commodity rather than an art form.

S: Well, the noncommercial aspect of my filmmaking is probably not intentional [laughs]. That's just the way things have shaken down. But I've been able to survive, and unlike most other independent filmmakers, I know I have a good "bread job," which is writing screenplays for other people [*Clan of the Cave Bear, The Howling, The Lady in Red,* among others]. So at times, when my career as a director, such as it is, would have stalled, I've been able to say, "Well, I'll just finance the movie myself, and I'll kind of stay in the game that way." No one has ever tapped me on the shoulder and said, "Go be a director, here's a lot of money." I financed my first film, *Return of the Secaucus Seven,* I financed part of my second film, *Lianna,* I was the only investor in *Brother From Another Planet,* and I was one of the few investors in *Matewan.* And all that came from screenwriting for other people. So there's a real aspect of vanity press to it, which is that I've been able and willing to invest in my own movies and that gives me a certain amount of independence as long as my movies don't cost much. And that's the second part of it, which is realizing that I have a sense of what's commercial in a thousand-print-release kind of way, and what's commercial in a forty-print-release kind of way. Since most of the movies I make go out with a hundred prints or less, at least to start with, and then build up word-of-mouth, I have to realize that it's a steep hill to climb and that I probably shouldn't spend too much on the production of the movie.

H: What kind of advice would you give to filmmakers trying to finance a project independently?

S: Well, be born wealthy. That always helps. I didn't do it, but you know, that doesn't mean somebody else couldn't [laughs]. I'd say that as you're figuring out how to approach things, be very honest with yourself, and that means you're going to have to do a certain amount of research. If you're going to go to somebody and say, "I want you to invest in this film," and they say, "Well, what do you think its financial prospects are going to be?" you should be pretty well versed in what they're going to be. You should be able to point to a half-dozen films that came out of left field, just like your film is going to come out of left field. You should be able to say why it will work if it's not an exploitation film, does it have sex in it, does it have violence in it?—all those things that investors look for when they're selling the videocassette rights. For instance, does the film have any stars in it? Show them that there are three films just like yours that made it, so they have such and such chance of making their money back. So I really think that you have to study the business side. You just can't say that you're going to create some art and expect all those business people to give you what you want. Because there's always a lot of money involved, you have to be shrewd or wealthy.

H: Did you pick a lot of this up during your days with Roger Corman?

S: I picked up the sense of what costs money and what doesn't, what you can do with just a lot of creative energy and labor working on your side, and what really is going to cost you cash. Working on his movies as a writer, and being on the set of a couple, and seeing how they turned out, I really got a sense of, well, this you can do with good intentions and a lot of labor and this is going to cost you money.

H: How do you wish Hollywood would change?

S: I wish the studios might show a little more courage and bring some diversity to the cinema. But directors also need to be more responsible. They've become too cynical. The studios lie about profits—nobody's percentage points are worth anything, so everybody wants everything up front. So now there's this cynical idea that once I talk them into making a movie, I've got them over a barrel: I can go over budget by five million dollars on a ten-million-dollar movie and they can't tell me what to do because we've already started rolling the cameras. Basically, your responsibility as a director is to stay in budget, and if you can't, ask for more up front.

H: Do you want to come back to Hollywood to direct?

S: Not especially. You know, I don't have anything against it, but to me it's just a location. If I were going to set something in Los Angeles, I'd go there. I tend to like to shoot things on location rather than in a studio. If I were going to go to Hollywood, it would have to be a regional film that took place in Los Angeles.

Filmography

1980   *Return of the Secaucus Seven*
1982   *Lianna*
1982   *Baby, It's You*
1984   *The Brother From Another Planet*
1987   *Matewan*
1988   *Eight Men Out*

DAVID CRONENBERG

Nothing to Fear

Canadian director David Cronenberg has galvanized audiences with his provocative horror films for nearly two decades. Fighting strict censorship laws in Canada, he has found popular acceptance in a country whose film tradition is firmly rooted in documentary filmmaking. Although some critics have berated him in the past for the graphic violence in his films, moviegoers continue to embrace his passion for the grotesque and macabre.

Cronenberg is an articulate, well-read scholar who is soft-spoken. On the surface he seems like any ordinary guy in plastic framed glasses and that he must mentally be as far removed from the subjects of his films as Dracula was from daylight, but after a few minutes in the same room with him, one can't help but get the impression that his glasses may be windows to some very bizarre fantasies. His body of work confirms this. *They Came From Within* (1975), *The Brood* (1980), *Scanners* (1980) and *Videodrome* (1983) are horrifying looks into a variety of psychotic worlds. They also happen to be films that have drawn accolades outside Canada. Both American critics and filmmakers like Martin Scorsese have praised Cronenberg for his original cinematic vision, comparing his films to the work of Luis Buñuel.

Born on the Ides of March in the middle of World War II, Cronenberg was raised by parents who enjoyed occupations in the arts. His father, a columnist for the *Toronto Telegram* and a contributing editor to *Detective* magazine, and his mother, a professional pianist, brought Cronenberg and his sister Denise up in a north Toronto suburb and encouraged both children to pursue creative endeavors. Enthralled by music, science, literature and movies, David grew up a voracious reader and wrote science fiction and fantasy stories, at a very early age, submitting several to a number of publications. Upon matriculating at the University of Toronto in 1963, he chose to enter the Honours Science Program. However, shortly after his writing abilities were recognized with Canada's prestigious Epstein Award, he changed his major to English Language and Literature, subjects he embraced so passionately that he finished first in his class at University College.

While considering an M.A. degree, he embarked on his first short film, *Transfer* (1966), a story about a psychiatric patient who becomes obsessed by his therapist. Perhaps making the film itself became a kind of therapy for Cronenberg, for he immediately felt so taken by the experience that he canceled all plans of graduate school and began work on his first two feature length films, *Stereo* (1969) and *Crimes of the Future* (1970). After a brief period spent in Europe on a Canada Council Grant, he returned to Toronto in 1972 to embark on a new series of feature films that culminated in *Rabid* (1977), the story of a woman who finds a monstrous growth on her body after a skin graft operation. The film, which consolidated his reputation as a horror filmmaker, ultimately led to his most provocative early work, *The Brood*, starring Samantha Eggar as a wicked femme fatale who gives birth to a litter of evil, ravenous creatures. While making *The Brood*, one journalist asked Cronenberg if the portrayal of the female antagonist had anything to do with his former wife with whom, at the time, he was fighting a bitter child-custody battle. In the same interview he was also asked if the slow painful deaths of his parents, both of whom succumbed to horrible illnesses, might have been an influence on his work. Offended by even the idea of taking an autobiographical approach to his filmmaking, Cronenberg only responded, "I don't know where the stories come from," although he does admit that making his latest film, *Dead Ringers* (1988), was in some ways "cathartic."

David Cronenberg's success in the United States, coupled with his persistent struggle to attain recognition in Canada, led to two of his biggest commercial successes, *The Dead Zone* (1983) and his popular remake of *The Fly* (1986), both of which were produced in Toronto with American financing. Recently, he directed *Dead Ringers*, his most provocative work to date and his first feature to transcend the horror genre. This frightening, disturbing work—winner of ten Genie Awards (Canada's equivalent of the Academy Awards) and the Los Angeles Film Critics' Award for Best Director—examines the psychological makeup of unbalanced, co-dependent twin gynecologists, a relationship loosely based on Bari Wood and Jack Geasland's novel, *Twins*, which is based on the true story of respectable twin doctors whose double suicide shocked Manhattan in the late 1970s.

HICKENLOOPER: Why do you find the horror genre most appealing?

CRONENBERG: Well, it was totally natural for me when I started to write, even before I thought about filmmaking. It seems natural to me to go where the primal energies and concerns are. With horror you are plugged directly and immediately into those things, there's no pussy-footing around. You draw the current from those sockets. It's very serious to me, I hope not in a boring way, but I couldn't make a film that felt frivolous. It doesn't mean I couldn't make a comedy. You can make a serious comedy I suppose, but it's so hard making a movie and it takes so long and involves such an incredible expenditure of energy that you really have to be plugged into a few sockets drawing on that current, or you just run out. Horror is not frivolous—it seems to cut away all the extraneous material and get right down to the basics. Of course, there *are* frivolous films within the genre, and why not?

H: Do you have reservations about adapting material directly from a novel, as opposed to indirectly, as you did with *Dead Ringers*?

C: I only had two experiences with any kind of book at all. One was *Twins*, on which *Dead Ringers* was based, and from that I didn't feel much need to use anything except the basic premise. The second was *Dead Zone*, and, ironically enough, it was by throwing the book away that I ended up making a movie that people thought was a most faithful adaptation of Stephen King's novel. And in fact, point for point, it's incredibly different from the book, but the tone somehow remains and it is the tone that people remember. If I had been faithful to the details, I would not have been faithful to the book. And I suspect that is always going to be true. If you try to do a literal adaptation of a book, you just get the husk, not the life.

H: Your films seem to evoke fears found in the collective unconscious. What might be locked up in your own unconscious?

C: If we are speaking strictly in Jungian terms, you only need to look into your own mind for the answer to that. If these fears are truly collective, then I am not the only one who has them. I don't feel that I'm a particularly paranoid person. I'm not a fearful or pessimistic person, and I know a lot of people who are heavy hitters on all of those accounts, but I don't live like that and I don't want to. So I don't think there is a direct correlation between what may be unique to my own unconscious mind and what I put on the screen. However, if you want to tap into the collective unconscious, then you only need to lose your inhibitions when you are writing and uncover what is covered up. That leads you to your natural instinct, and part of that is becoming very childlike. It's like what Miro said about trying to get back to painting the way he did when he was five years old. I think that's absolutely true. There is a certain sense of play on a film set when you get rid of all those layers of sophistication and cultural accretion and get back to some basics. That's the reason horror has such universal appeal. It translates better than any other genre from country to country because it is so innate.

H: Marc Boyman, who produced *The Fly*, pointed out that you are continually fascinated with the question of how long you can love someone who is changing, in this case changing physically.

C: It's a smaller part of a larger question relevant only to *The Fly*. The bigger question is that of identity. What does an identity consist of and is there a continuity of some kind in personality? Is there an absolute form of self from the beginning to the end of a person's life? Is it mental, is it physical? If you change yourself

THE RISING RESPECTABILITY OF THE B-MOVIE

extremely in a physical way and consequently change yourself mentally, then are you the same person? You have the sense that you are, but is that just an illusion? On a romantic, personal level is this transformation different from the way you or I change? How would it affect us if we're involved in this person's life?

H: Is that what particularly interested you about the twin charac-ters in *Dead Ringers*—their physical uniqueness?

C: Yes, the idea that being a twin was physically as close as you could get. This was my experiment. I look at each film as sort of an experiment in the lab. These twins that we're studying in this par-ticular experiment are my creatures. Now I'm being deliberately extreme and it sounds very cold, and of course I don't feel totally that way. But it's the only time we have two human bodies that are identical, as identical as bodies can ever get, yet their minds are obviously different. It's really a science-fiction movie except that it's loosely based on a true story. But the whole same-body/dif-ferent-mind construct launches you into endless meditation on all kinds of things, including sexuality. That's why I was never just interested in doing a movie about twins. It was when it was twin gynecologists, who are sort of fated to die together, that I was really excited about that premise?

H: With respect to twins, there are two controversial schools of thought in psychology. Many times those schools cross over but for the most part psychologists attribute the behavioral patterns of twins to either genetics or the environment . . .

C: You know, I've been in some debates with psychologists, par-ticularly regarding censorship, psychotics and the media, and every time I speak to one, my respect for them goes down.

H: There are some who still don't regard psychology as a science.

C: It isn't, but psychologists like to pretend it is. And that pre-tense, when you start to enter the arena of politics and censorship, can get a lot of people into trouble. But anyway, there are some elements of science in it, but most good science is art and when you get down to the basics they are the same. It's like Koestler's book *The Act of Creation.* I think it's totally true; the best artists are scientists and the best scientists are visionaries, and artists and scientists get their inspiration and make their connections in the same way. Where were we?

H: Heredity . . .

C: Right, genetics or the environment. If you look at it that way, it starts to become an old medieval discussion of free will and predestination. In recent studies on twins separated at birth who later meet each other when they are thirty-five, you find that they have married women with the same name, they have the same job, they drive the same car and so on. And it's freaky. Is there a gene that determines the name of your wife? You know, they were both Shirley, so how specific can genetic predetermination be? Then the next question is, does it really matter? The experience of life suggests overwhelmingly that freedom of choice and free will determine our personal makeup despite the fact that there is a lot of evidence to the contrary. With certain characteristics genetics holds eighty percent of it and environment has twenty percent. I don't think that twins are any different from anybody else. The unique thing about twins is that it's the only time we can get to see what the differences are very quickly, especially with twins who are separated at birth. If they're brought up in very different environments, you can then start to say, well, these similarities can't be accidents. These eccentricities, these odd mannerisms, these gestures, they can't have been derived from parental or cultural influences because they have been raised in totally different countries. There's the well-documented case of one twin who was raised in Palestine during the Second World War and another who had been raised in Nazi Germany and yet they were totally different and totally the same at the same time. It's phenomenal, but to me it just accentuates the mystery which is . . . well, it's like what Bertrand Russell said: "What's mind, no matter. What's matter, never mind." They are different and yet they are totally interdependent and it's a great mystery to see how a brain can be dissected piece by piece, yet you can never see the mind, never really know . . . it's very mysterious. My belief is that if your body dies, your brain dies, you mind dies, your soul dies, all of those things die.

H: Moving specifically into the production of *Dead Ringers*. I understand that it took you ten years to get it made. Why so long?

C: The subject is very bizarre, especially if you strip it down at a pitch meeting, a very depressing commercial process. When you don't have a script, but just an idea, and you're going to people for money to get to the position where you can have a script or write a script, you become dependent on two things: on the imaginations of the people you are talking to and upon your own ability as a storyteller. If one or both of those things is not working, then you don't make a movie. I think often, after the fact, people see the movie and they say, "Oh, that's what he was talking about. I wouldn't have minded making that." It was just one of those projects which was very difficult to sell.

H: In the past critics have questioned the sexual politics of your work. Canadian film critic Robin Woods wrote about how your projects have a dominant patriarchal ideology and that you have a tendency to place your female protagonists in submissive positions.

C: Is that on their knees or hanging by their toes? Listen, Robin Woods is a lovely guy, but I really think he's destroyed himself as a critic by becoming very schematic in a militant and political way. It's gotten to the point where you can predict what he is going to say about every movie because it's a political response rather than some other kind. I'm not saying that you can't have a political stance evident in your criticism, but I think it's become too rigid with him. You know, he ended up having to applaud directors whose movies he knew were no good, but which were politically correct. I really don't think that his analysis of my films stands out at all. I haven't read his response to either *The Fly* or *Dead Ringers*, so I don't know what he's saying now.

It's interesting that almost everyone asks me if anybody else has attacked me for *Dead Ringers*. But nobody attacks me! They say couldn't someone see this movie as being these two guys who have this wonderful relationship, and then this woman, portrayed as a kind of Eve, evil apple-bearing Eve, comes along and gives them drugs instead of apples and breaks up their strong male bond which inevitably destroys them. Of course, the people who say this don't actually propose it themselves because they usually know better. It's only been one or two reviews that sort of took that tone and I don't think it holds up at all. I mean, these two guys are strange right from the beginning. It's obvious that I'm not present-ing them as some kind of ideal. And look at the Geneviève Bujold character. She is very strong and very human and very textured and turns out to be a lot more self-aware than they are. It's meant to be ironic when Elliot says, "She's an actress, she's a flake, you never know who she really is." In fact, she ultimately does know who she is and it is they who don't know who they are. I think it's just the idea of having gynecology in the film that really sets a lot of people's teeth on edge. And they gird for war because gynecol-ogy is one of the quiet arenas of sexual battle these days. Even when it's a woman who is the gynecologist it doesn't seem to de-fuse that. I actually did do an interview with a guy in England who totally freaked out on his own TV show and actually walked off his own set.

H: I hope it wasn't live.

C: No, it wasn't live, it was for MTV, but he kept saying, "My God, gynecology, why gynecology?" And I said, "Well, if you calm down, I will tell you." I told him I wanted to discuss sexual politics and make the audience uneasy, and all he could say was "But I mean, gynecology, why gynecology?" And he kept saying this over and over again until he finally just walked off. His crew was totally bewildered. They said they had never seen him do anything like that before. That's sort of the closest I've ever come to being at-tacked for *Dead Ringers*. I was so befuddled by his outrage that I never actually figured out what it was. That, I have to say, is very rare, and I think that both *Dead Zone* and *The Fly* were instrumental in laying those things to rest. I think *Videodrome* really disturbed a lot of people because it was discussing those things very directly and had a scene in which Debbie Harry burns her breast with a cigarette. It was very provocative, especially to feminists.

H: How did you respond to their objections?

C: We had to discuss it very specifically scene by scene. When-ever I had a discussion with a feminist—and by the way, I consider myself a feminist. I mean, I don't see myself on opposite sides of the fence except when it's militant and extreme and it's someone who wants us all to pretend that women and men are the same in every way. I'm a feminist in the sense that I believe men and women should be considered the same with respect to job oppor-tunities, the basics. To me it's obvious that women and men are very different. And if you try to pretend that that's not true you only get into trouble. You can solve the problems that exist by accepting what the differences are and understanding what they mean to us in different cultural situations—so when it's a hot situ-ation to begin with, and when we start talking about what the movie means, then it always gets defused, and whomever I'm dis-cussing it with tends to realize it's not what they thought. If you're heavily into semiotics, there's always the danger of becoming an image policeman or woman and then the idea of just the image itself, of a woman burning her own breast with a cigarette, is for-bidden. If I ever get to talk to militant feminists or semioticians, it becomes hopeless. Because for them the film has no meaning, it's just a mass of imagery, and the imagery is bad. The fact that it shows men being tortured too doesn't seem to matter to them. However, when you have a scene where a woman is being whipped, it's bad because they immediately make a bunch of as-sumptions. Namely, you put that scene in because a) you want to whip women and b) you think your audience wants to see women whipped and wants to whip women. Those things all follow for them. There's no room for complication or discussion of the strange or of the psychology of the human heart. You can't talk about that. I get nowhere with those people. But then again, I don't run into them too often.

H: I read an article from 1981 which quoted you as saying "The more blood the better. It's the needed ingredient if you want to cause fear." However, a director like Alfred Hitchcock might have disagreed . . .

C: Gee, I bet you that I didn't really say that. Go ahead anyway.

H: Well, if you didn't, my question is moot. Is that something you believe?

C: Did you mention Alfred Hitchcock?

H: My second question was that a director like Hitchcock might disagree. He felt strongly that suspense created through montage was the best way to evoke fear.

C: My main purpose is not to cause fear. Frankly, that's why I don't think I said that, but maybe in a moment of flippancy I did. First of all, when people say that about Hitchcock, I say, "Have you seen *Frenzy*?"—not for the blood but for the scenes of excruciating on-screen violence, like raping a woman, strangling her to death with his tie. Now, I have never done a scene as rough as that in my whole life. And I have to say that part of Hitchcock's restraint was imposed on him by the censorship of the times. His later films are much more violent and graphic. Secondly, you really have to get into your relationship with filmmaking there. You see, Hitchcock liked to pretend that he was a manipulator of people, a master puppeteer, and that his movies were manipulating emotions. He liked to pretend that he was a scientist, very aloof and just pushing the buttons. I say "pretend" because it's obvious now that there's a lot more of him, his own strange psychology, in his movies than maybe he would have liked to admit. To me it just means that he's an artist. It also means that the public stance he took about his art was just a public stance. But we'll take it at face value. My relationship with my audience is not that—I don't feel that I am a manipulator. I feel like I am sharing an experience with them, I'm recounting it, I'm telling them the story. I'm waking up from a dream and saying, "Okay, I've got to share this with you, I've got to tell this incredible dream to someone." You know, everybody has had that experience. Why do you want to tell it to somebody? Well, partly to defuse it, to defuse the scary parts by defusing it amongst other people. But also it's to share the good parts. And to me, that's my relationship to the audience. I don't feel like a manipulator. Of course, there are elements of manipulation in any art. All that manipulation means on that level is simply that you try to define what kind of stimulus will get what kind of response. And then, of course, you must always remember that you're also making the movie for yourself.

H: With respect to violence, though, don't you think the law of diminishing returns applies? Once an audience sees gratuitous violence over and over again they eventually grow numb to it.

C: What if your purpose is to make the audience numb to violence? Then it's a perfectly acceptable thing to do. So what I'm really saying, not to be flippant, is that you have to figure out what your purpose is as a filmmaker in making this particular film. You can't make assumptions. For example, most of the violence in my films is phenomenal, fantastic. It's stuff that the audience cannot be expected to imagine if it weren't shown. To take the most famous example—the exploding head in *Scanners*—if I had decided to cut, allowing the audience to only hear an explosion offscreen, would you have know what had happened? The answer is no, of course not, because you have never seen that before. Now, of course I could have some third person say, "Oh my god, that guy's head exploded," but then you're obviously into a different kind of moviemaking. That's more like radio. I would also like to point out that later in *Scanners*, when the Patrick McGoohan character is about to be executed with a forty-five automatic, and the gun is put to the back of his head and the trigger is pulled, we don't see his head blow apart, and that's because the audience does know what it is. They don't have to see it, they understand. You could probably pick one or two instances where this is not strictly true, but in most cases, and *Videodrome* is a perfect example, there's no way that you're going to understand it if it's not shown because it's not within the audience's experience. I'm inventing stuff. It's phenomenal. It's really dream imagery, and it's not particularly realistic in a very basic sense. When a man puts his hand into his stomach, how do we convey that without showing it? It's a very straightforward problem. So when it comes to screen violence— not in every instance but in most of the most noted instances— there is no alternative but to show it.

H: Two of your most successful films were American productions, *The Fly* and *Dead Zone*. Could you tell me some of the differences between directing Canadian and American productions? Are there differences in creative freedom?

C: Well, they were both shot in Canada. I never shot a film any-where but Canada. I've never shot an IATSE [International Alliance of Theatrical and Stage Employees] film. I mean, IATSE is here as well, and it's not that I don't think they're any good, it's just that I've grown up with a union called the ACFC—Association of Canadian Film Crafts people—and so they weren't, strictly speaking, American productions. Technically there is a point system we use in Canada. Neither *The Fly* nor *The Dead Zone* officially qualified as a Canadian film in terms of our Canadian film awards, the Genies, which are the equivalent of the Oscars in the U.S. I think the only problem that we ever had on either *The Fly* or *Dead Zone* was that we had an American producer working up in Canada, having to make films the Canadian way, and at first being paranoid about it, and worried about it, and then loving it. In fact they came back to make other films. Certainly Deborah Hill came back a couple of times to Toronto after *The Dead Zone*. I know that Stuart Cornfeld, who was the producer on *The Fly*, has wanted to come back but he just hasn't had a film that worked that way. So really I haven't had American film production experience.

H: In the past you have compared the relationship between the U.S. and Canada to yin and yang, in the sense that what is worshiped in the U.S. is despised in Canada. What differences do you find between the Canadian and U.S. cultures?

C: Gee . . . I've said some very provocative things, haven't I? Well, I think it's obviously not so clear-cut, and that's always been a problem in Canada, in terms of our own identity. In fact, maybe here we've stumbled onto the reason that the real subject of most of my films is identity. Because I'm a Canadian, you see. And we are much more like Beverly and Elliot, the two twins in *Dead Ringers*. I mean, it all begins with our past and where we came from. We didn't have a revolution. We got our independence from England diplomatically and politically. When it came to opening up the West, we sent in the Mounties with guns, and only when the area was policed, did the citizens go in without arms. And that is perhaps one of the reasons that we have a totally different attitude toward guns and gun control here than you do in the States. We just don't expect citizens to have guns, that's all. We don't even think of it as a right or not a right. It's odd. Why would you want a gun? It's a completely different approach. And I think that gives you an idea of where many other things come from. In the States, independence and independence of action is revered almost to the exclusion of everything else, and in Canada, social groups are the preferred model for taking action. You never take the law into your own hands. You don't even think about it. You get a bunch of people together, you talk about it, and then you do something. This is not to say that we don't have people who worship independence, power and money in Canada. But it's the proportion I suppose. In Canada there is a very ambivalent relationship between society at large and stardom. People who are stars are exciting, but it's also considered a bit arrogant to be a star. Does that mean you are saying you are better than everybody else or are you trying to show everybody up by being so good? You know, we do have that sort of ambivalence, which is why we prefer that our stars come from somewhere else. Then it doesn't cause that problem.

H: Canada doesn't really have any kind of star system, does it?

C: Well, it's okay to be a star if you are Wayne Gretzky, but you see, Wayne Gretzky is on a team, right? And he spends a lot of his time telling everybody how great his teammates are and how he couldn't have done it without them, and that's a great Canadian star. He's a team player. That's our idea of a star. There's that old Chinese proverb, "The nail that sticks out the furthest is the first to be hammered down." There is that in Canadian culture and the bad part is that if you happen to be spectacularly good at something, you might have trouble getting a chance to express it fully in Canada.

H: Canada is more puritanical?

C: It depends. I don't think that Toronto is more puritanical than Pittsburgh, but I think in general, yes. Our censor board in Ontario has powers that would be considered totally unconstitutional in the United States. We censor films here before they are shown. That can't happen in the States, so I'd say there's a bit of

Scottish-Presbyterian background in Canada. That's where that tone springs from. But there is a good part of that, which is that Canada tends to be much more peaceful, more sane. For instance, Toronto is a much better place to bring up kids than in L.A. So I live in Toronto by preference because our social programs are better developed—it's just the way we think: Society and government should take care of people who can't take care of themselves. Obviously we're not perfect at it, but it's the proportions that really count. And overall, I think we do a good job. But I must say, I'm really glad that the U.S. is just right across the border. For me it's the best. You need the yin and the yang. And you need both halves to make a perfect home.

H: Because of your particular style, I understand that you found it difficult to find acceptance in the Canadian film industry.

C: Yes, I did. When I made *Shivers*, which in the States is called *They Came From Within*, it was a huge scandal in Canada, which had absolutely no tradition of horror filmmaking at all. Again, our tradition is more socially oriented. The National Film Board, a government organization, has always preferred the John Grierson tradition of documentary filmmaking. They see real people as people who sort of work the land, so if you're going to make a movie, a fiction movie, it should be about people like that. That's real moviemaking. And to make a film that's horrific, and even worse, fantastic in its inventions, well, that was unheard of. There was no tradition for that and people weren't able to deal with it, especially government agencies who put some money into the film. They were really under fire in the houses of Parliament because of *Shivers*. It was a big scandal here, a huge scandal. But that has settled down, mind you.

H: I heard that you're starring in a Clive Barker film.

C: Star? I don't know if that's the right word. I do have the third lead and that is a big role. We'll see after the fact whether I'm starring or mooning or something, I don't know.

H: You're not playing a gynecologist?

C: No, but I am playing a psychiatrist. You know, I'm getting typecast already.

Filmography

1966   *Transfer* (short)
1969   *Stereo*
1970   *Crimes of the Future*
1974   *Squirm*
1975   *They Came From Within*
1977   *Rabid*
1977   *Fast Company*
1980   *The Brood*
1981   *Scanners*
1983   *Videodrome*
1983   *The Dead Zone*
1986   *The Fly*
1988   *Dead Ringers*
1991   *Naked Lunch*

JOHN CARPENTER

The Banality of Evil

John Carpenter's youthful looks and fervent idealism may easily veil the fact that he's been making films in Hollywood for the past two decades. But the success of his career as one of Hollywood's most acclaimed horror/science-fiction directors hasn't in any way lured him into a life of complacency. A vocal epitome of many of the political and social values that came to characterize the sixties, Carpenter isn't inhibited about commenting on the current state of affairs inside and outside of Hollywood. His didactic thoughts steer our conversation toward the nation's new wave of post-Reagan conservatism.

"The Republicans are slowly continuing to kill us," he says, referring to the controversial obscenity clause that the National Endowment for the Arts has adopted under pressure from right-wing extremists. Many critics believe that the clause is a flagrant blow to the First Amendment. "We're surrendering all of our rights to fanatics and corporations," Carpenter adds. "The conservative tide has washed us from the 1990s back into the 1950s, excuse me, the 1930s, pre-Roosevelt." But John Carpenter isn't one just to sit by and let the world change around him without a struggle. Recently his outrage manifested itself in his 1988 film, *They Live.*

"I just didn't want to do another alien picture," he says. "I felt it was time to make a social satire about the state of things in this country." The film's premise is that a civilization of aliens is controlling the politicians, businessmen and media figures of America, who are in turn feeding the public subliminal messages that are keeping them mindlessly apathetic. "It was a film about the eighties; how Ronald Reagan dismantled the American middle class and eroded the moral values of society. He kept pumping us with the message that we were so great. The problem was that we were so busy gloating that we didn't see what was going on around us. Just look outside. I've never seen so many homeless in my entire life—and not drug addicts and alcoholics—I mean, respectable lower-middle-class people." Carpenter's expression turns sour. "But maybe that's why nobody was interested in seeing the film. Who wants to hear that your civilization is in decline. Instead of doing something about it, people would rather stay at home and watch "Cheers." It really depresses me, but you can't surrender to it."

Surrendering is something Carpenter has never been accused of. In fact, the director garnered a reputation for his resistance to authority while he was a student at the University of Southern California's film school. When the Department of Cinema discouraged him from expanding his short film, *Dark Star*, into a feature-length film, he stole the negative. "I was very ambitious. I wanted to take my film and get it seen in the real world. USC had nothing to do with Hollywood realities."

In 1978 he wrote the screenplay to the moderately successful thriller *The Eyes of Laura Mars*, but it wasn't until later in the year that he burst onto the screen with his own film, *Halloween*, a low-budget horror thriller that was soon to become the most profitable independent film of all time. Carpenter also received a substantial amount of critical support. Andrew Sarris called it "the most frightening film in years." Perhaps not since Alfred Hitchcock's *Psycho* had so many screams been heard coming out of theaters. Carpenter is delighted with the thought.

Born in Bowling Green, Kentucky, John Carpenter was raised by parents who encouraged him to be creative. His father, a music professor and studio musician who played back-up violin and viola for Roy Orbison, Johnny Cash and Brenda Lee, introduced Carpenter to music at a young age. "I started learning piano, violin and guitar at the age of five," he says. "I thought I wanted to be a musician until the day I saw *It Came From Outer Space* in 3-D. For me that was everything I ever wanted in life." At the age of eight, Carpenter got his first 8mm camera and began making home movies with his friends. "I kept telling everybody that I was going to go to Hollywood and become a famous director," he continues. Going to the movies also became a ritual for the young enthusiast. "Howard Hawks's film version of *The Thing* became my favorite," he remembers, speaking fondly of a film that he would eventually go on to remake in 1982.

In 1966 Carpenter enrolled in Western Kentucky University where he spent most of his time playing bass guitar in a rock and roll band. "If I'd stayed in Kentucky, I'd be a full-time musician today." But his passion for film prevailed, and it wasn't long before his father reluctantly let him venture to Southern California where he enrolled at USC's prestigious film school, the program which had just graduated fellow alumnus George Lucas two years before.

HICKENLOOPER: *Dark Star*, your first feature film, started out as a student short at USC. Tell me something about the origin of the project and how you expanded it.

CARPENTER: It was going to be a senior thesis film and began out of an unusual combination of elements: reaction to *2001*, which had been out about a year and a half earlier, and my interest in *M.A.S.H.*, Robert Altman's film, which was a funky, left-wing look at war. I'd always believed that machines fall apart, as opposed to what *2001* was showing—the glory of being able to fly, glory of space and so forth. Usually, these things fall apart very quickly. If you own a car, you know that. And that's what appealed to me in making *Dark Star*. Also, at USC and in movies coming out of Hollywood, nobody was doing any black comedy, nothing absurdist, not even science fiction. This was, of course, long before *Star Wars*. I teamed up with Dan O'Bannon, a classmate at USC.

H: Doesn't he have a featured role in *Dark Star*?

C: He plays one of the characters. We developed a short film— basically we were thinking about twenty minutes at the time.

H: To tell the entire story?

C: Well, twenty minutes involved simply showing the last act of the bomb, the phenomenological bomb, introducing the characters and so forth. It was going to be, at least in my mind, much more of a streamlined Hollywood film; in other words, it wasn't experimental. I had structure that would show a command and respect for the kind of Hollywood movies that have traditional narratives. We spent two years working on it and almost had it finished when we got an offer from a very small Canadian distributor, who thought it might be a good idea that could be expanded into a feature. He was willing to put up $10,000 to do this. This was the summer of '72 and it just seemed like a real good thing to do at that point. It would mean that one way or the other, whether it was a major distributor or minor distributor, there'd be a feature film to show for all the effort. So O'Bannon and I went through the movie and came up with a feature version of it. By padding and expanding the middle, we created a second act which deals with their bombing one planet followed by living aboard the spaceship before they come to the second planet at the very end. We also wanted to develop O'Bannon's character since he was available to us as an actor.

H: This was after you graduated from USC?

C: Well, I never graduated. I sort of drifted away.

H: You had a falling-out with the school?

C: It was over the way they treated students at the time; the way they still do from what I understand. You see they have a rather unproductive policy which states that a panel of faculty members, made up of Hollywood wanna-bes and has-beens, decides which students get to make what films. It's all very political and in the end the movies made are owned by the university. It's not exactly the most healthy environment for student filmmakers. Anyway, when we finally showed the expanded version of *Dark Star*, the then-head of USC called me up and said, "We want our movie back." And I said, "It's not your movie. You don't own it. It didn't sign anything that says that you own it. I paid for every frame of it. Who the hell do you think you are?" So Bernard Cantor, who's now deceased, went to their lawyers and said, "Why don't you go after Carpenter?" and their lawyers said, "We can't win. He's right." By the time we finished *Dark Star*, cut it all together, we realized we'd spent all the $10,000 that we had just shooting the new material.

H: What kind of critical response did your film get?

C: Kind of snotty. I remember my shock at reading *Variety*. They put it down as a kind of student spoof. They remembered the 16mm grainy origins and I thought, "My God, this is not what I had in mind at all." And at the time, I truly expected to be able to get some kind of directing job from it. I mean I was seeing other movies and saying, "I can at least do that." But I didn't get shit out of it—nothing, zero, goose eggs.

H: Why do you think the British press and audiences appreciated it more?

C: I don't really know. Europeans look at movies a little bit differently than we do. They have a different idea of cinema, at least critics do. I think the critical responses there are always helpful when you're starting out—to get somebody behind you and say this is worth watching. My film really appealed to them, much to my surprise and delight.

H: You've made films both independently and for the studios. Can you tell me something about your experience working under each?

C: It's very different, and then very much alike. After a certain point in filmmaking, the same problems start occurring over and over again. Even on a big film you have problems with time—you never have enough time. When you make a big-budget film, there is lots of pressure to be commercially acceptable. It better be great because you're spending all this money. So the risk taking, in terms of subject matter, the kind of treatment, or trying something offbeat, becomes overwhelming. In the end, you are forced to go with what the audience wants. So you tend to end up making formula films in big-budget movies.

In independent filmmaking, if you can really get control of the film—and that means getting the people who put the money up to let you have final cut and creative control—you can try to do something unusual. Sometimes you fail and sometimes you succeed, but at least you give it a shot. You still have to get good performances out of the actors, you have to get some complicated shot done against impossible odds—all the problems inherent in filmmaking. There's a lot less willingness to be quirky in a big-budget film. I enjoy each. It's really nice to have all the technical ability at your disposal when you're making a big film. When we were making *The Thing*, we shot the whole movie without any special effects and then spent almost eight months doing all the creature stuff in a warehouse. It was great to be able to do that. You bring back the crew, you rebuild the sets and off you go. On *Starman* we got to work with ILM [Industrial Light & Magic] in San Rafael, California, and they're terrific at special effects. With a big budget you can order it like pizza, but on a small budget, you're there at the end of the day with a big cucumber monster and you're trying to make it look good. So, it's more difficult. On the other hand, you have a lot more freedom in independent filmmaking. I think that's the most important thing after all these years, to have a certain amount of freedom.

H: At the time you made *Big Trouble in Little China* you seemed really bitter about the studios.

C: [laughs] O'Bannon had a great quote about his experiences making *Alien*. It was the same studio I had worked for, Twentieth Century-Fox. I'll try to paraphrase it: "Fox tried to do to me what prisoners do to each other in the prison yard." It's called sodomy. I couldn't have said it better. It was a really terrible experience. I truly, deeply love the movie and had a great time making it. Unfortunately, I was trapped between a regime change and was caught in a lot of political turmoil with some folks who represent the new breed of executive in America.

H: And what is that?

C: I don't know if it's changed a lot from the old days, but I think it has a little bit. They engage in what's called spite fucking.

There's a great deal of enjoyment in destroying people. I watched a lot of people around me destroyed. It's pretty vicious . . .

H: Do they care about movies?

C: No, not at all. They care about "your place." They think they know everything . . . I really can't say more. I might lose my temper. But I will give you an example. One of the times when I went for a meeting over in the executive building at Fox, there were armed guards around the place because there were death threats against the president. That's the kind of personality that you're dealing with.

H: You don't think they're concerned about the quality of the films they make?

C: Sure, as long as it grosses over fifteen million dollars in the first weekend. Money is the bottom line in this business now.

H: You touched upon something you said about your most recent film, *They Live*. You suggested that materialism and capitalism were running rampant at the expense of our humanity.

C: That's obvious, isn't it? That's not a great profound statement. It's just that nobody has the guts to say it. Unrestrained capitalism will destroy us—absolutely.

H: But that's not news either . . .

C: No, it's just that somehow in the eighties everybody just forgot everything about history. The hippies have gotten completely stupid. It's numbing. I look around and people say the most incredible things and I want to say, "Are you kidding? Do you know what you're saying?" I mean, I've been there before. I was even alive.

H: Do you think that the medium of film and television is responsible for perpetuating some of these values?

C: It's hard to say. A lot of people give movies a great deal of influence over folks in our culture. I'm not so sure about that. I suppose that you could say *Star Wars* and its return to a kind of action/adventure/romantic style set a tone for the formulaic eighties movies. But I don't really believe that. I always believe that it's a confluence of events. I think that the political landscape of the eighties had a lot to do with it. The culture confronted the bad old seventies and at the end of the seventies we got our hostages taken in Iran and we were embarrassed and we wanted to feel good again. And by God, we went at it. I think people got bitter about all the civil rights bullshit. You know, "I don't want to pay anymore."

H: The Supreme Court just overturned two civil rights laws. Affirmative action seems to be on its way out.

C: It's unbelievable and it's just that the times have really turned. Because the times are getting so bad now, people are licking their chops for revenge. We saw it happen in Nazi Germany. Now I'm not suggesting that we're all fascists, but, boy, we can sure jump that way. I think the humanity of the country really changed a lot during the eighties. And it's now being reflected in the kind of movies that are getting made.

H: Nietzsche referred to public apathy and ignorance as "the banality of evil." That by not caring, or not thinking, society's moral fabric breaks down and becomes insidiously cruel.

C: I think there's truth in that. You're right—people don't want to think today. I'll never forget my chilling experience with making *The Thing*. We previewed it to what they call a "focus group," which is a bunch of people ranging in ages. After the screening we had a discussion and this one fifteen-year-old gal said, "What happened in the end?" She was referring to the scene when the last two survivors are sitting out in the snow and neither one of them knows if the other is *The Thing*. "What happened?" I said. "Well, the interesting thing is that you have to have to use your imagination." And she said, "Oh, I hate that." I'm dead serious. I felt intensely depressed.

H: Was your version of *The Thing* more faithful to the short story "Who Goes There" than the Howard Hawks version was?

C: Yes. The Hawks version really had nothing to do with imitating "Who Goes There." It was a monster on the loose in the station and it was extremely well done. But at the time, and nobody seems to remember this now, it was vilified by all the science fiction writers. I mean, they hated it. They said it was a betrayal, a betrayal of its source material. Now, I just read this article in *The New York Times* which said it was obviously a classic. Well, it wasn't then. They hated that movie. Now it's become a classic for a variety of reasons. Because Hawks's style is so interesting and the way it was put together is so interesting: the overlapping dialogue and the visual style of it, and the fact that it has a lot of scary moments in it. But at the time, all the science fiction writers who now have amnesia said, "This is just another Frankenstein monster." I remember reading articles at the time, when I was a little boy, because I wanted to see it but my father wouldn't let me. I had to wait several years. They said Hawks just screwed up the short story. What I did in my version of *The Thing* was to try to get a better sense of that paranoia that goes on when you don't know if it's your best friend who goes there.

H: How did the Hawks film influence yours?

C: It really didn't. The Hawks film influenced *Halloween* more than anything else. I mean, I loved the original *Thing*. It's one of my favorite films of all time. I could watch it over and over again. It evokes the time it was made especially well, the early fifties and the McCarthy scare, that your best friend might be a communist. It also had a kind of western feel to it. The same kind of western tone that Hawks used in *Red River*. The western plains this time being a huge circle of ice. Howard Hawks is my favorite director, so there are a lot of things that appeal to me about the original *Thing*. But when I watched it, I realized that I needed to do it very differently. I knew I either had to show the monster or not show it, but put it in shadows. All the literary critics and all the left-wing folks think, well, you shouldn't show the monster because that's kind of tacky and poo-poo. Well, there's another way of going about it. And, boy, if you do it right, if you hit a home run, you create the greatest monster of all time. Look at *Frankenstein*—Boris Karloff, he wasn't in the shadows. So that's what we did. We decided to put it under lights and create a monster like no other seen before. Clearly, that brought the rage of the critics down upon my head. I remember one guy said, "He who lies with slime, rises with slime," or some-thing like that. He called me a pornographer of violence.

H: Did you get any critical support?

C: No.

H: Though *Halloween* was praised for its cinematic style, it also seemed to spark a slew of imitations, like *Friday the 13th*, which has been condemned for its exploitation of violence. How do you view *Halloween* as compared to *Friday the 13th*?

C: It's really hard for me to look at *Halloween* objectively. We went out and made it in twenty days for $300,000—it was a very cheap film. I had loved watching horror movies all my life, and in *Halloween* I was trying to do all the things I wished horror films would have done. Horror movies should definitely scare you. That means things jumping out of the dark at you, and I'd always thought that these guys always did it with the wrong timing. They'd have a shot of somebody looking around the room and you knew that the killer was in there, so they'd always blow it. I just wanted to do it once when it came out when you'd least expect it. The idea would be to turn the audience's expectations completely around. So there you're standing and bang! it happens. The whole idea of the Michael character sitting up in the end, the idea of him being evil which cannot be killed was very appealing. It all came into the idea of *Halloween*. So we did it, and the audience screamed and yelled at it. They had a blast, just like a roller coaster. And I think that was the element that was infinitely copyable, it's so easy to look at. My film just happened to be the first one out of the gate. When I took at *Friday the 13th*, the thing that bothers me about that series is that they intentionally do not try to define character. In other words, we make all the characters the same and we make them all stupid and we do that for the following reason: because we want the audience to yell at the screen. We want the audience to feel superior to these idiots who walk around about to get killed. Well, after a while what you're really doing is making por-nography, in a way. There's no feeling there, they aren't real char-acters that you care about. I think that's what people object to in horror films. It's not really the gratuitous violence, but rather the fact that the writers don't give a shit. That, or they don't know how to write real people.

H: Ken Russell and Michael Cimino both said they have their score in mind before they shoot a foot of film. Perhaps the most classic example of this was Sergei Eisenstein, who worked very closely with Prokofiev in structuring his shots for *Alexander Nevsky*. As a musician and composer, how do you work? Do you ever work on your music beforehand?

C: Never. I don't think about it at all.

H: It never influences your composition?

C: No. And you must understand how a lot of the composition is done. I cut the film and get it in its fine cut, then put it on video-tape. I go to the recording studio and synchronize the videotape with a 24-track recording. And it runs in sync. Then I sit at a synthesizer and without writing a note, I improvise a score. It's all done by watching the movie. It's all done by supporting what's there. I'd get real screwed up if I tried to do it the other way. That's why those guys are all geniuses and I'm not.

H: Many of your films seem to work in a similar way structurally. You start with your characters on one level and at some point you let your audience get ahead of them in the story. Would you tell me something about how you build your stories?

C: It really depends on what kind of movie you're doing. If you're doing a suspense thriller, it's always good to let the audience be a little bit ahead, because then they can get worried about what's going to happen to people. That's just the old-fashioned rule that goes way back to Hitchcock. Let the audience in first. Not always, but at certain points you want your audience to know what's going on and your character to be trying to find it out. Then there's a little tension. I tend to work in an old-fashioned way, in a three-act structure, and when I approach a movie, it usually has some suspense to it. I think the most difficult thing in any film is the character and how he relates to the story, what part of the story he is, if he is the story or serves it. That's always the difficult part.

C: *Starman* seemed to be a real departure for you. What kind of changes did you have to go through to enlighten your audience rather than terrify them?

H: Well, it's interesting. I made a three-hour TV movie in 1978 called *Elvis* with Kurt Russell. It was about Elvis Presley, and basically, in terms of being a director, it's extremely easy when you have good actors and you're doing a movie about people. There's really not much to it from a directorial standpoint—you just pay a lot of attention and do your best. And *Starman* was, in that sense, extremely easy because I had these great actors. I came into the business thinking I could do anything. I wanted to do musicals, westerns, war movies, dramas, everything, and it was a chance to do a big-budget romantic film. The kind of things that I've always been offered have been based on either *Halloween* or *Escape From New York*. And here this big studio said, "Hey would you like to do this?" I said, "Are you kidding? Let's go!" That's how it was done. We shot in the spring of '84 and because it was shot on the road, it was physically difficult. Karen Allen and Jeff Bridges were so good and we had a great time doing it. Everybody loved the project. It had a lot of sweetness and heart to it. It's probably my most optimistic film.

H: Why is that?

C: In most of my work I tend to tap into my pessimism, but not for *Starman*. My pessimistic side works in *The Thing* because it's about pessimism and solipsism, ego. It's about the end of the world and the evil within the superego. I wanted to make a film that would be an allegory about the fact that without trust, without human personality, you get people who are a lot like *The Thing*. But *Starman* is a love story like *The Philadelphia Story*. It's all the classic stories of star-crossed lovers, the lovers who can't live together, but who have an unbreakable bond, like in *Brief Encounter*. I hope that it works on that level, because it touches a little thing inside us. It's a departure because no one has ever seen something like this from me.

C: Tell me the difference between the way you direct a dramatic scene and the way you would direct a horror scene when you're working with an actor?

H: It's not how you work with the actor, it's in what your intention is with the audience. There's one basic thing a director always has to go back to no matter how much trouble he's in or what location he's shooting on, or how difficult the sequence he's doing. You have to put yourself in a dark room someplace and imagine a screen in front of you. Everything that the audience is looking at is on that screen, and you have to jump into that audience all of a sudden and say, "How am I viewing what I'm doing here. How is this going to be seen on the screen?" No matter whether the caterer is poisoning the crew, the producer's coming down, or the actor's throwing a fit. Dramatically, it all happens on a theater screen. So you jump back and say, "How do I want the audience to see what's going on? And how do I want the characters to respond?" That's the way you approach it. Now if you're doing a very emotionally poignant scene like the one between Starman and Jenny in the car when he's got his gun pointed at her—and this is a very dramatic turning point in their relationship—then I'm going to want to be close in on their faces. That's what I'll want to see on the theater screen. But if somebody is coming into a room where there's a psychopathic murderer and they're walking around the room looking for him, and the audience knows he's going to jump out, then that would be an entirely different approach.

H: Was it difficult to bring off *Starman* successfully in the wake of so many other science fiction films?

C: *E.T., Close Encounters, 2001, The Day the Earth Stood Still, The Man Who Fell to Earth, Alien*: you mean all those? No, the hardest part was looking for something very new to bring to it. That's what was scary from the studio's point of view. A lot of people were terrified of this project, but I thought it was a great opportunity for me. I could have never done *E.T.* I would have turned him into the Thing and had him eat Henry Thomas.

H: Do you ever feel pigeon-holed in the horror and science fiction genre?

C: Well, to me that question seems implicitly negative. I get asked it a lot and perhaps it's true. However, I can only respond by saying that I make all the films that I want to make. They all have different intentions and it disturbs me that most people find horror and science fiction suspect genres, not quite legit, especially among critics. People think I do nothing but beheadings, but there's no violence in *Halloween*—it's all implied. Every horror film is cathartic in two ways: being the victim and being the aggressor. In my films, I let you be both, so you get to work that out within yourself, within the safe confines of the theater, and you come out feeling better. Unless you're a critic.

H: Some of your films have been more successful critically than others. Does the negative feedback affect your future projects?

C: Nietzsche also said, "That which does not kill me makes me grow stronger." In another life I have a lot of revenge to take out on folks. I think you're always sensitive to criticism if you care about the movie you're making. If you don't care about it and you don't put your best into it, you don't really want it to be good and effective, it wouldn't mean anything. But no, I always care.

H: Do you have any personal nemesis in the critical world?

C: Critics—they're difficult. I think the Ayatollah was the ultimate critic. When he put the death sentence out on Salman Rushdie, that was it. I worry a little bit about critics. I went through this in film school. We use to have these great debates. The department was divided up into two sections: one was production and one was film history and criticism, and neither side understood the other. And we used to have these talks based around an Indian saying, which is "Don't criticize somebody until you walk in his shoes." And a very, very successful filmmaker friend of mine said, "Well, the critics shouldn't know how to make movies. They should just watch and respond to it." And the other side of the coin is they should try it once to see that it is an act of courage to make a film. They don't understand. So it's a tension. I don't think the standards of a lot of critics are very high. I don't think they go to school for it. In other words, they don't take film history and criticism, they don't major in it. They're kind of like restaurant critics. They can go sit at a table and eat, and if they like it, it's good. Well, wait a minute, there's a little more to it than that. That's my opinion. I know one critic, a very famous one, who sits and eats while he watches. Seriously, he has a big tray brought in and he eats food while he watches movies. Do you know who I'm talking about? Well, come on now. He also looks like it, he's chunky.

Filmography

1970   *The Resurrection of Broncho Billy* (short)
1974   *Dark Star*
1976   *Assault on Precinct 13*
1977   "Someone's Watching Me" (TV)
1978   *Halloween*
1979   "Elvis" (TV)
1979   *The Fog*
1981   *Escape From New York*
1982   *The Thing*
1983   *Christine*
1984   *Starman*
1986   *Big Trouble in Little China*
1987   *Prince of Darkness*
1988   *They Live*

GEORGE ROMERO

I Am Legend

It's the middle of the night in the remote countryside of western Pennsylvania. You find yourself in an abandoned farmhouse. Upstairs lies a corpse, its face partially devoured. You run downstairs, the nausea creeping into your gut. There's no time to rest. You're exhausted, but you've got to stay awake, got to keep moving. You must find wood, anything solid. You begin breaking up the furniture, hammering nails into door and window frames, anything to block passageways into the house. Just then, the phone dies, the lights go out and you find yourself all alone in total darkness. Or are you alone?

Suddenly, you hear a loud thump from outside, then a scratch, a rattle at the front door. A loud bang reverberates through the entire floor, a board snaps, glass shatters, and there they are—hands, a dozen, two dozen, reaching through the windows, groping, clawing at you from the outside. You see glimpses of their contorted faces, their decaying flesh as the foul stench of death surrounds you. Just then, the front door crashes to the floor. They push and stumble their way into the house. As if in slow motion, they drag their decomposing bodies towards you. There's nowhere to run. They're here, the walking dead. And they've come to eat you alive.

Night of the Living Dead (1968) may be the most psychologically terrifying film ever made. Shot on a shoestring budget in the counties north of Pittsburgh, its lurid content horrified audiences and

344

the media around the world. Shortly after it release, it was immediately banned in over fifty countries for its shocking portrayal of cannibalistic zombies, but at the same time it drew attention for its seemingly political content and unusual, frenetic camera work. In the United States the movie was only shown to late-night audiences, crowning its young creator, George Romero, the new cult hero of horror pictures.

In a decade monopolized by rather tame, low-budget monster movies, Romero's film brought something fresh to the genre. Through the use of high-contrast photography, setting up his camera in tight interiors and successfully giving the story a claustrophobic intensity—in addition to exploring a highly taboo subject, cannibalism—he was able to evoke the most primal fears from audiences as no other popular horror director had done before. With the help of a lot of controversy and a media campaign against the film, *Night of the Living Dead* soon made Romero's name a pop legend outside the midnight movie circuit, a reputation which he believes has limited his growth as a director.

"It's very difficult for me to get a film made unless it's got gore in it. I've been pigeon-holed," says Romero with a sad face. "It's a good thing that I like horror pictures," he finishes, adding a half smile. Over the last two decades Romero's reputation as horror director has endured. *Martin* (1979), *Knightriders* (1981), *Creepshow* (1982) and most recently *Monkey Shines* (1989) have demonstrated Romero's constant innovative approach to very original and always chilling tales.

Born and raised in the Bronx, Romero grew up feeling he had an artistic bent in him that he could not freely realize in his neighborhood. When he reached college age, he pursued his aspirations at the Carnegie Mellon Institute in Pennsylvania, alma mater to another pop visionary, Andy Warhol. Shortly after finishing his studies, Romero and a group of friends made a feature-length film and established their own commercial production house, The Latent Image. Shooting everything from industrial films to political campaign spots, the group secured enough financial success to embark on their first major undertaking, *Night of the Living Dead*. The outrage surrounding the film's content and its rising cult status paved the way for the movie's Pittsburgh-based director to embark on a slew of other projects, including two *Living Dead* sequels,

Dawn of the Dead and *Day of the Dead*, part of Romero's extraordi-nary horror trilogy inspired by Richard Matheson's short story "I Am Legend."

HICKENLOOPER: Does "I Am Legend" specifically deal with cannibalism and zombies?

ROMERO: No, no, vampires. It just dealt on an allegorical level with the idea of a new society stepping in and devouring the old. It's been made several times into movies. There was one called *The Last Man on Earth* with Vincent Price which was pretty good.

H: But *Night of the Living Dead* wasn't the first film project you did . . .

R: No, I had started a small company, The Latent Image, a few years before *Night of the Living Dead*. It was a time when there was literally no film production in Pittsburgh whatsoever. We had a couple of cameras and some lights, so we would shoot everything on location. It wasn't too long before we became a commercial house and started to do all kinds of local spots, sometimes political things, and we made money. We just went around to the advertis-ing agencies. There's a lot of industry there, so we got work . . .

H: Why did you find horror most appealing?

R: Well, we wrote a few scripts, and by this time we had already made a feature right out of school, *Expostulation*, which was never quite finished. It was an anthology film, five stories, written by different people. I'm sorry it never got done. Anyway, much of the film was related to horror so I knew it was a genre I could work with. So for $60,000 we went ahead and made *Night of the Living Dead*.

H: At what point did you decide to make a trilogy out of it?

R: The story I had written was in three parts so it basically was a trilogy from the beginning, although part one was preponderant, part two was about a page long and part three was just a para-graph. However, I always had it in three time periods. During the first phase the cannibalism began, but the humans still outnumbered the zombies, and then there was a point later in time when things fell into equal balance, then, in the end, it seemed as though the zombies were starting to run things. But in the very end you find out that, even though they're outnumbered, the humans still control the zombies. Nothing has changed after all of those revolutions—if you want to look at it on an allegorical level. Also, during the shooting of the first film, I should mention that Jack Russo stepped in to work on the script with me, so the screenplay was a solid collaboration.

H: Why did you choose black and white for *Night of the Living Dead* and color for the other two parts of the trilogy?

R: Initially it was a budgetary decision because we didn't have any money. We started to shoot, then about one week into the production, we raised more money and talked about switching to color and reshooting the material we had shot. At that point we made an aesthetic decision to continue in black and white. It gave it a very flat, somber look. I don't think it would have been as terrifying in color.

H: Were you upset about the video release being colorized?

R: I'm not militant about colorization. Maybe if I had made *The Maltese Falcon* I would be, but I'm not nearly as militant about that as I am about seeing a film cut savagely for syndication or whatever. I think that's much more of a sin than colorizing.

H: I understand that you originally had problems with the ending of *Night of the Living Dead*.

R: Well, we never changed the ending. We had a lot of people refuse to distribute it because the ending was so dark, but we refused to change it.

H: I think the ending maintains the film's integrity in its vision of horror. It's nihilism is honest to the tone of the entire movie.

R: I hope so . . . I'll tell you, the ending was the topic of weeks of arguing with some New York distributors who turned us down. In fact, while we were making the film, we were taking a big gamble in completing it without a distribution deal. American International refused to touch it unless we saved the hero in the end.

H: Did you ever consider having an alternative ending?

R: We talked about it a lot but none of them were ever really taken seriously.

H: What kind of direction did you give the zombies?

R: As little as possible, because if you say to some of them, "Walk this way," while you're raising one arm, then they'll all take it literally and in the next shot everyone's arm will be raised. So I just told them to do their best impression of a dead guy.

H: One of the better moments in the film is when the characters trapped in the farmhouse begin arguing over the most banal things while the world is coming to an end outside.

R: That was the whole thing I wanted to go into this film with. Once you accept the rather implausible premise, flesh-eating zombies, and then you just concentrate on the little things that people would get involved in, it gives the story some realism. I didn't want to put in any characters like a scientist, because it would come across as too artificial and staged.

H: A lot of critics have attempted to raise racial questions about the film because your protagonist is black. Was it a deliberate choice to use a black actor?

R: When we wrote the script, the guy's color wasn't described at all. The character was just "Ben." I guess in the script there was an assumption that all the characters were white. No color was mentioned for any of them in any of their descriptions. Duane Jones happened to be the best actor we knew, so we cast him. The only thing that we did consciously was not change any of the dialogue. After several brainstorming sessions, we decided that the hippest thing to do would be to leave it alone. I mean, it was 1968 and everybody with a conscience was thinking about racial problems and there was a temptation to try to make hay out of it. I never thought at the time we were being crusaders or politically correct.

But we took a little bit of pride in recognizing that we were willing to do this. In fact, if there's anything that is to our credit it's that we didn't change one word in the script after we cast it. Maybe that's a gold star, maybe just a silver star.

H: How did critics respond to the film?

R: At first they crucified it, particularly guys like Roger Ebert, who wrote a really scathing piece in the *Chicago Sun-Times*. He said, "How could people sink so low?"

H: But he reversed his position 180 degrees by the time *Dawn of the Dead* was released.

R: I know. I think the main problem was that some moron in Chicago decided to schedule *Night of the Living Dead* as a kiddie matinee and Roger just happened to walk into the theater and saw all these kids running around the auditorium, hysterical with fear. And usually what would happen with the old kiddie matinees was that the parents would drop off their kids and leave. So there they were, these poor kindergartners stuck in this theater watching this orgy of murder. Consequently, Roger wrote this piece, "What is Hollywood Doing to Children?" It killed us. Though eventually Roger did sponsor *Dawn of the Dead* for the U.S.A. Film Festival in Dallas and then went on to write *Beyond the Valley of the Dolls*. I think maybe he finally discovered how to have fun. The year 1968 was a time when there was all sorts of lobbying for a ratings code, and we got swept along in that rush of emotion. We were just in the right place at the wrong time or wrong place at the right time, to be one of maybe a dozen pictures that were constantly named as proof we needed a ratings system. I think all those things in total can be seen as a grab-bag of lucky things that happened to the movie, otherwise, I don't think it ever would have gotten the kind of attention it wound up getting. It took a lot of heat, critical heat. At the same time it was talked about as this radical, highly political film.

H: It stirred up the imagination of millions of people, enough to make it one of the most provocative horror films of all time. What is it about the film specifically that makes it so enduring?

R: I think once something is proven to be durable, it becomes indestructible, its afterlife is secured. I think it's an effective film, even though all I can see in it are its flaws. When it came out, it was the first film of its kind that didn't cut away when the zombie bit somebody. And in the political circles, it was one of the first films to have a black lead and some allegorical, sociopolitical content beneath its surface. I don't think we were revolutionaries, it's just that we were crazy enough to make a horror movie right at a time when everybody, including us, was talking about all this, so naturally it bled into the film. Plus it got critical attacks and attention from purists in terms of cinematic form; it was used as a whipping boy, and as an excuse for why we needed a ratings system—I think all those things just went together. Underneath it all, a movie has to be effective enough that you can sit and watch it no matter what your view is.

H: Do you think the movie works on a level beyond politics? Is there something that hooks into the collective unconscious, or something about cannibalism and the claustrophobia of being trapped in a house that works on a psychological level?

R: I can't really address any of the real esoterica, but I think it does hold some primal fears. You know, the neighbors have turned into ghouls, that kind of stuff. There's a lot of pure bogeyman stuff, unsettling angles and use of light that makes one feel paranoid.

H: *Dawn of the Dead* takes place in a shopping mall, and it was at this point that critics said your Living Dead films were a comment on American consumerism. You even said that your films were about society devouring itself.

R: Well, I think not society devouring itself so much as new societies devouring old ones, establishing what appears to be a completely new set of rules but what really turns out to be not very different at all. The second film was only about consumerism. There are certainly themes that I hit whenever I can in my films: American consumerism, religion, inability to communicate, the beast within. As far as the entire trilogy being about consumerism, I don't think it is. There's a sociopolitical allegory behind the whole trilogy, I would say, that after the new society has devoured the old, underneath all the pretense nothing much has really changed because the species stays the same.

H: *Dawn of the Dead* is a little more tongue-in-cheek than its predecessor.

R: Oh yes, much more. Again I think it just reflects the time that it was made. Everybody was out dancing in those days.

H: What about *Day of the Dead*, which seems to take on the same dark, ominous tone that you had in *Night of the Living Dead?*

R: That got a little darker because I think times are getting a little darker again.

H: What do you think goes on in the minds of your zombie characters and how have they changed through the trilogy?

R: I don't think they've changed very much, I think they've just operated on instinct all along. They're innocents. They're just infants. They start to learn how to do things and that's what screws them up. But the last time we heard from one of them in *Day of the Dead*, I thought he was a pretty good guy—when Bob walks off into the sunset. Maybe he'll find some new way of life and get by. In my mind they personify human potential, which is first just savage and depends on what they learn.

H: Why was there a ten-year lag between the making of *Night of the Living Dead* and *Dawn of the Dead* and only four years between *Dawn* and *Day of the Dead?*

R: Well, my smart answer is to say I spent five years avoiding it, and then five years trying to get a deal, which is not far from the truth. I did avoid it at first.

H: You didn't want to make a sequel?

R: I just didn't want to make another horror film. I was afraid that I'd get slotted, even though I love the genre. It's so easy to get pigeon-holed, which has happened to me. Happily, it's in a genre that I love, but unfortunately I still can't walk in with a script and get funding for a film that's not horror.

H: After *Night of the Living Dead* you made a film called *Jack's Wife* which had its title changed to *The Hungry*. At one time you said you'd like to remake the film. Would you tell me something about the project?

R: In fact, I just said yesterday to a friend that I'd like to remake that film. The problem with the original was that I was under-financed and then the company that was subsidizing the project went belly-up halfway through. We had a choice of either quitting there or trying to finish the movie somehow, which I did. Unfortunately, the film suffered, got lousy distribution and didn't get shown anywhere. But it's an idea that I still like today. It's a modern witchcraft tale about somebody getting caught up in the idea that witchcraft can change their life.

H: In the past you've said that your vampire film, *Martin*, has stood out as your favorite project. Why do you think it's personally your most successful film?

R: I thought it was the best translation off the page of any of my films. It was the most successful in terms of my ability to match the ideas I had written and executed. The situation just happened to be perfect. We got great locations, a lot of cooperation. On a craft level, I think it has some of the most successful sequences that I have ever realized. It may not be the most pleasant of my films or most accessible, and other people may not like it as much, but it's just one that I love.

H: Have you thought about doing a fourth part to the *Night of the Living Dead* trilogy or do you think you're finished with it?

R: I'd like to only because I was never able to do everything I wanted to do. I had written a script for the third part which was a much more expensive film than was produced. It would have cost a lot of money to make and I was basically told by the people who financed the picture, "Sure, we'll put up seven million but you have to deliver an R-rated picture. If you want to stick with this hardcore violence, you have to spend only three million." Because of that, I wound up cutting the script to make it more wieldy. I really love what *Day of the Dead* is, but to me it's not the ending, it's Act I of the ending. I wasn't able to take it all the way. There is potential there and I'd love someday to do it, but I sure don't want to do it now. And I don't want to have to do it under contract or with any sort of mandate.

H: Where would the fourth pick up?

R: I don't know. When I wrote *Day of the Dead* it was completely autonomous. I may never do it, and it would be really hard for me to get it going again. I don't want to do it if it's underfinanced. It would have to come at a point where I had enough money in the bank so I wouldn't have to worry about the light bills.

H: Are you trying to work outside the horror genre now?

R: I always have, and I've always had scripts that aren't horror. The couple of films that I have made outside the genre have been underfinanced and underbacked, and that's not served me very well. I haven't got the campaign or advertising money, so they haven't succeeded. There are many films that I've tried to get made; I just haven't been able to.

H: Your films are graphically very violent yet you've tried to disassociate yourself from the "slice and dice" directors like Tobe Hooper [*Texas Chainsaw Massacre*] and Sean Cunningham [*Friday the 13th*]. What are the differences between the way you approach violence and the way some of the exploitation directors might approach it?

R: I don't necessarily try to disassociate myself from those guys. However, there is a kind of film I try to disassociate myself from, which are those that get made because the violence is the only value in them. There are film deals that get made based purely on how much blood is in the script. I don't think that's any fun. That's like saying, "Hey, they were successful with a shark, let's use an alligator." I just think there are a lot of thoughtless people that make films who don't have an affection for the horror genre and/ or the skills to make an effective film. There are films that just prey on the fans of gore. I find that unfair, but there is a demand out there.

H: After your success with *Night of the Living Dead* you went on to direct some documentaries for ABC. What was it like going from feature filmmaking to documentary filmmaking?

R: It was really cathartic, it was great, there was no pressure. We were getting a salary. It was three years of coasting that allowed me to get my head back together. I had a business partner whom I trusted for the first time. We had a good time.

H: Your partner, Richard Rubenstein, has called you an editor first. Can you tell me something about your editing process? Does it affect the way you direct, or your composition?

R: A little bit, it has to. I guess I really was an editor. I always did both. I mean, I used to shoot, direct and edit. I'm always thinking about how it's going to glue together while I'm shooting it. So I think it's an advantage. I know when something's going to cut and when it's not. It can save you some money.

H: Do you need fewer cover shots if you know how it's going to cut ahead of time?

R: No, you need the cover shots. It's not always what you need, it's what you might like to have, but time costs more and more money year after year. You don't have the luxury of walking into a room and seeing something that you'd like to shoot. You may just not be able to afford to do it. That's the stuff that bothers me. It's improvising. It's all those happy little accidents which are to some extent like watercolors. You're not completely in control of what's going on. Now it's getting to the point where you really can't take advantage of the happy accidents that happen, because every minute costs several thousand dollars.

H: Because of the controversial nature of your work, distributors have asked that many of your films be tested by preview audiences. What are your thoughts about studio executives market researching a film?

R: The public doesn't necessarily know what they want nor are they always able to articulate what they want. So I think it's impossible to ask twenty questions to a thousand people and come out with the answers that are going to make your movie a hit. I think it's misguided, over-used. I mean, we're supposed to be the creators. When I say "we," I mean not just the filmmakers, but the producers and everyone who takes the responsibility for putting this material out for the public to see. We're the entertainers, we're the ones who should educate, we're the ones who should help make tastes rather than listening to fumbling, inarticulate requests for things people may not fully understand themselves. It's really like asking an infant to pick up its menu.

H: Sounds a little bit like feeding your zombies . . .

R: I don't mean to disparage the public quite that badly, but I think you get the drift of what I'm saying. I think what happens is that it's just another way for the executives to absolve themselves from responsibility. "Well, look at the preview cards. I had to do this." It's an unfortunate state of affairs. It may be the single factor for us being in the black hole we're in right now as far as cinema is concerned. I think we may be in one of the weakest periods in the history of film.

H: Didn't your most recent film, *Monkey Shines*, fall victim to this?

R: Right. The producers encouraged me to give it a more upbeat ending. They had screened the picture in preview after preview after preview, and when the whole world started telling them that they didn't like something in the film, the distributor can be in very persuasive position. So in this case, we changed the ending. It was very difficult to refuse them. I didn't have autonomous control over the picture, although Orion did say to me that they would respect whatever my call was. But then there's the whole other side of the coin where you want the distributor to have faith in the product too. You can cut your own throat and insist on your ending and the next thing you know the film opens on some airline flight. It's all part of the game-playing process. I was not pleased, I would have preferred to have the original ending, but at the time I did it willingly and without anyone twisting my arm.

H: What is it about Pittsburgh that particularly draws you to want to make movies there?

R: I happen to be sitting here right now, so it's a lot easier for me to go out and make movies on Grant Street than it is for me to go to Century City. It's as simple as that. I just like to live here. I like the people here. I like the work style. I like the fact that we're a little island under slightly less scrutiny. There's a work ethic here that's really nice.

H: Do you ever think you're at a disadvantage?

R: Probably in some ways, but not too much. I mean, we have the same equipment. It's really more in postproduction that you would be at a disadvantage, and I've always done it either in New York or L.A. anyway. The only other advantage of being "there" is if you need a big stage, sure. You have no choice. But there's a sameness that comes with living in L.A. You know, "How are they shooting interiors these days? What kind of gels are they using on the windows? What's the ratio?" Everything starts looking the same.

Filmography

1966	*Expostulations*
1968	*Night of the Living Dead*
1973	*Hungry Wives*
1973	*The Crazies*
1978	*Zombies*
1979	*Martin*
1979	*Dawn of the Dead*
1981	*Knightriders*
1982	*Creepshow*
1985	*Day of the Dead*
1989	*Monkey Shines*

ROGER EBERT

A Star Beneath the Screen

Roger Ebert and Gene Siskel may be the most visible film critics in the history of American cinema. Their syndicated television show "Siskel & Ebert," which has gone through many metamorphoses since it was first aired over ten years ago as "Sneak Previews," has made them better known in American households than many film directors and stars.

Ebert maintains a sobering perspective on his celebrity status. He circulates with friends he's known for years and leads a fairly private life in Chicago, where he has been the resident film critic for the *Chicago Sun-Times* for over two decades. "It would be a lot worse if I lived on one of the coasts," he says about his role as a celebrity. As one of America's first television "star" critics, the recognition factor was something neither he nor anyone else had ever anticipated upon entering his profession. "A film critic should be one of the most inconspicuous fellows on the planet, sitting in the back of a dark theater, quietly scribbling down notes," says Ebert from his *Chicago Sun-Times* office. "Now, being on television has sort of mutated all that. Suddenly, we have thousands of television media celebrities . . . and it's unnatural. More people are wearing mirrored sunglasses and playing the role of star than ever before. And the public recognizes them. It's not meant to be in human nature that somebody recognizes you who has never seen you in the flesh before."

The often superficial accolades that come with appearing on television do not daunt Ebert from taking film criticism seriously. In addition to writing for the *Sun-Times*, from which he is syndicated in over two hundred newspapers, he teaches at the University of Chicago and has written several books, including an annual compilation of his reviews (*Roger Ebert's Home Movie Companion*), a laugh-out-loud, ribald account of his years spent at the Cannes Film Festival (*Two Weeks in the Midday Sun*) and others. Ebert, who appears frequently at international film festivals, often gives seminars to the public that include scrupulous film analyses.

In an era when the media has saturated the American public with virtually every aspect of Hollywood films and filmmaking, the critical eye of the film reviewer has recently been looking into the front side of mirrored sunglasses, seeing his reflection and asking the question, "Who said we had the right to own a pair of sunglasses?" The author of this new query is Richard Corliss, who in a recent debate with Roger Ebert and Andrew Sarris, turned the spotlight on his own profession, asking the question: What is state of film criticism and is there a future? The mirrored sunglasses are what Corliss uses to illustrate the cult status of the television film reviewer, and how his rising popularity is occurring at the expense of serious film criticism. "Movie criticism of the elevated sort," writes Corliss (*Film Comment* March–April, 1990)," . . . as practiced over the past half century by James Agee, Manny Farber, Andrew Sarris and Pauline Kael . . . in the mainstream press and in magazines . . . is an endangered species. Once it flourished; soon it may perish, to be replaced by . . . performers who must create a stern and goofy TV personality and look natural while cribbing from a TelePrompter." Specifically citing "Siskel & Ebert" as nothing more than "a sitcom starring two guys who live in a movie theater and argue all the time," Corliss fears not just for the future of serious film scholarship, but for intelligent "readers with the vigor, curiosity, and intelligence that Agee demanded of film critics . . . To understand pictures, we still needs words."

How does Ebert respond to all this? Well, the man whose stout figure has become the trademark of America's most popular critic agreed to answer my questions in his office, a veritable warehouse of videotapes, posters and film books, where I hoped to get a better look at the whole picture.

HICKENLOOPER: Would you talk about how you became inter-ested in films growing up?

EBERT: Well, I grew up in Champaign-Urbana, Illinois. And it was one of the last areas in the country to get television, because these two local newspapers were fighting over who was going to get the channel. So, as a result, I probably went to the movies more than other people my age, because we didn't have television. And in grade school, I think, the week centered around the Saturday matinees at the Princess Theater on Main Street in Urbana, where I saw countless movies. And then starting in high school, Cham-paign got the Art Theater which was a member of the Art Theater Guild, and there I saw my early Bergman and Fellini films, the British angry-young-men movies, *Citizen Kane*, and so forth. And in college there were film societies. I just became a lover of film that way. I never took any film classes, because there weren't any of-fered at the University of Illinois in those days. But I went to the movies a lot, and I also wrote about them for the college newspaper.

H: Would you talk about the origin of "Sneak Previews?"

E: Well, in 1975 a woman named Thea Flaum approached [Gene] Siskel and myself and asked us if we'd like to do a monthly show reviewing the new movies for the local PBS station. Our orig-inal feeling was—at least my feeling was I didn't want to work with Siskel. I didn't know him or like him. We were so competitive, and we weren't on speaking terms. But nevertheless I didn't want any-body else doing it, so I agreed. And it started out as a once-a-month series, later developed into every other week, and then fi-nally weekly on PBS, going from local to regional to national. And then eight years ago we went into commercial syndication with the Tribune Company and four years ago we switched from Tribune to Buena Vista, where we are now. The names of the shows over the years were "Opening Soon at a Theater Near You," "Sneak Pre-views," "At the Movies," and now "Siskel & Ebert."

H: How improvisational is the show?

E: I can tell you exactly how improvisational—when we're lead-ing into a clip package it's scripted. Most of the voice-overs over the clips are scripted, although we have now started ad-libbing to screen about one shot-by-shot commentary per packaging. And coming out—this is our new format that's only two shows old—is immediate ad lib. But I would say about sixty percent-sixty-five percent of the show is ad lib.

H: Have you and Gene Siskel grown to like each other?

E: We've grown to tolerate each other. There's some grudging affection, I suppose.

H: Were you aware of what kind of impact your show would have?

E: Not really. The entire show is a phenomenon. It's still aston-ishing to me that a national television show like this is coming out of Chicago. When I was growing up, and certainly when I started out as a film critic, New York and Los Angeles were the centers for national film criticism. And it was ironic, indeed, that at one time no less than three national television shows about the movies were coming out of Chicago. As we left "Sneak Previews" and "At the Movies" they continued to produce shows with hosts who were hired to replace us. Both of those shows are now off the air, but nevertheless at one time Chicago was the national capital of TV movie reviewing. It still is, I guess, except there's only one show instead of three.

H: Do you think that your show might have been a catalyst for what seems to be a very popular interest in not only films themsel-ves but in the film industry, for example, the success of *Premiere* magazine and "Entertainment Tonight"?

E: I don't know if we were a catalyst or if we just came along early on the crest of a wave that was already headed for shore. It's obvious, on television anyway, that movies are an art form that works well with television because you can show film clips. And that's why television stations have movie critics, but they don't have book critics. It wouldn't be very exciting on the news to show a printout of a paragraph of a book. So I'm realistic enough to

know that one of the reasons movie reviewing worked on television was people like to see scenes from movies, and they like to see
their favorite movie stars. At the time we started the show in 1975,
the morning television shows had movie critics, like "The Today
Show" and "Good Morning America." And some local television
stations also did. But since then there's been an amazing boom in
entertainment journalism, including trade coverage. It's a fairly
recent phenomenon, for example, that the weekend box office
gross is now big news every Monday in the newspapers and on
television. And I suppose we might have had something to do with
it.

H: Do you feel that your work, in print criticism, is taken less
seriously now that you're a celebrity?

E: No. For one thing the television has allowed me to find more
readers for my print criticism. I'm syndicated in two hundred papers now all over the country, and my book *Roger Ebert's Home
Movie Companion,* is now entering it 6th annual edition, so that I
think more people read what I have written now than ever did
before. It might be interesting for you to know that in terms of my
professional life I've spent about eighty percent of my working
time in print and only twenty percent on television.

H: Frequently at film festivals you are known to offer seminars
in frame-by-frame analysis, most notably your scrupulous examination of *Citizen Kane.*

E: I've been through it with the stop-action film analyzer many
times. I've read the screenplay. I've seen the movie in theaters. I've
seen it on television. I've seen it on laser disc. I'm as familiar with
that film as it's possible for me to be with a film. And yet every
time that I walk into a room and the movie is on I find the same
phenomenon. I'm unable to tell you what scene is going to come
next. I think this is true of most people who have seen the film.
The flashback structure is so complex. The narrative structure of
the film involves emotional continuity rather than temporal continuity. For example, when you see Charles Foster Kane being
splashed by mud in front of that pharmacy and Susan Alexander
laughs at him, how many people remember that that is part of

Joseph Cotten's flashback? Particularly since he wasn't there. And that's why the movie maintains such a fascination to people, because they can't memorize it. I'm very familiar with other movies that came out around the same period of time that I've looked at also an equal number of evenings, such as *The Third Man, Notorious, Rebecca, Gone With the Wind*. With these films I can sit there and tell you what the next scene is going to be. With *Citizen Kane* there are still those surprises. It's like trying to catch lightning in a bottle. It's a film that still lives, it's still elusive to the grasp, still squirms away from you, it still has an interior dynamic of its own that cannot be reduced to familiarity no matter how many times you've seen it. I'll bet we could gather a convention right now of the twenty-five *Citizen Kane* experts of your choice, and put up a big blackboard at one end of the room, and everybody together could try to construct the series of scenes that make up that movie. You'd just have a big fight.

H: You, Andrew Sarris and Richard Corliss recently published a series of essays in *Film Comment* (March–August 1990) which turned into a well-publicized debate over the state of film criticism. Richard Corliss, who wrote the first essay, was lamenting the loss of serious print criticism. He felt threatened by television critics like you and Siskel, and felt that those shows were being created at the expense of print criticism. He said that because of the TV critics, fewer people were taking the print critics seriously.

E: There's much more print criticism than there ever was before. I think that Richard was writing primarily out of an autobiographical impulse. His article was in the form of a farewell to *Film Comment*, which he basically put on the map, and he said a few things. And I think that he felt as you do, when you succeed at something and then finish with it—the kind of feeling that he should have done more. I think that a lot of those feelings were involved in his article. I think I was able to demonstrate in my article that there is a lot more written about films now than ever before. Daily newspapers find the salaries to hire more full-time film critics now than twenty years ago. So that many local communities have their own local film critics, whereas before the paper would have typically carried only some kind of syndicated Hollywood gossip column. One point that I made in my article was that the key turning point in newspaper film criticism was the Twentieth Century-Fox ban on Judith Crist after she knocked *Cleopatra*. And there were probably less than half a dozen American newspapers with serious film critics at that moment. And the publicity over that suddenly made it fashionable or trendy for a newspaper to have a film critic with an outspoken personal voice. And the repercussions of that have been phenomenal. Within a few years many newspapers, many more newspapers, had film critics. Now Richard deliberately misread that paragraph in order to say in his rejoinder that during that same year there had been Andrew Sarris's article on auteurism and Pauline Kael's "Circles and Squares" article. Obviously the key word in my sentence was *newspaper* film criticism, and the articles he was talking about appeared in *Film Quarterly* and other film magazines. The key word was *newspaper, newspaper, newspaper*, and I asked him about that at the Cannes Film Festival, and he kind of grinned and said, "Well, I butted it a little bit." But he was really making a spurious point, because I think that Richard probably doesn't take newspaper film criticism very seriously. And yet as I pointed out in my article, there are a lot of very good local newspaper film critics around the country—a lot of them. And they do a very good job. And in terms of words written, they write a lot more than the academic or weekly or quarterly or monthly critics. I think you'd be amazed at how many words of good criticism are written each month by people like Peter Rainer, Sheila Benson, Vincent Canby or Darren James. It's a lot of good, perceptive commentary that's out there. And in addition to this, look at the boom in film magazines, you know, the original *Film Quarterly* and *Film Comment* and *Cinéaste* have been joined by *Premiere*, which is by and large a pretty serious and constructive magazine. And just look at *Entertainment Weekly*, the Time/Life publication, which is mid-cult.

I think Richard's just demonstrably wrong, and I got a lot of letters from colleagues after that exchange appeared, saying that they agreed with me that actually there is a lot more constructive criticism and peer discussion of movies around today than there was twenty years ago.

H: Except in universities, where you talked about the death of film societies.

E: Yeah. It's ironic that the growth of film academic studies has been accompanied by the death of film-loving or film-going on campuses. I myself am unmoved by the more arcane versions of film scholarship in which the language of film is analyzed as if it were linguistic.

H: The Deconstructionists?

E: Well, deconstructionism is an intellectual game that can be played. It doesn't have any connection with the daily experience of people who go to the movies. The thing that really has killed movies on the campus is home video. It used to be that if you were a college student the only way you could see old movies or classic movies or cult movies was to go to an auditorium where they would show them to you on 16mm, and this would be known as the campus film society. Today home video makes it possible for you to program your own TV and so, as I pointed out in the article, campus film societies have fallen on hard days.

H: It's amazing what you say about university film societies. I helped run the Yale Law School Film Society which had been around for thirty years, and that was just four years ago. And at that time there were six other film societies. And I called a friend back at school recently, and he said there was one film society left.

E: It's just devastating. There was once what was known as the film generation. You know, the sixties *Blow Up* period. Now there's the postfilm generation. Young people today are completely illiterate when it comes to classic films, because they literally do not see them or know about them. We're going back into the dark ages—kind of like the burning of the library at Alexandria or something. When I was going to college, part of your experience consisted of finding out who such people as Federico Fellini, Akira Kurosawa, Ingmar Bergman, Vittorio DeSica, Orson Welles, Alfred Hitchcock, Howard Hawks and John Ford were. Today the big deal is to rent *Batman* and show it in the rec room of your dorm. These movies are out there on home video, but with the exception of the unusual student who is really interested in movies, it's not part of the common experience.

H: How do you think print criticism has changed since the days of James Agee? Do you think there's been a change since the 1940s and 1950s? Obviously Andrew Sarris and Pauline Kael had an impact on print criticism.

E: Well there is no such thing as print criticism. There are only critics who work in print.

H: Okay.

E: And each one has his own voice. I think there was a time when there was very little serious written about movies. And we go back to those pioneering works in film criticism by people like Otis Ferguson, James Agee, Graham Greene, Robert Warshaw, and then suddenly right when the studio system was collapsing, you had the rise of these tremendously individual key figures such as Kael, Sarris, and Dwight MacDonald who all through the late fifties and into the sixties was writing a monthly column at *Esquire* that was tremendously influential. It had the largely spurious controversy over whether or not the auteur theory was valid. I think the auteur theory was primarily in America, and I think most reasonable people in this country believed that the auteur theory was valid. If there was a fight between Kael and Sarris [see *Film Theory and Criticism*, edited by Gerald Mast and Marshall Cohen], I'm not sure what it was about, because if you read Kael's criticism it is very director oriented.

H: When Truffaut left *Cahiers du Cinéma* he said that he felt he had been much too hard on directors and that he felt that basically as a film critic he was nothing really more than a frustrated director. And I know you've been involved with writing scripts. Do you feel that there might be some truth to that statement, that a lot of critics are just frustrated artists?

E: There's a lot of truth to that statement as far as Truffaut is concerned. He was a frustrated director. And he proved it by becoming a director. Some people are directors who start as critics. Other people are critics who start as critics. The notion that the critic is supposed to be able to direct or produce or act or write is completely apart from the function of a critic, which is to be an ideal member of the audience. The good critic has to be the ideal viewer, not the ideal director or writer or actor. He has to be presumably the most interested and alert and involved person in the audience. And he has to be able to write about what he has experienced in such a way that the public and the artist can learn something about what happened by reading his piece.

H: In your rebuttal to Richard Corliss in *Film Comment*, you wrote that you felt part of the problem today was that Hollywood was in the midst of a power shift back from director to star and agent.

E: There's no question about that.

H: Could you elucidate?

E: In deal after deal you find that the film can't be made unless they can get the right star. In case after case you can talk to screenwriters and directors who are given the A-list of a given Hollywood studio and told the project is a "go" if we can cast somebody off this list. There was a period in the seventies when unique pictures could be made without star power.

Look at *Taxi Driver*. Certainly Robert De Niro was not a star when that movie was made. Look at *2001*. There weren't any stars in it. Today if you're not going to have a major star in a major studio film you have to have one of two other elements: It either has to be the kind of film where the genre is the star, such as a horror film, or it has to be the kind of movie where the subject matter is telling enough that it overrides other considerations. For example, a film like *Platoon*. It didn't have any stars who had any back-up or clout. And yet the subject matter was the star. But generally speaking, you've got to have a star. The stars are getting enormous salaries—ten, fifteen million dollars. Packages are being put together by agencies with the stars, the screenwriter and director who are all clients of the same agent. Consequently, the agent has usurped some of the power of the studio in terms of putting together a film.

H: You also wrote in your rebuttal that you felt that many of the interesting directors who were working today emerged in the seventies, like Martin Scorsese.

E: That's true. And I just saw *GoodFellas* yesterday. It's more true than ever. Scorsese is a standard-bearer right now. But I want to elaborate on the previous point a little bit. There was a time in the so-called Golden Age when packages were put together by the studio heads. They would assign a writer, a director, and the cast to a movie. They would pick the project. They would put a writer on it. They would put a director on it, and they would say these are the stars. Today an agent is likely to put together the screenplay, the director and the stars. And everybody knows about many movies that have been cast out of one agency. Wouldn't it be a good argument to say, "Well, in the Golden Age this process seemed to work, why isn't it a good idea now for one person, and if he knows something about the movie, to assemble these packages?" And the answer is no, it isn't a good idea, because they're being put together with an eye on a different goal. You see, when a studio chief put together one of these packages, he did so trying to make a movie that would make as much money as possible at the box office, in order to increase his studio's profit and to make his job secure. The problem is an agent gets his money up front, so that the agent puts together the project in order to get his fifteen percent from everybody's salary, a fifteen percent that is paid whether or not the movie makes money. As a result you've had some very bizarre films. Michael Ovitz at CAA [Creative Artists Agency] is particularly notable in this respect: packages put together primarily just to make everybody money, and then when the movie comes out it's a spectacular disaster because his primary responsibility was not to the movie's ultimate commercial success. As a result of this, some of his clients have suffered, because they've been put in packages that were attractive rather than movies that were attractive.

H: There are some who believe that the 1970s was a very hopeful time in the American cinema because directors were at the height of their powers, as creative and political forces in the industry. This of course may have been a direct result of the auteur theory. When do you think this began to change? When did the power begin to shift back toward the studios and agents?

E: Some say that the directors' days of glory ended with *Heaven's Gate*. Personally, I think the turning point may have been the rise of the blockbusters, the super-blockbuster films, the hallmark films. Once studios started seeing a hundred and fifty and two hundred million dollar grosses being possible, the directors turned away from making the profitable smaller pictures. For example, the whole black exploitation movement, which produced a lot of films that were more than exploitation films, died because our studios weren't interested in spending six million dollars to make twenty million dollars. They were interested in spending twenty million dollars to make two hundred million dollars. And so black films, which existed from the late sixties until the mid-seventies, ended almost as soon as they begun. A less visible victim of the same process was the smaller, ambitious, original film. The studios aren't that interested in making films like that. A *Taxi Driver*, a *Hardcore*, a *Five Easy Pieces*, a *Last Picture Show* could not be made today. There's no market for these films today.

H: Could the seventies have been another Hollywood Golden Age?

E: I think as we look back on American film history, the seventies will be seen as the decade when American directors flowered in the sense that European directors did in the sixties.

H: Are you hopeful about the future of American filmmaking?

E: For twenty-four years I've gone to every movie of any note that's made in America. And I've seen most of the films overseas that made it over here and got any attention at all. The average level of satisfaction I have in terms of, take a hundred movies, how many of them did I enjoy, would probably be a downward curve. Out of a hundred movies, fewer of them are interesting today than were at any previous year that you can choose. It's steadily going down. Part of that is my own increasing familiarity with genres, so that I'm no longer able to be surprised by movies that might have surprised me the first time I saw some of these conventions—archetypal situations. From that point of view, I just mentioned to myself as I walked in to see the Scorsese film yesterday, "Well, thank God, I know I'm going to see something interesting." I feel the same way about Woody Allen. I always felt that way about Robert Altman. I hope he starts making films regularly again.

H: Has film criticism lowered its standards to compensate for the seemingly rising tide of mediocrity in filmmaking?

E: Well, film criticism does a couple of different things. Daily reviewing of the sort that I do is the real reason that anyone reads a review in a newspaper—to find out if they should go see that movie on Friday night. And so an effective critic is going to, at some level, be able to communicate to his viewers whether or not he thinks they would enjoy the film. He cannot tell them if they would or not. He doesn't know them. I have a rule with my criticism that I never, ever use any kind of language that says this will be enjoyed by person X, Y or Z. On the other hand, my review should be descriptive and evocative enough that a person could read it and say I think I'd like it even if he didn't. Or I don't think I would like it even if he did. So that's the one thing that you've got to have. And if you do that, then it isn't your standard that matters so much as the standard of people reading your review. I'm quite aware that every time I review a *Friday The 13th* movie, I sell tickets to it. Because the worse I say it is the more its audience is probably going to think they'll enjoy it.

H: Horror pictures used to be the B-movies of the forties, fifties and sixties, and in the last decade they seem to have become the A-movies. They have big studio budgets now. Would you talk a little bit about the evolution of the genre?

E: Well, Hitchcock said that he liked to play the audience like a piano. And I think that horror pictures have that as their ambition. In other words, a horror movie often acts just like a ride at Disneyland. It causes emotion to happen, and it does so with a very predictable efficiency. This is why people go to such movies. Today we live in a time where tone of voice has been raised, the noise level has been raised, and impact and input levels have been raised, so when you go to a movie, frequently there's an average goer going to the movies because he wants to have a movie that can give him those sharply experienced emotions. Generally speaking, one underlying factor why everyone from any background or any level of sophistication goes to a motion picture is to have their mood altered for two hours by having a voyeuristic, escapist experience through sharing in some way the lives of the people on the screen. This is more important than their critical motivation, their social motivation to go in and sit down. The lights go down, and for a couple of hours it's like living someone else's life. We're living in a time of speedup. It used to be that people would sit through a movie in two hours and have an appreciation of its entire structure. Now we have an artificial climax every six minutes. Television commercials are thirty seconds long, fifteen seconds long, five seconds long. We have little sound bites. We have nuggets of information. The horror movie, by its nature, is more suited to this speedup, because it consists of a series of fairly easily manufactured emotional climaxes.

Books by Roger Ebert

1984   *A Kiss Is Still a Kiss: Roger Ebert at the Movies*
1987   *Two Weeks in the Midday Sun: A Cannes Notebook*
1990   *Roger Ebert's Home Movie Companion* (annual edition)

ABOUT THE AUTHOR

George Hickenlooper graduated from Yale College in 1986 with a B.A. in film studies. He has written for *Billboard, L.A. Style,* and *Cineaste* magazines. In 1988 his short film "Newark Needs Insurance" was honored in the Canadian International Film Festival. The following year he directed a documentary about director Peter Bogdanovich and author Larry McMurtry. He recently co-directed a documentary about filmmaker Francis Coppola and the making of *Apocalypse Now.* The documentary was honored at the 1991 Cannes Film Festival.